An eth^T   102 045 071 1   all far

MANCHESTER
1824

Manchester University Press

New
Ethnographies

Series editor
Alexander Thomas T. Smith

Already published

The British in rural France:
Lifestyle migration and the ongoing quest for a better way of life Michaela Benson

Chagos islanders in Mauritius and the UK:
Forced displacement and onward migration Laura Jeffery

Literature and agency in English fiction reading:
A study of the Henry Williamson Society
Adam Reed

Devolution and the Scottish Conservatives:
Banal activism, electioneering and the politics of irrelevance
Alexander Smith

An ethnography of English football fans

Cans, cops and carnivals

Geoff Pearson

Manchester University Press
Manchester and New York

distributed in the United States exclusively
by Palgrave Macmillan

Published by Manchester University Press
Oxford Road, Manchester M13 9NR, UK
and Room 400, 175 Fifth Avenue, New York, NY 10010, USA
www.manchesteruniversitypress.co.uk

Distributed in the United States exclusively by
Palgrave Macmillan, 175 Fifth Avenue,
New York, NY 10010, USA

Distributed in Canada exclusively by
UBC Press, University of British Columbia, 2029 West Mall,
Vancouver, BC, Canada V6T 1Z2

British Library Cataloguing-in-Publication Data is available

Library of Congress Cataloging-in-Publication Data is available

ISBN 978 0 7190 9540 5 *paperback*

First published by Manchester University Press in hardback 2012

This paperback edition first published 2014

Printed by Lightning Source

Man lives in remembrance of one festival and in expectation of the next.

Roger Caillois

Contents

List of tables

Acknowledgements

This book has been developed over a long period and I would like to express my gratitude to everyone who has assisted towards its publication over the past sixteen years. Inevitably some that should be mentioned have been unintentionally overlooked, so this list is by no means exhaustive. I would like to thank the two academics who have been the most influential in the way my research has progressed. First, Professor Michael Salter, now at the University of Central Lancashire, who supervised my Ph.D. at the University of Lancaster, taught me the value of participant observation as a research method and the veracity of descriptive approaches to popular culture generally. Second, Dr Clifford Stott of the University of Liverpool, with whom I have worked on various projects since 2001 and whose application of the elaborated social identity model of crowd behaviour provided a theoretical anchor for many of the norms of football crowd behaviour I had identified.

I have been fortunate to receive support for my research from both the University of Lancaster's Law Department (1995–99) and the University of Liverpool's Football Research Unit and Management School (1999–2011), both financially and in allowing me the time and freedom to carry out my fieldwork. I would therefore like to thank the relevant staff at both institutions for their assistance in this, in particular Murray Dalziel, Rogan Taylor and Rory Miller. I would also like to express my gratitude to the University of Lancaster Law Department's Iredell Studentship award and the UK Home Office for financially assisting in data gathering.

I would also like to thank those involved in the Liverpool and Keele Ethnography Symposium for their enthusiasm, interest and encouragement for my work, particularly Frank Worthington, Mike Rowe, Matthew Brannan, Jason Ferdinand and Manuela Nocker. The Symposium has been invaluable in improving my knowledge of ethnographic theory and enabling me to discuss the various concepts that appear in these pages. Thanks also to Garance Marechal and Arianna Sale for their assistance, particularly in light of my woeful lack of French or Italian language skills.

I would also like to thank the commissioning editor at Manchester University Press and Dr Alex Smith, the *New Ethnographies* series editor for both enthusiastically supporting the publication of this monograph and for their helpful comments, criticism and guidance. Along with the external reviewers, their efforts have helped to improve this book significantly from its initial drafts. Thanks also to Rachel Johnston for her proofreading and stylistic comments at such tight deadlines.

In the field, I would like to acknowledge those who have carried out observations with me not already mentioned, including Roger Levermore, Andy Davies and James Hoggett. On the non-academic side I would in particular like to thank Aidan Green, Tim Davenport and Matthew Rollinson for their patience in sticking with me when I was off 'looking for interesting data' when all they wanted was a quiet drink or (rarely) an early night. Thanks also to those people from the Football Supporters' Federation, England Fans, the Independent Manchester United Supporters' Association and the Manchester United Supporters' Trust who have assisted me in gathering data. Particular mention should be made of the administrators of the Red Brigade [pseudonym] message board for allowing me to use their excellent forum to gather data, and for assisting me in gaining informed consent from their members. Thanks also to those police officers who have taken time to chat to me about my work; as many of the quotes have been used anonymously, again I cannot express my gratitude individually.

Finally, the most important people to thank for their contribution to this book are the hundreds of fans whom I observed and talked to in the course of my research, both unwitting and consenting. Particular thanks to anyone who has assisted me in gaining access to data in the field (e.g. introducing me to characters or groups), who has helped me along the way in practical terms (e.g. getting hold of tickets) or has got me out of the occasional 'scrape'. For purposes of anonymity I cannot thank them by name but their contributions have made this book possible.

Series editor's foreword

At its best, ethnography has provided a valuable tool for apprehending a world in flux. A couple of years after the Second World War, Max Gluckman founded the Department of Social Anthropology at the University of Manchester. In the years that followed, he and his colleagues built a programme of ethnographic research that drew eclectically on the work of leading anthropologists, economists and sociologists to explore issues of conflict, reconciliation and social justice 'at home' and abroad. Often placing emphasis on detailed analysis of case studies drawn from small-scale societies and organisations, the famous 'Manchester School' in social anthropology built an enviable reputation for methodological innovation in its attempts to explore the pressing political questions of the second half of the twentieth century. Looking back, that era is often thought to constitute a 'gold standard' for how ethnographers might grapple with new challenges and issues in the contemporary world.

The *New Ethnographies* series aims to build on that ethnographic legacy at Manchester. It will publish the best new ethnographic monographs that promote interdisciplinary debate and methodological innovation in the qualitative social sciences. This includes the growing number of books that seek to apprehend the 'new' ethnographic objects of a seemingly brave new world, some recent examples of which have included auditing, democracy and elections, documents, financial markets, human rights, assisted reproductive technologies and political activism. Analysing such objects has often demanded new skills and techniques from the ethnographer. As a result, this series will give voice to those using ethnographic methods across disciplines to innovate, such as through the application of multi-sited fieldwork and the extended comparative case study method. Such innovations have often challenged more traditional ethnographic approaches. *New Ethnographies* therefore seeks to provide a platform for emerging scholars and their more established counterparts engaging with ethnographic methods in new and imaginative ways.

Alexander Thomas T. Smith

Introduction

Locating the carnival fan

Why would a football fan travel hundreds of miles to a city where their team is playing without a match ticket? Why would they not wear the team's colours, and why might they avoid using their club's official travel package for the journey? Why would they ignore instructions not to drink alcohol or to avoid certain areas frequented by the local fans? Why do they make these journeys and why do they repeat them time and time again? One explanation has been that these fans may be 'hooligans', travelling to matches in the hope of confronting like-minded rival fans, but this is not a book about football hooligans. Nor is it about the occasional football fan, who might buy his or her club's replica shirt, watch Sky's 'Soccer Saturday' religiously and attend the occasional match. This book is about the loud and noisy subculture of wider football fandom who attend matches home and away, who spend a huge amount of their time and money following their team, who help to create the chants that form the 'atmosphere' at matches but who provide a constant challenge to the football authorities and police through their attendance and modes of expression. It aims to provide a deep ethnographic account of these supporters, their interpretations, attitudes, motivations and behaviour. This book does not attempt to judge these fans, although it does make recommendations as to how these groups can be understood and managed, particularly in situations where there is a risk of disorder or violence. Fundamentally it aims to provide a window into the world of the 'carnival fan' groups and produce an account that will be understandable to those outside this subculture, but also recognisable to those within it.

Defining the subject matter for this book was a difficult task, as is explaining why it was that I chose to research this subculture of football support. Academic interest in the activities of match-going fans developed largely in the 1970s, but focused not on the majority of fans, but instead on the activities of the 'football hooligans', who, it was claimed, vandalised property and fought at matches. As the work of the 'Leicester School', Stanley Cohen (2002) and Geoffrey Pearson (1983),[1] among others, demonstrated, fighting and disorder had always occurred at football matches and in other social environments. It is also probable that the media response to the disorder or 'hooliganism' that occurred during this time exaggerated its prevalence and severity (Hall, 1978; Pearson, 1998). However, the increasing number of fans travelling to away matches from the 1960s onwards certainly provided more regular opportunity for confrontation between rival fan groups. Most importantly for the purposes of this book, it is likely that many of those labelled 'hooligans' at the time were merely part of travelling groups of fans, some of whose members were engaged in this 'hooligan' activity. Many of these travelling fans, although not becoming involved in disorder or violence themselves, would have become impervious to the disorder that accompanied away matches, and some would have enjoyed the notoriety of being associated with a 'hooligan' fan group.

This book returns to this independent, hard-core, 'home and away' fan element at the turn of the century. I have labelled those within this culture 'carnival fans'. Defining and labelling the subculture that was the focus for this research was a challenging task, and not one which I believe lends itself to a quantitative judgement in terms of, for example, the number of matches attended. The fans with whom I carried out the research certainly attended many games, but typically they were more than just 'obsessives' who attended every match, 'trainspotters', 'ground-baggers' or 'anoraks' (King, 2002). One key element that these fans had in common was that they attended matches away from home as well as matches in the home stadium, but not everyone who travels to an away match is a carnival fan. Football 'tourists', who would stand among the travelling support and be ridiculed as they took photographs of their favourite players for ninety minutes were particularly evident in my latter work with fans of Manchester United. Additionally, travelling support will also contain 'anoraks': obsessive fans who would try to attend every match, purchase every programme and piece of memorabilia. Some, but by no means all of these 'anoraks', fell within the carnival fan subculture. A club's away support would also be bolstered by 'exiles' who were now living in the locality of the match and who only occasionally attended matches.

Using the label carnival fan for those in this particular subculture was the result of considerable deliberation. Originally, I intended to use the term 'hard core' to describe this type of fan, as I had in my Ph.D. thesis (Pearson, 1999), but the connotations with football violence were not appropriate for the majority of the research participants and the term suggested that these fans would be found at every match. While some of the carnival fans did attend all matches, this 'ticking off' or collection of matches and grounds was not as important a part of the subculture as it was for other fans. 'Mavericks' (Williams *et al.*, 1989) or 'rogues' were briefly considered, but discounted due to the connotations with disorder and the fact that the activities of the subculture formed a central part of the wider crowd's expression of support for the team, rather than being in some way marginalised. Borrowing the 'Ultras' label which originated in Italian football support was also considered, but the motivations of the Italian 'Ultras' were very different, with a primary focus on supporting and representing the team inside the stadium (Dal Lago and De Biasi, 1994; Sale, 2010).

As the research progressed, it became clear that for this group of fans, there were a number of shared motivations that differentiated them from other fan groups, be they 'hooligans', 'anoraks', 'part-timers' or 'armchair' (i.e. non match-going) fans. Heavy alcohol consumption, 'piss taking' and collective expressions of fandom were all essential to their match-day experience. For these groups, creating a 'carnival' at and around the match appeared to be as important as the match itself, unlike motivations of violence or 'ground bagging' that may appeal only to some. As we will see, viewing football fandom as an expression of carnival is not original (see Giulianotti, 1991, 1995; Brown, 1993; Hughson, 2002; Jones 2006), but not all fans have this motivation behind their expressions of support for a team. My research suggested that carnival fans were a subculture within the wider body of football fandom (both match-going and non match-going). Other fan groups participated occasionally in such expressions of carnival, but for those I have labelled carnival fans, attending football was *primarily* an expression of the carnivalesque. Following the rediscovery of Mikhail Bakhtin's work, there has been some criticism of the use of carnival as a 'mode of understanding' or 'episte-mological category' (Stallybrass and White, 1986: 6) in popular culture. However, my findings suggested that for a large number of fans, the experience of going to the match took on the form – and possibly the functions – of the now suppressed and over-regulated festive ritual of carnival.

The fans that were the focus for the research fulfilled a number of criteria. They attended matches, including away games, with regularity. But, equally importantly, they made an emotional investment in what it meant to be a football supporter (in addition to the emotional investment in the team they supported). For the carnival fan, supporting the team was not just about sitting in the stadium watching the match. It involved a physical and emotional demonstration of support for both the team and the club, most obviously demonstrated through football chants to urge the players on. It also involved an engagement with other carnival fans of the club. For this subculture, the football club was not just the players on the pitch, or the club's badge and history, but also the club's support. Carnival fans 'bought into' a culture of support, with its own rules, norms and even dress code; they were proud of this culture, reinforced it and celebrated it.

It should be noted here that I did not initially choose to research this particu-lar subculture; instead, during my observations of match-going fans more generally it became apparent that this subculture existed. They then became the focus of my research for a number of reasons. First, it was this subculture that was implicated in the 'hooliganism' associated with travelling support in the 1960s, 1970s and 1980s that received so much academic and media attention. Had the 'football specials' existed today in the form that they took in the 1960s and 1970s, then the fans I researched would probably have used that mode of transport, irre-spective of any disorder that might occur around them. Returning to this 'hard-core' travelling fan after the days of the reported mass disorder at football matches is therefore an interesting comparative endeavour (indeed some of the fans who were observed were part of that previous era). Many of the fans I carried out research with would also have been known as 'Category B' fans by the police in the late 1990s and early 2000s. This overly simplistic system of fan categorisation rated fans as Category A (posing no risk of disorder), Category B (might engage in disorder if it occurred) and Category C (those who travelled with the intention of fighting). During this project, it was rare for the research participants to be involved in disorder, but on occasion some became involved. This potential risk of disorder from the type of fans I observed is also recognised by the Leicester School, who identified 'maverick' fans (i.e. those who did not travel on official transport or packages) as tending to be 'at the centre of disorders' (Williams *et al.*, 1989: 202). Williams *et al.*'s scheme to reduce disorder abroad involving English fans recommended that the mavericks 'should be prevented completely from gaining access to matches' (*ibid.*: 205). While I fundamentally disagree with both the categorising system and the draconian recommendations, this type of fan – who in the post 'football-special' era prefers to travel independently – does pose a risk of being caught up in disorder even if they have no intention of causing trouble.

Second, this subculture was of interest in terms of social control and crowd management. My research initially focused on policing and legal responses to 'hooliganism', and large groups of travelling supporters provided potential targets for local hooligans, as well as being tightly regulated by local police forces. Usually the hooligan groups (which in Chapter 4 we will see were typically defined as those who travelled to matches with the intention of confronting rival 'firms') were quite distinct from wider supporter groups, but this was not always the case. For low-risk fixtures there was often insufficient interest in a 'firm' assembling, while at higher-risk fixtures, policing tactics or local practicalities sometimes resulted in the 'hooligans' and the carnival fans sharing or being corralled in the same location. Additionally, many of the 'hooligans' and the carnival fans knew each other and on the occasions that the boundaries between the groups were blurred, they chatted, drank and even sang together. A handful of the carnival fans were considered to be occasional 'hooligans': often young fans trying to establish a reputation, or older fans who were largely 'retired' from fighting at football. As a result, although I attempt to differentiate between the groups, this distinction was not always clear or absolute for all participants. For the police (and occasionally local 'hooligans'), of course, this distinction was even harder to make, especially where the carnival fans dressed like 'hooligans' and ended up in the same locations.

Finally, it is important to recognise the social impact of this group of fans upon football fandom more widely. In terms of creating 'atmosphere', their significance far outweighed their numbers; this subculture was largely responsible for creating the chants that became popular at matches, and also provided a focus for the chants of home fans. Their networks enabled them to promote their own style of support to rival fans and television viewers as the way that fans of their team behaved more widely, through song, dress and usually unspoken rules of behaviour. Their impact upon how English football supporters behaved was more significant than the smaller hooligan firms, or the larger number of occasional fans, and yet their behaviour has received comparatively little academic attention. Although carnival fan subculture forms a minority of match-going support as a whole, it dominated the away support of the clubs under observation; attending matches as a visiting supporter, it was simply impossible to escape it.

In observing these groups over a sixteen-year period, this book will also touch upon the seismic changes that have transformed football fandom since the mid-1990s. When I began my research at Blackpool FC in 1995, four sides of the stadium were terraced, with adult access costing £7. Blackpool now has an all-seater stadium, with tickets for the same section of the ground in 2011 costing £25. Policing and the law has also changed; in 1995, around 400 fans were subject to 'football banning orders', but this number now exceeds 3,000. Technology has also prompted a huge change in fan culture. Mobile phones and the internet played no recognisable role in carnival fan culture when my research began but in latter observations, nearly every supporter possessed a mobile phone and the majority posted on internet fan forums. When meeting a new member of the Manchester United carnival fans in 2011, they were just as likely to be introduced by their message-board 'handle' as by their real name. In practical terms, the changes in stadium development, pricing, social control measures and technology have revolutionised how the carnival fans behave. However, in analysing this culture over this period it was also noticeable how much remained static, and the way in which fan culture resisted the commercial development of football is also a theme in this book.

While this book will consider the changes that have swept through football and detail how the fans responded to these changes, it does not claim to be representative or comprehensive in terms of detailing the transformation of football. It provides a longitudinal and, it is hoped, thickly descriptive (Geertz, 1973) ethnographic account of the carnival fan, based on observations with fans of three different clubs. During the sixteen years of study I attended over 250 different match events and spent more than 2,000 hours in the field. However this is but a fraction of football matches occurring in this period and my findings cannot claim to provide a representative view of all football supporters (even at those clubs), or the 'carnival fan' groups of all football clubs. What I hope it will do is contribute significantly to the academic understanding of football fan behaviour, and maybe dispel some of the inaccurate and potentially harmful myths about football supporters.

Previous research into 'hooliganism'

There has been considerable academic research into the behaviour of football supporters since the 1970s, resulting in a number of theories explaining fandom and fan behaviour (mainly sociological, but also from criminology, psychology and socio-legal studies). It should be noted that until the 1990s almost all of these contributions focused purely on criminal and quasi-criminal fan behaviour at or around matches. From the late 1960s onwards, the disorderly actions of groups of football fans became known as 'football hooliganism' in the media and as hooliganism became perceived as a significant social problem, academic interest in the phenomenon increased.[2]

A history of the study of football hooliganism itself could fill an entire chapter of this book but I do not intend to go into the debates in detail, especially as this book is not primarily about hooliganism. More in-depth accounts of the different approaches and theories can be found in Armstrong (1998: 14–20), Giulianotti (2000: ch. 3), Frosdick and Marsh (2005: ch. 6) and Stott and Pearson (2007: ch. 3). The disagreements between various camps have been well documented, in particular those surrounding the 'Leicester School' (led by Eric Dunning at the Sir Norman Chester Centre for Football Research at Leicester University), which was the dominant source of academic thought on the topic during the 1980s. In his reply to critics of the research, Dunning (1994: 128) argued that the 'Leicester School' label was misleading as not all of his colleagues fell under the structural figurationalist umbrella influenced by Norbert Elias's work on the 'civilising process' (see Elias, 1978; Elias and Dunning, 2008). While my own findings on the causes and nature of football crowd disorder contrast sharply with the figurationalist approach, they do draw upon some of the previous work from the Leicester School, in terms of their socio-historical work on media representations of football crowd disorder throughout the twentieth century in *The Roots of Football Hooliganism* (1988), and the empirical findings set out in *Hooligans Abroad* (1989). The (pre-1991) Leicester School approach argued that incidents of hooliganism resulted from the actions of rougher sections of the community that had not been incorporated into the 'civilising process'. 'As one can see, in Britain at any rate ... football hooliganism is related in a complex way to the class structure ... At its roots, if we are right, football hooliganism is ... a long-established subculture of aggressive masculinity that is predominantly but by no means solely working class' (Murphy *et al.*, 1990: 12–13). The class-based element of this explanation was soon criticised as not explaining why some 'hooligans' did not come from these 'rough working class' subcultures or why disorder only occurred at a minority of matches.

The criticism that the Leicester School approach did not adequately explain why disorder did not occur more regularly came particularly from the social–psychological approach, which began to gain pre-eminence in football crowd research in the early 2000s and was soon influencing public policy and policing tactics across Europe. Drury, Reicher, Adang and Stott were the chief proponents of this school of research into crowd behaviour and policing, developing and applying the elaborated social identity model (ESIM) of crowd behaviour. Between 2000 and 2006, much of my fieldwork was carried out with Clifford Stott, some as part of a series of projects investigating good practice in the policing of English fans abroad funded by the UK Home Office and the Economic and Social Research Council (ESRC). The social identity model stated that mass disorder at events such as football matches was made possible by the existence of a shared social identity among participants within the crowd which was radically affected by intergroup interaction (Stott and Reicher, 1998; Stott *et al.*, 2001, 2007). The theory suggested that changes to this social identity were caused not by the internal psychology of those with a predisposition to 'hooliganism', but by external influences upon the crowd, that could lead to otherwise good-natured crowds becoming disorderly. This departed significantly from the Leicester School's explanation which, it was argued, failed to grasp the intricate dynamics of why crowds were at times disorderly, but at other times entirely manageable. To the social psychologists, the Leicester School's arguments suggested that while the culture of 'aggressive masculinity' remained predominant in football crowds, disorder would usually occur, which it clearly did not. The ESIM account also put forward compelling arguments as to why, in football 'riots' abroad, it was typically not the 'known hooligans' who were involved and arrested, but fans with no previous criminal convictions. For my research into predominantly non-hooligan fans, this was an exceptionally important body of work and although I approached the subject from a different discipline, I found the ESIM account compelling and have been heavily influenced by it.

Participant observational and ethnographic accounts of fandom and hooliganism

There have been a number of ethnographic descriptions of football fans and football 'hooligans' (see Hughson, 1998) that have provided extensive data against which the findings from this research can be tested. The major ethnographies of football fan groups thus far have provided findings recognisable to my own experience with carnival fans and have challenged many of the accepted media-led understandings of what it is to be a fan or a hooligan. Many of these authors have not been afraid to 'get their hands dirty' when it comes to their fieldwork, and a number have put themselves in harm's way in order to gather data. However, while the findings are valuable and some of the analysis provides us with the tools with which we can understand the culture (e.g. Marsh's 'rules' of disorder and Giulianotti's use of 'carnival') the picture is by no means complete. Some of the work, particularly that carried out before the Taylor Report of 1990 transformed football stadiums and led to the pricing out of large sections of the traditional football support, is now highly dated. I will also argue in this book that recent technological developments have also been playing a huge part in defining and shaping fan culture – this has not, to date, been seriously addressed. Furthermore, there are some significant disagreements with previous findings on issues such as causes and severity of violence, and the role of drugs and alcohol.

The first major ethnography of football fans came from Marsh, Rosser and Harré (1978), who carried out interviews with, and observations of, fans of Oxford United in the 1970s. It would appear that their observations were carried out by use of a video recorder set up outside the terrace under scrutiny, and thus provided incomplete access to the field in comparison with later ethnographies based on extensive participant observation. However, their efforts did provide an attempt to access and describe the life-world of the fans through more than merely a selection of 'white room' interviews, so their work is fundamentally ethnographic in nature. They found that terrace life was rigorously structured, with 'career' paths for younger fans, and that violence was not as serious or dangerous as it may at first appear, with clear rules of what was 'acceptable' and a general fear of unregulated violence. Marsh's findings are undoubtedly dated, both in terms of the physical changes to football stadiums and the changing nature of 'hooliganism', but much of the data is still relevant in explaining the structure of the football terrace and the relative lack of serious injuries and fatalities in football crowd violence. In the early 1980s, John Williams carried out participant observation with fans of England and English clubs abroad, the findings of which are set out in *Hooligans Abroad* (1989). Williams's data told a story of English football supporters being routinely attacked by local fans, being poorly policed and then becoming involved in disorder. In that sense his findings were similar to the data uncovered by my own research with Clifford Stott detailed in *Football Hooliganism: Policing and the War on the English Disease* (2007). However, the subsequent analysis of this data indicated that the figurational structuralist approach of the Leicester School (as it was) was superimposed onto the actual findings even when they did not support it.

The 1990s saw a number of ethnographies of fans and hooligans that developed the debate over fan behaviour and 'hooliganism'. Gary Armstrong's ethnography with Sheffield United's 'Blades' (1998) is the most comprehensive study of a 'hooligan' group to date. His findings echoed those of Marsh in questioning whether football hooliganism was as serious a social issue as it had been portrayed. Armstrong also demonstrated that rather than being 'mindless' thugs, being a member of 'the Blades' provided significant, and useful, social currency. Armstrong was heavily criticised by Dunning *et al.* for downplaying the seriousness of violence at football matches and 'going native' (discussed in Chapter 1), but my own findings suggest that Armstrong's data authentically portrayed the levels and severity of football crowd violence. Richard Giulianotti's ethnography of supporters of the Scottish national team at the 1990 World Cup and 1992 European Championships casts light upon the 'tartan army', who, in contrast to their English neighbours, were largely perceived as peaceful and good-humoured travelling fans. Giulianotti revealed how Scottish supporters travelled independently in huge numbers, were often drunk and rowdy but yet rarely became involved in disorder. Giulianotti used the metaphor of carnival to explain the behaviour of these fans, and his focus not on 'hooligans' but on ordinary supporters (albeit ones who Williams *et al.* would have defined as 'mavericks') indicated a change of focus in the 1990s in the study of football supporters.

In line with Redhead's argument that 'serious study' of football fandom should not merely concentrate on 'football hooliganism and macho posturing' (1993: 5), other ethnographers have also focused on football supporters expressing 'traditional' forms of fandom, most notably Adam Brown (1993) and Antony King (2000, 2003). Both detailed how Manchester United supporters behaved, particularly at European away matches, during the 1990s, highlighting serious problems in the traditional explanations for the causes of 'hooliganism', and the lack of a clear differentiation between the 'fan' and the 'hooligan'. King (2002) also identified the phenomenon of traditionalist football supporters resisting 'new-consumerist' fandom, a theme which reoccurs in this book. Other ethnographic work of note in this field includes Millward's (2006) study of fan viewpoints on European away matches (of particular relevance to this study due to its analysis of the behaviour of fans on internet message boards) and Rookwood's (2008) intensive and thorough research into the views of fans (particularly of Liverpool FC) that reflect a number of my own findings from Manchester United fans. Finally, a more detailed ethnographic account of the events in Marseilles, Charleroi, Munich and Rome described in this book can be found in Stott and Pearson (2007).

Fan confessionals and 'hoolie-lit'

There have also been a large number of books written in the first person by fans and self-confessed 'hooligans' about their own experiences. I have treated these self or auto-ethnographies, particularly by those professing to have been hooligans, with extreme care due to concerns about authenticity and bias. This is not to discount their value completely; although verifying specific incidents was usually impossible, some accounts were instantly recognisable to my own experiences and observations as being reflective of the wider subculture. Colin Ward's *Steaming in: The Journal of a Football Fan* (1994) is one such work, which I found to portray the subculture of the hard-core travelling fan in a manner instantly recognisable to my own findings. The same can be said for the likes of Kurt's *As the Reds Go Marching on* (1995) and White's *Are You Watching Liverpool?* (1994), which both detailed a Manchester United fan culture also reflected by research participants in this study. One of the most influential fan auto-ethnographies remains Nick Hornby's Fever Pitch (1992). Growing up, he was a middle-class, out-of-town fan who hated football violence and expressed a liking for all-seater stadiums – opinions that were the antithesis of what the carnival fans (many of whom were also middle class and out of town) believed watching football was about. This demonstrates the difficulties in viewing football fans as a homogeneous body with similar motivations and interpretations of what being a football fan is really 'about'.

Hornby prefaces his account by bemoaning the lack of true 'fan' accounts in contrast to books written, 'for want of a better word, by hooligans' (*ibid.*: 12) and nearly twenty years on from its publication, fan auto-ethnographies such as *Fever Pitch* are overwhelmed by the amount of hooligan confessionals on the market (see Redhead, 2010). Some of these works, most notably Tony O'Neill's *The Men in Black* (2006) and *Red Army General* (2005) were 'must reads' for the research I carried out with fans of Manchester United. Although I could not verify the accuracy of most of the incidents detailed in O'Neill's accounts, their pages have become something of a bible for those United fans who had no experience of the current hooligan 'scene' or the activities of United fans in the 1970s and 1980s. In order to understand how many of the United fans view 'hooligans', books such as O'Neill's had to be understood as their contents formed the accepted historical reality of United's following, even if it was not always an authentic account of what actually occurred. Similarly, an understanding of the 'accepted wisdom' (whether accurate or not) about notorious hooligan gangs around the country (such as Chelsea's 'Headhunters' or West Ham's 'ICF') was also important when carrying out research with fans following the England national team.

For the most part, however, I felt unable to use the confessions of hooligans or former hooligans (the term 'hoolie-porn' has been disparagingly used to refer to this genre, 'hoolie-lit' might be more appropriate) as it was difficult to verify much of the detail within them. I found that those who claimed to have been involved in football violence (or claiming to be 'in the know') often told wildly varying tales. Most hooligan reports were of miraculous victories over rivals (usually against superior numbers); very few admitted when their firm had lost these confrontations. Disputes arose about the numbers involved and who 'won' the battles. Even when the same account of events was agreed on by the rival groups, there were often wildly differing interpretations of whose reputation was enhanced. For example, one famous incident of crowd violence involving West Ham United fans at Old Trafford in 1985 captured on film for the documentary 'Hooligan' (Thames Television, 1985), was described by United fans as an over-whelming victory and proof that West Ham's hooligans had never come to Manchester and 'got a result'. West Ham fans on the other hand claimed the result belonged to them as they stood their ground against overwhelming odds.

However, even if we can verify the accuracy of individual incidents, the hooligan confessionals simply do not provide an accurate version of the behaviour of football crowds (or even the hooligan groups themselves). Most of the accounts focus purely on when it 'went off', rather than giving a balanced account of times when 'the lads' chose not to fight, or could not find anyone to fight, or were prevented from fighting by the police. Hoolie-lit therefore provides a very unbalanced version of football crowd disorder that may suggest that hooliganism was more prevalent than it was. The assumption seems to be that hoolie-lit is not bought by readers who want to read about how games passed off peacefully – it is to provide entertainment in the form of describing exciting and dangerous crowd disturbances, and as such tends towards the sensational. Of the Brimson brothers, prolific writers of 'hoolie-lit', Redhead writes that they 'maintain that hooliganism has not completely disappeared [but] struggle to convince their readers that their examples of rucks and riots are really from the 1990s rather than earlier eras' (1997: 10). The view that such accounts were likely to be inaccurate was also one shared by participants in the current study:

> Dave: I take them [hooligan 'confessionals'] with a pinch of salt . . .
> Moston: They're exaggerated.
> Dave: Of course they are.
> Moston: Whether it's like they're purposefully exaggerated . . . I think sometimes in the heat [of the moment] you probably think it's ten times worse than it's . . .
> Freddy: Yeah. All that said, for as much bullshit as they are . . .
> Moston: They've got to fucking sell their books haven't they?

The media and popular press

There has also been substantial journalistic comment on the behaviour of football fans, and in particular 'hooligans', usually in the form of news reporting of incidents of crowd disorder, although occasionally through features where journalists go 'undercover' to discover the 'secret world' of the hooligan. One famous example of this was Donal MacIntyre's undercover investigation of Chelsea hooligans ('MacIntyre Undercover', aired BBC, 09/11/99). Unfortunately, the media has not always been a source of reliable data about the behaviour of football fans. The main criticism of media accounts of football crowds has been their tendency to exaggerate and sensationalise the nature, scale and seriousness of 'hooliganism'. Far from playing a passive role in simply reporting facts, the media – and the popular press in particular – have played an active role in constructing the phenomenon of football hooliganism (Pearson, 1998). In the 1970s, in particular, sensationalist reporting of hooliganism led to a moral panic over the problem (Cohen, 2002). This in turn led to an 'amplification spiral' (Hall, 1978) of increased public interest in the issue and pressure for newspapers, particularly the tabloids, to print more and more stories in increasingly sensationalist terms.

Reporting on incidents of football crowd disorder often used the metaphor of hooliganism as being a disease or sickness (Pearson, 1998) and other sensationalist reports on incidents claimed that incidents brought 'shame' upon the fans, the club, the game of football itself and even – with English fans abroad – the nation. It is generally accepted by the differing schools that have researched the phenomenon of football crowd disorder that between the mid-1960s and 1980s, the media over-reported (at least in contrast to previous levels) and sensationalised the problem beyond the actual reality of match-day disorder. While this problem has diminished since the 1980s, incidents of violence where video footage is available (such as the disorder between West Ham and Millwall in September 2009) are still reported in highly sensationalist terms. Conversely, other incidents of football crowd violence and disorder which were observed to occur regularly around domestic matches, but where footage was limited or unavailable, was typically not reported. As a result, media reports provide little assistance in helping us gauge the actual levels, severity and causes of hooliganism.

We should also be careful when relying upon the media to help us to understand what happened in individual incidents of disorder. As we will see, media reports of the violence in Marseilles in 1998 contrasted starkly with what was observed on the ground, both in terms of the events and their causes. One of the most outrageous examples of media misreporting of 'hooliganism' followed disorder in Stockholm in 1989 when England played in a World Cup qualifier. Newspapers reported huge numbers of England fans (one estimate put the numbers at 1,000) rioting in the streets: 'It's war' was the banner headline on the front cover of *The Sun* (07/09/89). Other reports explained how 500 England fans 'looted' a department store, and that at one stage English hooligans overturned a double-decker bus. The explanations for the disorder in Sweden simply did not tally with those from my own observations with England fans that started ten years later. Had the culture of supporting England abroad changed so dramatically in this period? The answer appeared to come from the only newspaper that departed from the sensationalised line on the disorder, *The Guardian* (08/09/89). The paper sent a reporter to Stockholm after the match to speak to the police, eyewitnesses, and – significantly – the bus companies and owner of the department store that was reported as being looted. According to these witnesses, the numbers involved in the disorder were significantly lower than had been reported, no looting had taken place, and all double-decker busses remained accounted for. Furthermore, the explanations of England fans returning after the match – which were dismissed by most commentators at the time – seemed to match the way in which disorder at England matches observed in later years developed: attacks on the English by local fans, ticketing problems, and one minor incident leading to an overreaction by riot police that rapidly escalated disorder.

I am aware that in analysing what happened on this occasion it appears that I am essentially taking one media explanation as being more reliable than others. However, as my research progressed, the reports of mass looting and unprovoked rioting seemed increasingly absurd in contrast to my own findings. Nevertheless, whether the explanation of the disorder provided by the fans is true or not, the reporting of the 1989 disorder clearly demonstrates the problem with relying on media reports of football hooliganism. In short, it was in the commercial interest of both the popular press and the hoolie-lit authors to give the impression that football hooliganism was more serious and dangerous than the reality. It is for this reason that ethnographies of match-going fans are so important in attempting to provide an impartial and (as far as is ever possible) value-neutral description of what does happen when large numbers of carnival fans travel to support their team.

Notes

1 No relation to the author.
2 This is not to claim that football crowd disorder was a new phenomenon or one deserving of such media attention. *Hooligan: A History of Respectable Fears* (Pearson, Geoffrey, 1983) details how similarly disorderly groups to 'football hooligans' caused concern among the media throughout the twentieth century and before. Stanley Cohen's *Folk Devils and Moral Panics* (2002: xxxiv) contends that the media have exaggerated instances of disorder to create moral panics that are disproportionate to the actual seriousness of the problem. The 'Leicester School' also carried out extensive historical research that revealed instances of football crowd disorder taking place with regularity throughout the century (Dunning *et al.*, 1988).

1

Ethnography: theory, method and practice

What is ethnography?

This monograph aims to provide an ethnographic account of the subculture of 'hardcore', home-and-away English football supporters that I have labelled carnival fans. An ethnography is the result of a two-stage process. First, I needed to try to access the intersubjective 'life-world' (Husserl, 1931) of the supporter groups, spending time with them and trying to understand their behaviour, motivations and their interpretations of the world around them. Second, I then needed to try to describe this world in a way that would be understandable to those outside 'the field'; i.e., those who may have no, or limited, experience of football crowds. I also wanted to present my findings in a manner that would be largely understandable to the research participants. I felt this was important to verify my account of the culture as 'authentic'; an academically impenetrable account could never be tested against the understandings of research participants. Although in some parts of this book academic jargon was unavoidable, my aim was to keep descriptions accessible. Providing a description that (a) explains to a non-football supporter what the subculture is like; and (b) research participants will read and recognise, was a difficult and sometimes impossible balance to achieve.

Although I have attempted to follow the tradition of classic ethnographic works of subcultures operating on the edge of legality or acceptable behaviour, such as Whyte's *Street Corner Society* (1973) or Polsky's *Hustlers, Beats and Others* (1969), stylistically, the book is also influenced by more modern works. These include Armstrong's *Football Hooligans: Knowing the Score* (1998), Bourgois's *In Search of Respect* (2006; crack dealers in East Harlem) and Fonarow's *Empire of Dirt* (2006; fans of the 'indie' music genre), all of which detail in largely non-judgemental terms the culture, rationale and actions of the groups under observation. I have also attempted to avoid making 'moral' judgements about the behaviour of the research participants. The book neither condemns nor condones criminal activity, disorder or violence. It does, however, attempt to explain why these activities occur and also engages with policy debates about law and policing. At times it is certainly critical of legal and policing responses to football fans, but these criticisms assessed the law, strategies and tactics on whether they achieved their own stated objectives, in the manner of an immanent critique (Adorno, 1982), rather than being based on an external, value-based or moral judgement. I have sought to highlight areas where, from my experiences in the field, a particular piece of legislation, or a particular police tactic fails to achieve its own aims (usually of reducing the likelihood of disorder or increasing fan safety). As we will see, from my observations and interviews with fans, a number of social control strategies imposed upon football crowds actually *increase* the likelihood of disorder and violence.

One of the first questions the research participants asked of my work was what ethnography meant. At the most basic level, ethnography is a written representation of culture (Atkinson, 1994; Van Maanen, 1988). Ethnographies are predominately descriptive accounts (Emerson, 1983: 17) of groups, cultures or subcultures which reflect the intersubjective reality of those on the inside, but in a manner understandable to those on the outside. The idea of 'intersubjectivity' developed from phenomenology (Husserl, 1931, 1964); the belief that certain subjective states can be shared by individuals in a particular social group with shared cultural values and understandings (Berger and Luckmann, 1962). These values and understandings may be alien to those outside the culture, and the ethnographer's task is to try to make them comprehensible. As Van Maanen explains, 'The trick of ethnography is to adequately display the culture ... in a way that is meaningful to readers without great distortion' (1988: 13). The term derives from the ancient Greek for 'folk/people' and 'writing' and Herodotus' *The History*, completed in 400 BC, is credited by many as being the first ethnography (Willis and Trondman, 2000: 5). People are therefore the focus for ethnography and their experiences, actions and views should be central to the tale. Ethnography is also more than a mere research methodology, as is sometimes claimed (e.g. Dunning *et al.*, 1991: 469), and it is true that it can be as much an *art* of cultural description as well as a scientific mode of enquiry (Frake, 1983: 60; Atkinson, 1994).

Willis and Trondman explain ethnography as being, 'a family of methods involving direct and sustained social contact with agents, and of richly writing up the encounter, respecting, recording, representing at least partly *in its own terms*, the irreducibility of human experience. Ethnography is the disciplined and deliberate witness-cum-recording of human events' (2000: 5). Ethnography should provide what Geertz famously called 'thick description' of cultural and social activities (1973; 1983), rather than merely detailing what is apparent on the surface. An ethnographer must be able to identify and understand the motivations, intentions and interpretations of those he or she is researching, recognising that the same physical or observed action may have different meanings or motivations. It is therefore a complex process requiring a significant amount of time in the field uncovering and interpreting this 'flow of social discourse' (Geertz, 1973: 20). Ethnographic description is also inevitably microscopic (*ibid.*: 21). This ethnography is of a certain 'type' of football fan; it cannot claim to be representative of the lived realities of all fans, either at the clubs under observation or more generally.

We also need to recognise the limitations of ethnography in ever being able to provide 'pure' description of a culture or subculture (Atkinson, 1994). No matter how deeply the ethnographer is immersed within the field, and attempts to understand those within it, he or she can never exactly reproduce the lived reality of the culture. As Emerson points out, 'an ethnographic description can never be an exact, literal picture of some "thing" such as an event or a social action. It is always a theory-informed *re-representation* of that thing' (1983: 21). For a start, the ethnographer will always make choices, conscious or otherwise, about what is important enough to be recorded. The ethnographer's account will always itself be an interpretation of the observations made in the field; trying to rescue the 'said' of social discourse 'from its perishable occasions and fix it in perusable terms' (Geertz, 1973: 20). Phenomenological approaches to the study of cultures acknowledge that accessing the subjective reality (or stream of consciousness) of social actors under observation is unachievable (Schutz, 1972: 99). While ethnographers may attempt to understand and describe the interpretative processes of the social actors as they construct their reality around them, they are essentially hamstrung by their own interpretative processes and 'fore-meanings' (Heidegger, 1962). As a result, their account is merely one of their *own interpretation* of the life-worlds of the social actors, mediated through their own prejudices (Gadamer, 1989: 277–300). An ethnographic account can therefore never be totally authentic. Ethnography's aim may be to provide a pure description of the field, but in reality it provides only a representation of it, based on the interpretation of both the ethnographer and then, ultimately, the reader. Nevertheless, a rigorous ethnography remains the best way available to social researchers to cast light on the intricacies and complexities of the life-worlds of subcultures such as the carnival fans.

Ethnographies are best constructed from qualitative interviews and participant observation. Other methodologies such as external observation, structured interviews and questionnaires have been used to supplement findings for ethnographic discourse, but these on their own are usually insufficient to gain a true understanding of the complexities of a particular social group or culture:

> Gathering data in what ethnographers call 'white room' interviews – that is, in the researcher's environment, not the [research participant's] – takes very little time and commitment on the part of the researcher. Ethnographers don't work that way. When we enter a scene, we stay there, for months or years ... No ethnographer worth his or her salt would believe for a moment that informants' words spoken in thirty-minute, white-room interviews are even close to being sufficient to understand the complexities of and motivations for real-life behaviour. (Fleisher, 1998: 53)

Coming from the outside of a social group with no understanding of its workings (or with an understanding based entirely on previous external research) and asking questions in an interview or questionnaire will produce extremely limited results. Without an understanding of the group in question, how does the researcher know which questions to ask? Or what the answers given actually mean? For example, if, without having entered the field, I were to ask travelling football supporters on their opinions of 'football hooligans', how could I be sure that my view of what constituted 'football hooliganism' was one shared by them? If there were differences in their understanding of the term, then my interpretation of the data I received would be wholly inaccurate. Would I even be able to interpret the answers given without knowledge of the construction and understandings of those inside the field about what happens around them? Even in the most mundane situation or in the performance of everyday tasks it is necessary to understand how people construct, interpret and define the world around them (Garfinkel, 1984), and for a complex social field such as the football crowd, this is not easy to accomplish. Additionally, as we will see, there are many practical reasons why research participants may be unwilling to discuss sensitive issues with outsiders, or may even deliberately mislead them.

As a result, in order to gain any kind of meaningful understanding of a social group such as carnival fans it is necessary to enter into that social environment, observe the behaviour of those in it, speak with the actors and allow them to explain to you what is happening. Over a period of time the researcher utilising these methods hopes to gain an understanding of the actions, norms, motivations and understandings of that group: 'Ethnographers usually live in the community they study, and they establish long-term, organic relationships with the people they write about. In other words, in order to collect "accurate data", ethnographers violate the canons of positivist research; we become intimately involved with the people we study' (Bourgois, 2006: 13). In a field as open and accessible as the football crowd, given sufficient time, gaining an understanding of the field and the actors within it is the (comparatively) easy part. More challenging is being able to describe what is happening to those on the outside. This needs to be done in a way that is understandable to outsiders without this inside knowledge and which does not overlook significant findings due to the researcher 'going native'.

On the one hand, the ethnographer must provide *authenticity*; their findings must be as accurate to the experience of the research participants as possible. However on the other the researcher must retain the *distance* necessary to be able to interpret this experience to the audience. This requires the ethnographer 'to be in two places at the same time' (Pearson, Geoffrey, 1993: ix), the 'here' and 'there' as Geertz describes it, in an act of 'ethnographic ventriloquism' (1988: 145). The ethnographer will inevitably have the audience in mind when he or she is in the field, and can therefore never be a complete participant nor produce an account of pure description free of the researcher's own interpretations and (mis)understandings. Neither, as we will see, should an ethnographer try to be distant or in some way 'objective', or else they can never hope to understand their research subjects or produce authentic 'thick description' of the field. Geoffrey Pearson sums up all that the ethnographer can hope to achieve:

> What is required of an ethnographer is neither full membership nor competence, but the ability to give voice to that experience, and to *bridge* between the experiences of actors and audiences, 'authenticity' and 'distance'. Just as a boxing commentator does not need to slug it out over twelve rounds to bring a fight to life, so the ethnographer must remain content to 'talk a good fight'. (1993: xviii)

Ethnography has proved particularly useful for describing social groups that are perceived as falling outside the 'norm', as it would be recognisable to the established order (e.g. academics, the media, politicians and the police). In particular it has seen considerable use in the study of 'criminal' or 'deviant' groups (Atkinson 1994: 29),[1] where policy makers have expressed bewilderment about 'why they do what they do'. Adler and Adler make reference to the use of ethnography by the Chicago School of sociology to describe these groups, and claim that 'these first ethnographers interpreted early-twentieth-century urban life for us' (1998: xii). As ethnography developed as a discipline, its use in gaining an understanding of these types of groups became clear; 'field research remains, no matter what the risks, the essential research method for uncovering the situated meaning of crime and deviance, for exposing the emerging experiential web of symbolic codes and ritualized understanding which constitute deviance and criminality' (Ferrell and Hamm, 1998: 9). In contrast, 'research methods which stand outside the lived experience of deviance and criminality can perhaps sketch a faint outline of it, but they can never fill that outline with essential dimensions of meaningful understanding' (*ibid.*: 10).

I must admit to some discomfort in using the terms 'criminal' and 'deviant' to describe the groups with whom I carried out this research. The criminal activity engaged in by these groups was – in the main – at the lower end of the legal spectrum of severity and in terms of potential harm to others substantially less than, for example, those who drive over the speed limit. And yet it is unlikely that car drivers who speed would be described as a 'criminal' group. Likewise, the term 'deviant' is extremely loaded, although there is no doubt that the groups under observation did deviate from the norms of social life when they attended matches. Indeed, as I will argue, this deviation from the humdrum of everyday life, in the search of the carnivalesque became the very reason why these groups gathered together and attended football matches.

Participant observation

Without rigorous fieldwork of a particular kind it is impossible to engage in the practice or discipline of ethnography. If we want to get anywhere near being able to describe the intersubjective 'life-world' of the groups in question, and the '"nitty-gritty" of how social actors experience and attempt to penetrate and shape their conditions of experience' (Willis and Trondman, 2000: 14), we need to find a way of gaining access to the field and of understanding the interpretations and understandings of those within it. Ethnographers do this by attempting to immerse themselves within the field in order to identify, adopt and reproduce those understandings. The method of participant observation provides the most rigorous way to achieve this internal understanding of such social groupings (Bruyn, 1970: 69–70, 204; Sellitz *et al.*, 1965: 283). This method of investigation, 'involves the researcher … taking a particular role within a culture in order to examine at first hand the social situation from a participant's point of view' (Burgess, 1991: 98), and is especially effective, 'for studying the subtle nuances of attitudes and behaviours and for examining social processes over time' (Brabbie, 1989: 285).

Additionally, participant observation can overcome problems which seriously hamper interviews, most obviously 'the discrepancy between real and verbal behaviour' (Friedrichs and Ludtke, 1975: 6, see also Becker and Greer, 1970: 138–9) and between what is *directly observed* and what is *recalled* in an interview situation (Sellitz *et al.*, 1965: 201). Mistakes, exaggerations and lies by interviewees are therefore circumvented. This is particularly important when carrying out research into groups where criminal activity is taking place, where bravado is common and where sudden emotional pressure can lead to spontaneous and uncharacteristic behaviour. All these apply to the football crowd. The phenomenon of fans 'acting tough' and exaggerating their involvement in hooliganism was well known among the research participants in this study. On occasion I was informed that certain individuals were 'bluffers' – claiming for the sake of bravado that they had been involved in incidents they had not. As Freddy, a Manchester United fan, pointed out during the course of my research: 'If they're telling you to begin with, that's a good indication. Most of the people who would do that [hooliganism] on a regular basis – and I don't know a lot, I know a few – wouldn't go on about it'. Furthermore, fans wanting to exaggerate the importance of their team's hooligan element would often provide misleading information on the duration and seriousness of violence and the numbers involved. Conversely, 'hooligans' who participated in serious criminal violence were unlikely to confess their crimes to me for fear of being reported to the authorities. On one occasion, the author of a hooligan 'confessional' explained that his book did not contain half of the activities that he had been involved in, due to his fear of repercussions. Additionally, football hooligan 'gangs' have previously been targeted by undercover police officers and journalists and during my research I was mistaken for both.

Finally, even when the risk of deliberate deception was not a problem, the answers research participants would give in 'white room' interviews about how they and others behaved in the field may not reflect what actually occurs. 'There are interesting discrepancies between what people say in isolation and the way in which they behave when they are under group pressure' (Festinger and Katz, 1953: 72) and this is particularly true in areas with a strong influence of intergroup interaction and where decisions are highly spontaneous. Fans who, under a calm interview situation, claim they would never become involved in disorder, may act very differently in a crowd causing such disorder, when they are influenced by a sudden change in emotion, a passionate crowd, the influence of drugs or alcohol or the influence of aggressive rival fans or various policing strategies. Another warning of the dangers of relying purely on interviews rather than observations, can be found in Marsh's account of an interview with a group of Oxford United fans, who initially provided a very graphic account of the prevalence and seriousness of crowd violence at matches. Marsh then played the recording back to them, but upon hearing their own account, one interviewee said, 'Well, it sounds a bit bad doesn't it? It's not always like – not always as bad as that'. They proceeded to give a different account of the seriousness of the disorder, highlighting the fact that disorder did not always occur and that very few people were actually injured (1978: 93–5). Marsh's conclusion was that 'football fans construct not a single reality but two distinct realities. On the one hand they view events on the terraces as being bloody and dangerous and on the other they see the same events as orderly and safe' (*ibid*.: 95). It also demonstrates the potential dangers of relying purely on interviews (or 'confessionals') to investigate the behaviour of football crowds.

Another reason why participant observation is beneficial for ethnographic study is that an observer will report forms of behaviour which may be alien to him/her, but which would seem 'normal' – and thus unnecessary to explain – to a member of that field during an interview. There are many types of behaviour that research participants may 'take for granted' and which would escape awareness and 'resist translation into words' in an interview (Sellitz *et al*, 1965: 201–2) and yet such behaviour may be significant. Participant observation, on the other hand, allows the researcher to make their own choice as to which behaviour to describe. However, although this is beneficial, it is also worth noting that where a participant-observer also becomes *accustomed* to the same types of behaviour, the problem of 'taking it for granted' re-emerges (*ibid*.: 215) in the form of 'going native' (discussed below).

The second defining feature of this type of empirical research is the requirement of *participation* within the field. The advantages of observation involving some kind of participation lie in the researcher being able to merge into the environment and thus lead to as little distortion of the 'natural' situation as possible. In other words, participation by the researcher results from their desire to avoid obtrusiveness or reactivity by those under research (Friedrichs and Ludtke, 1975: 34). Additionally, more information may become available than to a non-participating observer. As a participant, I was welcome to 'hang around' with groups of fans and learn about experiences and attitudes from what was heard and seen. In other words, I was able to learn the 'answers' without having to ask questions to this effect (Whyte, 1973: 303). As a participant I was also more likely to be personally affected by responses to the behaviour of the group, and feel an emotional response that was I hope comparable to that of others in the field. To take an obvious example, participating in heavy alcohol consumption with the fans meant that when confrontations occurred, there was a greater chance I was experiencing how these 'felt' to the drunken fans, rather than being a sober observer trying to interpret why drunken fans were reacting in such a way. Another example came from an incident where I was assaulted by stewards, falsely accused of a criminal offence and then ejected from a stadium. While I had heard and also witnessed such instances, participation provided me with an opportunity to actually *experience* what was a constant threat for carnival supporters at matches away from home.

Covert versus overt participant observation

Participant observation within a football crowd provided an excellent 'strategic position' for securing relevant and accurate data, providing the 'least limited entrée to relevant situations' and causing 'the fewest changes in the field' (Friedrichs and Ludtke, 1975: 22). Avoiding 'distorting the field' is a key element of successful participant observation. An ethnography is meant to be a description of how a particular group or culture behaves, not merely of how they would behave if they knew they were being observed. Standing in a football crowd as an overt observer may significantly influence how members of that crowd would behave; some may try to impress the observer while others may tone down unlawful activity for fear of being reported. Indeed, many police forces use overt 'spotters' and handheld camcorders to control as well as merely monitor 'risk' supporters.

Furthermore, an overt observer in a football crowd also has the potential for influencing how police and stewards may act towards the crowd. My own experiences, and O'Neill's ethnography of police at football matches, indicate that police officers do not always 'play it by the book' when it comes to the policing of football crowds. Some officers adjust tolerance limits upwards at matches, allowing fans to swear, goad opposition supporters and generally 'let off steam' (O'Neill, 2005: 69) in a way which in other contexts may lead to censure or even arrest. Other officers may lose their temper with fans (*ibid.*) and during my research I witnessed numerous incidents of unlawful assaults on supporters by officers, along with more persistent bullying, harassment and provocation of football crowds. Would these officers have behaved in this way had they been aware of my role in observing the crowd? On the limited evidence I could gather from instances of policing when the police knew I was present to those where they did not, it was impossible to make a definitive claim on this, but the potential for distortion of the field is clear. In short, the overt participant observer 'can't help but contaminate the ... environment in some degree' by their presence (Polsky, 1969: 128).

Therefore the best way to conduct participant observation – in terms of gathering undistorted data – is to not reveal that you are an observer to the research participants. In this case, to pretend to be a normal football fan, sharing only the aims and objectives of those around you, so that your presence does not alter the field. The technical advantages of covert research methods are recognised[2] but the method requires an element of deception of those around you, particularly when it comes to answering questions about your job, or when it comes to making notes of observations. As such, there are very serious ethical problems with covert participant observation as a research method which have been debated in detail (e.g. Bulmer, 1982; Crow *et al.*, 2006; Erikson, 1967). The codes of ethical practice in the social sciences caution against the use of covert methods. The Statement of Ethical Practice for the British Sociological Association states that the use of covert methods may only be justified in certain circumstances (for example where access to the field would otherwise be prohibited), and the ESRC Research Ethics Framework states that, 'Deception (i.e. research without consent) should only be used as a last resort when no other approach is possible'. The British Society of Criminology Code of Ethics goes further, ruling that covert methods are only justifiable where the topic under study is of 'exceptional importance' (although how this is defined is not explained). However, despite these misgivings, the ethical codes and committees in the social sciences largely suggest that covert research can be justifiable 'in situations where the field would otherwise be closed to research, where overt techniques would unduly distort the field leading to inaccurate results, or where the safety of the researcher is at stake' (Pearson, 2009).

In the last decade, the authority of the research committees in the social sciences has been called into question by a number of researchers. Hammersley (2006: 5) for example has expressed concern about the content of the codes and the role of the committees, arguing that they rely upon medical and psychological models of ethics (based upon the principle of 'informed consent') that are often inappropriate for research in the social sciences (see also Coomber, 2002) and suggesting that ethical committees are not always in the best position to determine what research should proceed. Crow *et al.* contend that the creation and implementation of 'hard-and-fast' rules are not always the best way to approach questions of methodology and ethics in the social sciences, particularly in fields where access is impossible by overt methods (2006: 88, 95). The drive towards increased ethical regulation of academic conduct in social research, beginning in the late 1970s but only 'fully taking hold' in the 1990s is described by Adler and Adler as 'The Dark Ages' for ethnographic research and has 'made ethnographic work on criminal and deviant groups almost impossible to conduct' (1998: xiv). This increasing drive by ethics committees towards restricting covert methods, means that academic researchers, 'are steered towards topics that are as "mundane" as possible' (Crow *et al.*, 2006: 89), which in turn limits the power of researchers to 'make a difference' to areas that are not easily accessible. As Taylor and Bogdan note, 'As researchers, we recognise the fact that to withdraw from all morally problematic situations would prevent us from understanding and, indeed, changing many things in the world in which we live' (1984: 71).

My early research into football crowds was conducted from a completely covert position. To the fans of Blackpool FC, I was merely a student at Lancaster University studying law (not a Ph.D. student studying legal responses to football hooliganism) and when asked about where I came from, I provided an address of some relatives living in the town, so as not to appear an outsider. As a result, I was both deceiving and spying upon the fans, acts I justified in three ways. First, I wanted (as far as possible) undistorted data that I felt could not been obtained had my intentions been overt. Second, I was concerned that if I was open about my research role I would not have gained access to the field, or my access would have been curtailed due to the fact that many football fans are mistrustful of academic researchers (Armstrong, 1993: 23–5; Stott *et al.*, 2001: 364). Stories of previous researchers and undercover journalists being attacked also made me aware of a potential safety risk of revealing my true intentions. Finally, I believed that my observations would not be harmful to the research participants and that instead I would be giving voice to many of their concerns about issues such as unfair legislation and abusive policing practices.

Revisiting my initial justifications as a more experienced academic, they now appear overstated. Although I maintain that I could not have gathered data on Blackpool in particular without remaining covert, and that my covert nature meant I was less likely to come to physical harm from those I was researching, my other justifications were more problematic. As my research progressed and I started to disseminate my findings in conference papers, academic publications and in the media, it became clear that my covert research *did* possess the potential to cause harm to some of the research participants. Although participants were anonymous and no individual was directly harmed, my findings occasionally had an impact upon how fans were policed. While I was pleased that the work carried out as part of the wider ESIM project made some matches (specifically games at Euro 2004) safer and more enjoyable for most fans,[3] it could potentially cause indirect harm to the 'hooligans', who utilised indiscriminate and aggressive policing to help to create disorder, but who had never given me permission to research them.

Regarding distortion of the field, the deeper I became embedded with the fans, the more my own role as 'participant' had the potential to effect what went on around me. Although I tried to act in adherence to field 'norms', on occasion I found myself altering events. For example, in an incident during Manchester United's visit to Istanbul in 2009, one of the research participants, Denis, went to confront another fan. My reaction as a good participant-observer should have been to allow the confrontation to occur, but my instinct was to prevent it as I knew that violence would occur and that he might be identified and arrested. My attempts to prevent the confrontation ultimately failed, but I could have seriously distorted what would have 'naturally' occurred (the delay I caused to the confrontation may well have distorted the field irrevocably anyway). On another occasion, when Martin was 'glassed' in a pub in Wolverhampton, I instinctively called for a first-aid kit from behind the bar and bandaged his bleeding head up. This played an important part in enabling him to attend the match, again, distorting the field. As a researcher, should I have stood back and observed what happened in both of these occasions?

I also had suspicions that when I was identified as a researcher by police (which happened regularly during the latter stages of my research when my role became known to several police 'spotters') this may have on occasion changed the way that the crowd I was in was policed. Judged against my objective of not distorting the field, the Istanbul and Wolverhampton incidents were technically weak pieces of fieldwork, but they were atypical of the role I usually took. Normally I tried to be a 'follower' when it came to decisions on, for example, pubs to go to, cities to stay in on Euro aways, where to stand in the away end, etc. and to act only in a way that reflected the norms of the groups with whom I was researching. As such, my actions in Turkey and Wolverhampton were precisely what I thought others in the group would have done had they been in my position. However, the more embedded a researcher becomes in a group, the more their presence will disturb the field and influence the actions of those around them. While I maintain that covert observation possesses technical advantages over overt methods in terms of field distortion, the influence of a well-embedded field research over research participants is inevitable. This was one of the reasons why, in the summer of 2009, I 'broke cover' for good with the Manchester United supporters I was researching.

A number of the supporters of the group I intended on researching for the 2009–11 seasons were already aware that I was an academic with an interest in football (in addition to the police officers who were also aware of my work as an academic researcher in football crowd regulation). Some knew that I had already published one book on football supporters and that I had utilised my trips with United to gain data for this. However, in search of additional data for this book I decided to spend the 2009–11 seasons gathering more in-depth data for specific theories that I had developed in the preceding years but for which I was lacking verbatim evidence. For this I would need to record more conversations and inter-views, something which would be difficult to do while remaining covert. Increasingly I also felt an ethical obligation to inform the group that I would be observing them throughout the season and, crucially, I no longer felt that 'going overt' would restrict my ability to gain good data. I was already accepted within the group as a genuine United fan and appeared to be trusted despite my profes-sional role. As a result I did not think I would risk my access to the field by announcing I intended on carrying out ethnographic research and that this announcement would not unduly distort the field. Having already observed the group over a period of time, I believed I would also be able to recognise any major changes in behaviour as a result of my revelation.

As most of the group under research posted on a specific internet discussion forum, revealing my intentions was relatively easy. After a discussion with a number of members of the group about whether they thought my proposal would be accepted, I started a 'thread' announcing my research plans, explaining how this would affect them, reassuring them of anonymity and asking for people who did not want to be involved to contact me so that I could ensure I did not record their activities or conversations (whether virtual or real). I also asked the moderator of the site to keep the thread prominent so that new users would be made aware of it. Responses to the thread were overwhelmingly positive, with fans saying how they thought it was a great idea, that they looked forward to reading the book and they did not need reassurances about anonymity. Only one member of the group expressed concerns and asked not to be included (although they later changed their mind). Of course, this did not mean that informed consent of all research participants had been granted. As the group was a fluid one with new or casual members appearing all the time (some of whom who did not post on the forum), it was impossible to ensure that all members knew exactly what I was doing, why, and how it could affect them. Furthermore, as most of this group's activities involved relation and communication with external groups (other United fans, rival fans, bar and hotel staff, stewards, police, etc.), it was always going to be impossible to ensure that everyone under observation knew of my purposes. For example, the stewards who assaulted me (see Chapter 5) did not know that they were being observed at the same time. Informing all those under observation at any one given time was impossible and any attempt would have seriously distorted the field. Insisting that informed consent should be compulsory in observational research into social groups is pointless if observations of this group include the wider social context in which it conducts its activities.

Choosing the research participants

My research into football crowds began as an investigation into legal responses to 'hooliganism', but, as it developed, my focus changed from the small, tight-knit hooligan 'firms' (who were not always present), to the activities of supporters who travelled home and away and fitted into the traditional English fan stereotype – enjoying drinking, singing and being boisterous. These carnival fans vastly outnumbered their hooligan counterparts, and – for matches abroad in particular – were as likely to be involved in disorder. For the carnival fans, what happened on the pitch was often secondary to the fun to be had off it and the key elements of a successful trip tended to be congregating in large groups, alcohol consumption, the creation of 'atmosphere' and the engagement in, or witnessing of, humorous events that could be retold and even relived in the future. Significantly for debates on 'hooliganism', carnival fans did not travel to matches with the intention of 'causing trouble' (although on occasion *some* of the fans did become involved in violence).

As was stated in the Introduction, my use of the label carnival fan in this book is fairly fluid as it was not always easy to differentiate hooligans, carnival fans, 'anoraks', 'new consumer' fans or occasional fans. The fan groups were in a state of constant flux, with members coming and going and sometimes acting in different ways depending on the time of year or the match in question. Furthermore, in terms of the motivation to create the football carnival that I describe in these pages, some research participants were less driven by this motivation than others. The following traits were also common throughout the groups under observation (although not shared by all participants):

1 An enjoyment of away matches (particularly those abroad) ahead of the routine of home games.
2 A preference for travelling either independently or on packages that were not official (unless the official package was significantly cheaper).
3 At matches they preferred to stand rather than sit.
4 The wearing of colours was less prevalent than with other fan groups (where colours were worn, they were more likely to be unofficial or 'retro').
5 They would regularly engage in low-level criminal activity; indecent chanting, breaching of alcohol controls and on occasion throwing of (usually harmless) missiles and invasion of the pitch.

In other words the carnival fans were, to a greater or lesser extent, the breakers of rules and expected norms.

From my observations, carnival fan groups accounted for a small proportion of those who attended home matches, but a significant proportion of those who travelled away (for Manchester United and England, carnival fans made up the majority of travellers). Their rule and norm-breaking often made them a risk to public order, particularly at away matches; their travel (and drinking) arrangements, not being controlled by the club, meant they were often present under the radar of the police. They could also be mistaken for 'hooligans', and targeted either by local gangs or police (particularly abroad) as a result. Therefore for those concerned with managing football crowds, reducing public disorder and improving crowd safety, it is important to understand the behaviour and the motivations of these groups. Furthermore, understanding the subculture of these groups is of interest in itself, especially due to their unrepresentative influence on football fan culture generally.

At this stage it should be noted that this is not primarily an ethnography of *youth* culture or *working-class* culture. The age range of the fans in the groups varied widely (from the late teens to the late fifties), and attending large numbers of football matches is not easy for those on low incomes or welfare support. However, as we will see, what might be considered traditional 'working-class' values permeated much of the activities and interpretations of the fan groups, while many of the expressions of the carnivalesque at football could certainly be viewed as 'juvenile'. Most of the fans from the three teams under observation came from professional 'white-collar' jobs. While the majority of participants following Blackpool, and around half of those following United came from the immediate locality of the home stadium, both supports drew fans from further afield (both 'exiles' and 'out-of-towners'). Fans following England were drawn from all over the country.

Research at Blackpool FC

Between 1995 and 1998 I carried out covert participant observation among fans of Blackpool FC. Fieldwork for home games would typically start in the pub before the match, or sometimes when I actually entered the stadium, and would usually end at the clubhouse afterwards. For away matches, fieldwork would start when I either travelled to Blackpool to catch the coach to the match, or when I intercepted the train carrying the carnival fans, and end when I travelled back to Lancaster University (usually on the last train). Fieldwork was regular and intensive: in three-and-a-half seasons I attended seventy-eight matches, thirty-four of which were in the first season of my Ph.D. The existence of terraces at most grounds meant I could position myself where any incidents that interested me were occurring, or could approach fans I thought would speak with me. The major weakness of my research at this time was that in only viewing fan behaviour at and around matches, I was observing them out of their wider social context. In contrast with Armstrong's (1998) ethnography of the Blades, I was not living in the locality of the fans under observation and did not get the opportunity to witness their behaviour when matches were not taking place. As Armstrong notes, the groups involved in football 'hooliganism' are not just limited in their activities to matches involving their team, and their behaviour can only be properly understood when placed in its historical and social context. For Blackpool, where incidents with rival supporters away from matches have been reported as occurring with regularity (particularly in the holiday season), this was of particular relevance. The fact that I was not involved in social activities on non-match days meant that opportunities for really 'getting to know' the fans was curtailed and that I was unable to understand the dynamics of how a club with no regular 'hooligan firm' (at the time of my research) could produce a sizable group of 'hooligans' every couple of seasons for high-profile derby matches. Finally, my relatively short time in the field meant that I was unable to explain why Blackpool's reputation for hooliganism had diminished from the 1970s and 1980s.

During the period of my research, Blackpool played in the third tier of English football, averaging home gates of around 4,500 and taking around 1,000 away (increasing to around 4,000 at local derbies). The location of the team, in northern England's premier seaside resort, made them a popular draw for visiting fans, although the relatively high levels of unemployment (particularly out of season) meant that many of their fans were 'exiled' elsewhere. As a town, Blackpool's reputation was, and remains, as being a 'party' – and carnival (Stallybrass and White 1986: 179) – town and popular tourist resort, attracting around 10–13 million visitors a year.[4] It is a town with a reputation as a place of hedonistic abandon, popular with stag and hen nights and with this thriving night-time economy, a reputation for drink-fuelled violence and disorder. Sinclair (2009) describes it as 'Britain's Wildest Town'. As a result of this, Blackpool FC have tended to attract larger crowds of travelling supporters than other clubs at their level, and along with this travelling support (and fans of other teams who may be present in the town) this leads to an increased possibility for confrontation. Much of their supporters' identity was tied to the seaside location, and popular chants included, 'Sea-sea-seasiders', 'We are the nutters, we come from the sea', 'You've only come for the 'lumies' (i.e. the Blackpool illuminations) and 'Day trippers go home'. Another vital aspect of the club's identity for their fans were the team's colours of tangerine and for high-profile matches they would make a particular effort to show their distinctive colours with flags, balloons, face paint and even hairspray to complement the usual hats, scarves and replica shirts. Blackpool's home matches were played at Bloomfield Road, and during the period of the research, the ground was seriously dilapidated (it has since been completely rebuilt) with terraced areas on all four sides and a capacity of around 9,500. The 'atmosphere' at Bloomfield Road came primarily from the South Stand, with a seated upper tier and a terraced paddock (the 'South Paddock') below. The South Paddock had a reputation among the rest of the ground as being 'rowdy', and would frequently engage in crowd 'surges' and pitch invasions following important goals (if the team won the coin toss, they always chose to attack the South Stand in the second half).

Blackpool fans were chosen for research largely for practical reasons: their geographical proximity to Lancaster University, the ease of accessing tickets, and knowledge I had gained of their culture from attending games socially during my undergraduate degree. I was also aware of their 'reputation' for football-related disorder: the first reported murder as a result of 'football hooliganism' occurred in Blackpool in 1974, and during the 1970s and 1980s, their 'firm' was described as large, 'up for it' (Brimson and Brimson, 1996: 22) and 'headline seeking' (Allen, 1989: 84). Although by the 1990s the Blackpool fans themselves were not especially notorious for football violence, their fans had been involved in a number of disturbances in their local derbies against Preston and Burnley and I had seen numerous instances of violence and disorder in and around Bloomfield Road prior to 1995. As a result, I believed that Blackpool would have an organised hooligan 'firm', and that if I were to 'hang around' in the right places for long enough, I would meet them, enabling me to observe the effectiveness of legal responses to football violence.

Participant observation with Blackpool fans was usually a full-day experience, beginning the moment I was in the company of carnival fans and was thrust into this football subculture either through the fans' recognition of myself, or of my 'colours'. After this initial acceptance, it was expected that I was able to demonstrate a certain amount of knowledge accessible only as part of the culture of being a Blackpool fan. My integration into the group was also helped by my own physical characteristics and dress which enabled me to 'fit in' (Taylor and Bogdan, 1984: 32). Burgess notes that access into some groups is limited by the physical 'identity' of the researcher and many areas are 'off limits' to women, especially areas on the 'fringes' or 'depths' of society where 'masculine attitudes' are dominant (1991: 91). For the carnival Blackpool fans, such attitudes were the norm. As part of the group, I was expected to indulge in heavy beer drinking, swear, engage in masculine and sexist chants and adopt an aggressive pose should confrontation occur. The showing of emotions other than anger upon defeat was largely seen as 'feminine' and unacceptable. All these activities make up what is stereotypically considered to be overt masculine behaviour which the Leicester School argued was a major cause of football-related disorder (Murphy et al., 1990: especially ch. 6). Similarly, I was also helped by both my skin colour and my age. Physically I was therefore fortunate in being able to fit the 'criteria' of the typical home-and-away fan and was able to integrate into the subculture of carnival fans with little observable effect upon the group's behaviour. Other aspects of the fans' subculture were more difficult to pick up without previous access to this knowledge; slang terms were expected to be understood, along with knowledge of Blackpool's history (and that of local rivals) and their songbook. Additionally, an unspoken code of conduct existed which was necessary to follow so as to disrupt the field as little as possible. It was only acceptable in certain circumstances to boo Blackpool players or start a racist chant and pitch invasions only took place under certain circumstances. There was a wealth of implicit subcultural background 'language' and 'knowledge' which it was essential to pick up to be accepted (Taylor and Bogdan, 1984: 51–2) but once I was in possession of this currency, I was accepted by people who otherwise were total strangers. This language or knowledge also enabled me to conduct informal interviews as common interpretative ground was in place (see Becker and Greer, 1970: 134–6).

My participation involved staying with the group and 'shadowing' their actions; this usually meant drinking in a pub and discussing football, before going to the ground just before kick-off. Inside the ground, I would engage in chanting, crowd surges and the occasional pitch invasion in order to 'fit in' with the fans, before leaving the ground with them and at away matches either travelling back by coach or train (sometimes stopping at more pubs along the way) or at home matches simply going to a pub or club. The more matches I attended, the more I became accepted as a 'known face' and the easier it became to obtain data, particularly through informants. As a known face I would be kept informed as to what was happening both on and off the pitch, including rumours of potential confrontations and even sexual liaisons involving the few female fans in these groups. One of the drawbacks of participant observation (particularly covert observations) is that contemporaneous recording of data is difficult (Frankfort-Nachmias and Nachmias, 1992: 275; Sellitz, 1965: 210) due to practical issues and dangers of distortion. The vast majority of my observations were recorded as soon as possible on the day of the match to prevent information being lost or confused. Inevitably, trying to recall everything of note that had occurred during the entire day was impossible and much useful data was almost certainly forgotten.

Research with the England national team

Between 1998 and 2006 I undertook participant-observational research with fans of the English national team, mainly away from home, three years of which was carried out as part of a wider externally funded research project investigating the policing of English fans abroad. In terms of immersion in the field, away matches with England provided an opportunity to carry out highly intensive (albeit short) observations of carnival fan groups. From the departure lounge of the airport (usually the day before the match), until the flight back (usually the day after), I had the opportunity to observe and talk with England supporters. In the host city I would inevitably bump into the same fans in town squares, bars and restaurants, and would engage in conversation, be introduced to friends and generally 'hang around' with, and as part of, the fan groups. For international tournaments, this physical immersion in the field often lasted for a number of days at a time. On several occasions I found myself camping on campsites or fields near the host city, surrounded by English supporters for the days immediately surrounding the match. Here, fieldwork was a twenty-four hours a day ordeal, where interesting observations or conversations could occur while brushing your teeth or queuing for the shower. Even asleep in my sleeping bag my fieldwork was never truly on pause as being woken by a drunken fan tripping over the tent or launching into a chant could occur at any time during the night. An additional strength of my research with the England national team was that for a period it was carried out as part of a wider research team which meant that it was possible to be gathering data from more than one location at once, and that when incidents occurred I usually had another pair of eyes to assist me interpret what was happening. Working in pairs or small groups also assisted when carrying out covert research as I felt I 'stood out' less than if I was observing alone.

Fans of the England national team had both a historical and contemporary reputation for becoming involved in large-scale 'hooliganism' and when they qualified for the 1998 World Cup in France, disorder and violence was widely predicted by the media. I travelled out for the first two weeks of the tournament for what would become a pilot study for a series of observations with fans of the national team that would take place over the next eight years. My research with England was to be of a different nature to that with Blackpool. Instead of a single longitudinal study running over a period of years, each trip with England proved to be a different, short but very intense ethnography with different groups of fans. Typically I would travel out, often with a colleague, one or two days before England were playing, find where large numbers of England fans were gathering and join them. Occasionally I would meet the same individuals, but usually each trip would see me among a different group of England supporters. This meant that observational data was limited as it took the supporters out of their social and economic context and focused only on their behaviour over a short time period. However the intensity of these observations provided excellent data about how the carnival fans of the England national team conducted themselves abroad, and how effective social control policies and practices were upon them.

My observations with the national team took in four major international tournaments: the 1998 World Cup in France, the 2000 European Championships in Belgium/Holland, the 2004 European Championships in Portugal and the 2006 World Cup in Germany. Additionally observations were also carried out at a number of World Cup and European Championship qualifiers and friendly matches in England, Germany, Holland and Poland. In terms of my research on hooliganism and policing, this period was a fascinating one. During my first observation, in Marseilles, I witnessed arguably the largest riot involving English football supporters, and two years later in Charleroi I observed another major incident of disorder, and the first reported use of water cannon on English fans. Incidents of serious disorder and violence were also witnessed on a number of other occasions during this period, providing excellent data about why 'hooliganism' was occurring. However of equal interest was the fact that such instances of crowd disorder were relatively rare. Indeed, despite the much talked about risk factors of large crowds, lack of tickets, excessive alcohol consumption, the presence of rival supporters and poor results on the pitch, the majority of matches passed off without violence or disorder and the fans merely revelled in the carnival atmosphere.

Research with fans of Manchester United

From 2001, as part of the same project, I also began carrying out observations with fans of Manchester United on their European away matches. In 2007, I extended these observations to include domestic matches and provide a better overall picture of the subculture of United's extensive carnival fan groups. As a club, Manchester United also provided a stark contrast to Blackpool. Whereas Blackpool had been a lower-division club starved of on-pitch success, Manchester United during the time of my research were one of the most famous sports clubs in the world, winning the European Champions League in 2008. This success was also reflected in a match-going support, and carnival fan groups, that dwarfed Blackpool's; during the period of research, United's home attendance averaged around the 70,000 mark, with the majority of matches sold out and tickets, particularly for away matches, difficult to obtain.

My research here was initially assisted by the fact that I am a Manchester United supporter, although at the time I embarked upon my research not what I would call a 'carnival fan' or active within the groups I ended up researching. This meant that I already had access to the cultural currency of a knowledge of their history and chants and also, having been born in Manchester, had to work less hard to gain respect from other fans who were often dismissive of 'out-of-towners' and 'glory hunters'. Second, of course, it gave me the excuse to spend more time, and more money, watching United matches and talking about my team. That said, carrying out an ethnography of supporters of your own team is not as ideal as it may initially appear. Working with United supporters limited my enjoyment of the social experience, as I had to be more wary of the activities I engaged in, particularly to avoid distorting the field and also had to constantly be 'switched on' to making observations, looking for opportunities to interview, and recording field notes. The amount of time I spent paying attention to the team's performance on the pitch inevitably reduced. I also had to be careful not to research, or be seen to be researching, United's hooligan groups. By this point in my research, I was not primarily interested in the activities of 'hooligans' and I also did not want to be suspected of being a 'mole' should police intelligence on them lead to arrests for conspiracy. There was also, of course, no guarantee I would have been accepted within the 'firm' even if I had wished to focus my research upon them, certainly not without engaging in serious criminal activity.

In 2007, a visit to a match in Kiev brought me into contact with a distinct group of carnival fans who called themselves the Red Brigade. This group had its own internet forum on which fans would discuss previous football trips and plan future adventures. The group was by no means exclusive, or self-contained, and many members drifted in and out of it, but it provided an excellent focus for an ethnography of carnival fans. Over the next season, I got to know more and more of the members of the Brigade, and they began to trust me and know about my work until, in 2009, I asked if I could focus purely on their activities for the following season in order to gain more data for a book that would pull together the work I had been doing over the previous fourteen years. One outcome of this is that there is an undue amount of interview and verbatim conversational data in this book gained from the 2009–11 seasons in comparison to the seasons before this, when the data is largely only observational and recorded after the event.

The strength of my research with United fans, particularly the Brigade, was that I was now able to gain data about their behaviour outside the immediacy of the football match. Living locally gave me access to a wider and more varied life-world of some of the individuals; I could attend nights outwith the Manchester-based members of the Brigade, and also gain an insight into their 'normal' lives outside of football. This gave me a much better idea of how their behaviour around football changed from their behaviour in other contexts, which proved invaluable in interpreting their purposes when they attended matches. The major weakness of my research with United fans was the danger of bias in terms of how I interpreted and reported my observations. The ethnographic danger of 'going native' in particular would be more acute than my research with either Blackpool or England.

Going native

One major criticism levelled at ethnographic research and participant observation is that it is less 'objective' than experiment or non-participatory observation (Durkheim, 1964: 15, Friedrichs and Ludtke, 1975: 19, Sellitz, 1965: 214). Many researchers, particularly those managing quantitative data, argue that the observer's 'scientific role' should demand an emotional distance from the research subjects and that by becoming a participant in the field, the observer might lose sight of their role as a 'neutral' researcher and instead incorporate the values and prejudices they have learned as a participant, into their findings. The researcher may become so engrossed in his field that they go native and lose their research perspective and 'scientific detachment' (see Burgess, 1991: 266; Frankfort-Nachmias and Nachmias, 1992: 275). Friedrichs and Ludtke also note the 'intrasubjective problem' of 'taking on the values and semantics of the observed' as common 'observer errors'. They add that, 'the higher the degree of involvement ... the lower his impartiality towards [the subjects] and to the incidents which he is to observe' (1975: 30). Trow also highlights the problem of 'going native', 'to the point of accepting his subjects' view of their world uncritically in a manner detrimental to objective analysis' (*ibid.*: 342). Empathising with subjects within the field is an almost inevitable result of participant observation (Taylor and Bogdan, 1984: 20), but this can easily morph into the adoption of a 'sympathetic stance' where the views or values of the research subjects are promoted (Johnson 1983: 215) thereby negatively affecting the results of the research, which is considered undesirable (Silverman, 1993).

In a research field such as football crowd behaviour, where strong prejudices and opinions exist, and where close ties between observer and participant are forged, going native is a potential problem. In particular, it may be that my accounts of 'what happened' in certain situations were based on my own sympathies, or upon reputations of others that I became aware of (Friedrichs and Ludtke, 1975: 26). For example, if there was a general belief among carnival fans that the police abused their power, after a time immersed in the field, would my empirical view of police behaviour be prejudiced in this way? Likewise, would exposure to low-level disorder and instances of violence in football crowds lead me to normalise this behaviour? The Leicester School accused both Armstrong and Marsh of playing down the seriousness of football violence by judging it by the standards of the hooligans themselves (Dunning *et al.*, 1991: 464) when in fact the violence described by them sounded more serious than they claimed (1991: 466). The Leicester School 'suspected' that Armstrong in particular:

> may have succumbed to one of the most obvious pitfalls of participant observa-
> tion – the danger of 'going native'. Indeed, there are indications that he may have
> been 'native' from the outset. Thus, if he shares the values of the Blades, this
> would help to account for the fact that he was unperturbed by the violent
> behaviour they sometimes engaged in. (*ibid.*: 467–8)

However, being able to adopt the values of the research group is *essential* to any ethnographic study if the researcher is going to have any hope of entering into the 'life-world' of the groups under research. In other words, 'going native' *in this respect* is not just unavoidable, it is also necessary if the researcher is to truly understand the social reality of those in the field and achieve interpretative validity relative to the research participants. If an ethnographer's findings are not set in a conceptual framework that is recognisable by the participants, then how can it be argued that they are an authentic account of the experience of those within the field? When we put aside the 'myth' of objectivism (Lakoff and Johnson, 1980: 159–60) and attempt to gain an insight into intersubjective expe-riences, immersion and participation within the field of research is the only method capable of achieving this aim (Burgess 1991: 78). Attempting to discard sensation that is 'too subjective', and trying to objectively define the phenomenon in question by the use of 'common external characteristics' in order to remedy participant observation's difficulties in obtaining 'objective' and 'scientific' data (Durkheim 1964: 14–46) is to miss the point. The accessing – as far as is ever possible – of unmediated intersubjective experience at the expense of naïve notions of 'objective' and 'external' meanings is an essential feature of ethno-graphic fieldwork and the more 'native' the researcher becomes, the closer their experience will be to those lives they intend portraying.

As a result, the notion of 'going native' in the traditional anthropological sense should not concern us. The real danger for ethnographers is that they will *remain* native when attempting to disseminate research findings once outside the field; losing the ability to differentiate that which the research participants consider the norm from that which those outside the subculture would consider worthy of record. The ethnographer's task is a difficult one, to be able to 'go native' in the field, but also to retain the critical awareness when writing and disseminating the fieldwork to avoid overlooking issues that he or she may normalise while in the field. The ethnographer must be able to understand that an issue, for example abuse by police forces, heavy alcohol intake, or low-level fan-on-fan violence, has been normalised by the research group, without normalising this when writing the account. My own reading of Armstrong's analysis of the levels of violence engaged in by the Blades was that he had achieved this. Armstrong detailed the instances of violence witnessed and did not discount them; his view was simply that these levels did not match the accounts of the severity of 'hooliganism' expressed more popularly. However, going native was a danger I needed to be aware of, and on at least one occasion during the previous sixteen years I have realised that I had fallen into the trap of not reporting, or dismissing, events due to them being normalised by the partici-pants. All an ethnographer can do is be as reflexive as possible about their findings and continually discuss and disseminate findings in order to try to identify, and prevent the reproduction of, native assumptions.

Ethical issues surrounding criminal activity

Although the research participants were not 'hooligans' (in the sense that they travelled to matches with the intention of engaging in violence or disorder), most were involved in low-level criminal activity on a regular basis. This included offences such as entering a football ground while drunk, possession of drugs, indecent or racist chanting, ticket touting, theft, making off without payment, disorderly behaviour, criminal damage and breach of by-laws such as drinking on the streets, smuggling alcohol on to 'dry' trains, and refusing to pay public transport fares. More serious offences were also committed on occasion, including fraud,[5] drug dealing, assault, affray and even violent disorder. As a participant-observer I witnessed all of these offences being committed and, as part of my role as participant (particularly in a covert role), committed some of the offences myself. As a result there are two specific ethical dilemmas that must be confronted.

First, as a witness to both criminal offences and plans to commit criminal offences in the future, did I possess a moral or civic duty to inform the authorities of what I had witnessed? Did I owe a duty to the state to follow, and force others to follow its established laws, or are there 'universal' moral rules in a Kantian sense that I should be measuring my conduct as a researcher against? I did not consider that either of these should provide a guide as to my own ethical conduct, particularly as my research was originally investigating the effectiveness and legality of the laws that were in place to regulate football fans (many of which were being regularly broken). To enter into the field with the intention of respect-ing and upholding the very laws that I was meant to be analysing seemed to be casting aside all pretence of neutrality. However, other ways of confronting the dilemma of ethical behaviour when researching in fields of deviance and crimi-nality have also been suggested. Reynolds (1982) contends that the researcher should not feel bound to any external moral code and should instead determine themselves how they wish to 'serve society' (i.e. whether knowledge itself is an end or whether personal morality is of greater importance). Another approach is for the researcher to adopt the ethical code of those under research, over and above any external view of ethical behaviour. This tactic was undertaken by Hobbs during his study of 'wheelers and dealers' in London's East End. Hobbs participated in the field even when this meant he became implicated in criminal activity. He argued that research of this nature required 'a willingness to abide by the ethics of the researched culture and not the normative ethical constraints of sociological research' and had he failed to follow those norms, access to the research field would have been closed (1996: 7).

Of the aforementioned methods of approaching the issue of ethics in the field, Hobbs's view was the closest to my own position. I did not adopt the ethics of the field completely; in some cases, I would not participate in criminal behaviour in the field for personal moral reasons (this was particularly the case with regard to racist chanting), and in others I was not sure that should a highly serious criminal offence be committed (e.g. a murder of a rival fan) I would be able to justify not reporting it. However, this personal moral compunction was unlikely to cause a problem. In the first example, by no means did all football fans in the groups I was researching engage in racist chanting, meaning that I was still adhering to the ethics of *some* in the community. For the second example, the chances of my witnessing such an occurrence were minute, due to both the rarity of serious violence and the fact that I was not specifically researching the 'hooligans'. My own ethical standpoint when it came to witnessing criminal offences carried out by research participants was that I owed a duty to the participants not to cause them harm through my presence. One important ethical principle is that social research should never injure the research participants (Brabbie, 1989: 474), either during the observation itself, or through the utilisation of the findings. This duty is even more fundamental for covert research. As we have seen, there are considerable ethical concerns about the use of covert research techniques because research participants have not provided informed consent. As a result, any researcher going 'undercover' needs to be especially careful not to cause harm to those who are being observed and the ethical codes of practice state that the primary concern for a covert researcher should be to avoid harming the participants. This places researchers under pressure not to report crimes that have been committed or are in the planning stage (Feenan, 2002; Norris, 1993). As far as I was concerned, it was only through my decision not to reveal details of individual criminal offences that I could justify utilising covert observation. This view is a commonly held one among those carrying out ethnographic studies of 'deviant' groups and has led to some researchers being faced with legal action over their refusal to provide evidence to the authorities (Ferrell and Hamm, 1998: 6).

Second, there was a practical reason why I did not report crimes or planned crimes to the authorities. My rationale for undertaking participant observation in the first place was so that I would not distort the field. Had I gone to the authorities and they had acted on my information, I could have distorted the field unrecognisably by preventing some instances of disorder and by providing evidence that would have helped the police remove 'troublemakers' from the field in the future through criminal conviction and/or banning orders. A final reason why I did not discuss criminal activity witnessed with the authorities was because 'grassing' could have placed myself in danger of violent reprisals, particularly if I wished to continue researching, or indeed watching, football in any capacity. So, despite academic arguments that researchers have a duty to 'blow the whistle' on illegal activity (Ferdinand *et al.*, 2007), at no stage was any specific criminal act or plan reported to the authorities. This was even the case on the occasions that I was assaulted by other fans. The one occasion where I did make a formal complaint, against a steward who assaulted me at an away match, was a decision made based on a number of factors. First, that without the complaint, I ran the risk of causing harm to myself and another fan due to being 'blacklisted' as a troublemaker; second, that a complaint against the steward was in line with the possible responses that a fan assaulted in that way would have undertaken; and, finally, for practical reasons relating to my professional role and the links my institution had with the club in question. On another occasion, I was the victim of an unprovoked assault which also led to head injuries being suffered by another fan when she was attacked with a crutch. I was asked to give evidence at the subsequent court case but fortunately I was able to avoid another ethical dilemma due to the fact that the speed and unexpected nature of the attack meant I could not identify the assailant who had attacked me, and due to being held in a headlock by another unidentified fan, I missed the second assault.

The second dilemma I was faced with was how to act when pressured to commit criminal offences personally. Polsky warns of this danger when carrying out covert fieldwork in criminal or 'deviant' groups: 'in doing field research on criminals you damned well better *not* pretend to be "one of them", because they will test this claim out and one of two things will happen: either you will ... get sucked into "participant" observation of the sort you would rather not undertake, or you will be exposed, with still greater negative consequences' (1969: 124). When the research participants committed offences I came under pressure to also become involved in the illegal activity, particularly when carrying out covert research. A refusal to have participated could have resulted in my being 'outed' as a non-participant, resulting in a loss of access to the research field, or worse, a physical assault (if the fans thought my refusal was because I was a journalist or undercover police officer). My refusal to participate in an illegal group activity could also have distorted the field, potentially influencing those around me to 'think twice' about the legality or morality of their actions. In the latter stages of my research, when my role as a researcher was known, a refusal to participate in some activities certainly had the potential to distort the field in this way, or make the participants suspicious about whether I could be trusted to be present when they were committing offences. Some participation at least was the path of least resistance when it came to being accepted and trusted by the group even in overt observations.

At the same time, I was aware that to completely cast aside all attempts to abide by the law would have potentially serious consequences personally and for my work. Football matches are highly regulated and an arrest by the police could have led to my being banned from attending games, and would also have been embarrassing for my institution and research funders. As a result, I approached the dilemma of which offences to participate in from a practical point of view in terms of the minimal amount of criminal activity I could be involved in without restricting the effectiveness of my methodology. This required a two-stage process of identifying the crimes that I considered the least harmful in a utilitarian sense, and that were less serious in terms of likely legal response. These offences I would have fewer qualms about committing in order to maintain my research position and avoid distorting the field. The second stage required me to determine which offences I could avoid committing without distorting the field and which ones were necessary. So, for example, if the group with whom I was travelling all 'jibbed' a train, I was not going to delay them by paying at the ticket machine. Likewise, if a crowd invaded the pitch and ran towards their rivals, I needed to be present in that law-breaking crowd in order to observe what was happening (Pearson, 2009: 247). However, when a crowd were chanting racist abuse, I would be able to avoid participating because it would be unlikely that my abstinence would be noticed.

I was helped in this process by the complex nature of the make-up of the carnival football crowd. While almost all of those I researched committed some of the offences detailed above, few would commit all. The fans generally picked their own level of participation with illegal activity in order to achieve their version of a football carnival. For some, drug taking and the use of prostitutes were an essential part of a European away match, but this was not the case for all. Furthermore, while some fans enjoyed chanting racist songs, others refused to join in and would object to the singing of them by others. Finally, when it came to the (rare) instances of violence, the levels of participation varied dramatically, from those who were happy to fight, to those who would pose and posture, to those who would move away from the disorder. As a result, it was often possible to 'pick and choose' the offences I participated in while remaining immersed in the overall crowd (see *ibid.*).

Anonymity of research participants

A final important ethical issue for a researcher carrying out fieldwork into sensitive areas is that the anonymity of the research participants should be ensured. Again, this is increasingly important where research is covert and participants have not provided informed consent, due to the obligation on the researcher not to harm those under observation. This book details the committal of many criminal offences, or of quasi-criminal behaviour that could be sufficient to lead to a football banning order (James and Pearson, 2006). Therefore it was important that the names of those involved were disguised to minimise the chances of action taken against offender. Furthermore, the importance of anonymity is not restricted to the occasion that offences were committed. During the course of my research I witnessed many other instances where research participants were involved in activities which had the potential to cause them harm or embarrassment should their names be revealed. For example, it is a relatively common practice for carnival fans to visit lap-dancing establishments or even brothels during visits to matches abroad. This was a finding that needed recording, but one which had the potential to harm the family lives of named individuals.

As a result of this, pseudonyms are used throughout this book. Additionally, all the internet usernames have also been changed (including my own), due to the fact that many fans know who posts under which username and that posts can be tracked to home or work IP addresses. All field notes, recordings and references to original names, along with any keys assisting me to connect individuals to pseudonyms were destroyed prior to publication. In a few cases, individual research participants will appear under more than one pseudonym. This was necessary as a result of some situations during my time researching Manchester United fans where an individual could be identified by other supporters by his/her actions and where this individual has also committed an action, or made a statement that I have used, which he or she would not want to be known to the rest of the group. While my ethnography highlights the cohesiveness of groups of carnival fans, the relations between individuals and cliques *within* these groups are also important. During my time in the field, individuals within the groups fell out with each other, criticised friends behind their backs, and even entered into secret sexual affairs. Where it was important to include this data in the book, complete anonymity was vital as I did not want my actions to disrupt the cohesiveness of the groups or relations between individuals within them. The true name of the forum www.RedBrigade.net has also been altered so that the forum does not gain any unwanted attention. Finally, on some occasions where crowd control measures were illegal and/or could result in harm resulting to police or stewards who had not given informed consent – and this abuse was not already in the public domain – I have attempted to hide the identity of the club/police force in question (if it is possible to do this and deliver accurate ethnographic data).

Notes

1 E.g. Armstrong (football 'hooligans' 1998), Drury *et al.* (anti-roads protesters, 2001), Hobbs (armed robbers, 1995; petty criminals, 1996), Hobbs *et al.* (bouncers, 2003), Patrick (gangs, 1973), Thorne (draft-dodgers and anti-war resistance, 1983), Bourgois (2006), Jacobs (1998) and Williams *et al.* (crack users and dealers, 1992).

2 E.g. the First Re-Statement of Research Ethics for the Socio-Legal Studies Association (6.6.1).

3 Research carried out as part of wider Home Office and ESRC-funded projects into the policing of English fans abroad fed back into police practice at the 2004 European Championships in particular (see Stott and Pearson 2007). Informal discussions with police officers and club officials that took place in course of my wider academic work also had the potential to alter how fans were regulated and policed.

4 www.bbc.co.uk/news/uk-england-lancashire-11061823; accessed 20/09/10.

5 In printing/distributing counterfeit match tickets and 'jibbing' into football grounds.

2

The football carnival

Football as carnival

My fundamental contention is that for many English football supporters, matches (particularly away from home and especially abroad) provide an opportunity for expressions of the 'carnivalesque'. It is this that has led to my labelling of the participants as 'carnival fans'. As we will see, there were many differences between the ways in which the hard-core home-and-away fans of Blackpool, Manchester United and England interpreted the environment around them, expressed their identity, and behaved at and around matches. However, one of the major unifying themes was the desire to step away from the ordinary and the everyday and to try to create a space – physically, socially and psychologically – for a version of carnival. This desire may not have been present in all fans at all matches, but it was a key feature of a particular subculture of home-and-away match-goers, and for many of them the most important part of following their team.

Football has been compared to a religion (Bromberger *et al.*, 1993; Morris, 1981: 22–4; Percy and Taylor, 1997), but for the vast majority of research participants this did not explain their attitudes towards football, nor their motivations for attending matches. To be religious in the traditional sense undoubtedly requires dedication and a sense of duty, and attending Rochdale vs. Blackpool on a wet Tuesday November night may seem, to some, akin to attending church. However, for the fans I observed, attending football was not primarily about going to the match and 'worshipping' the club or the team. Research with England and United fans in particular demonstrated that watching the matches was often secondary to the 'craic' of the trip itself. Many England fans travelled to international tournaments with no tickets and no intention of getting into a stadium; attending purely for the party surrounding the matches. Some commentators in the media have mistaken this type of fan for a 'hooligan' who attended to cause trouble with no intention of going to the game, and some police and magistrates still use the lack of a match ticket as evidence that a fan is a hooligan,[1] but from my research this is to misread the motivations of these supporters. It is the carnival that surrounds the match that is of fundamental value, and this becomes increasingly important in situations where tickets are scarce.

Meanings of what constitutes 'carnival' vary and my own usage of the term is not intended to reflect modern-day street carnivals (such as the Notting Hill Carnival) that are often highly stage-managed, regulated and regimented. Nor does it reflect the remnants of traditional medieval carnivals that are still played out in the likes of Dusseldorf or Cologne, where local participants will typically party for certain nights but will make constant returns to the normality of work and home life in between. Instead, my use of carnival as a tool by which to explain the motivations of the research participants is drawn from the descriptions of social historians, who highlight the importance of feast days and festivals for the populous of early-modern Europe in providing a welcome break from the comparative struggle and oppression of life for the ordinary population. Carnival was the largest of the festivals, running usually from Christmas (or even earlier) until Lent, and involving music, singing, fancy dress and excessive eating and drinking (Burke, 2002: 183). The major themes of carnival were, according to Burke, 'food, sex and violence', with the 'carne' prefix to 'carnival' making reference to the first two through its translation as 'flesh' (*ibid.*: 186).[2]

While the traditional Christmas to Lent carnival was popular in early-modern Europe in Southern and Central Europe, this elongated period of festivity was not as popular in Britain and Scandinavia, and other shorter festivals and feast days, 'performed its functions and shared its rituals ... It is closer to the truth to think of the religious festivals of early modern Europe as little carnivals than to think of them as grave sedate rituals in the modern manner' (*ibid.*: 199). My contention is that these intense periods of celebration and hedonism are closely akin to the type of fandom observed during the course of my research. Kolve described one such festival in England, St John's Eve, as being an occasion where, 'people danced, sang and leapt with great pleasure, and did not spare the bagpipes ... many loads of beer were brought ... what disorder, whoring, fighting and killing and dreadful idolatry took place there!' (*ibid.*: 195).

In the last few centuries, the spectacle of carnival has been suppressed (Stallybrass and White, 1986: 178–9) and eliminated as a 'real social practice' (Stam, 1988: 134). It has been argued that its remnants remain in symbolic carnival expressions in the likes of Brazil (*ibid.*) and central Europe, but that in Britain the true expressions of the carnivalesque were marginalised to seaside resorts such as Blackpool (Stallybrass and White, 1986: 178–9), to the contemporary night-time economy (Winlow and Hall, 2006), bank holidays and Friday nights (Presdee, 2002: 34). Presdee argues that the meaning of carnival is now 'threaded through our culture' (*ibid.*: 44) and that 'explosions' of the carnivalesque appear from the 'fragments' and 'debris' of carnival which are increasingly criminalised (e.g. warehouse raves). The phenomenon of carnival has been used frequently by postmodernists to describe and deconstruct aspects of contemporary culture, following its academic rebirth, which appears to have been sparked by the 1965 publication of *Rabelais and His World* by the Soviet philosopher and literary theorist Mikhail Bakhtin. It has also been suggested that the use of carnival in this way, or at least Bakhtin's interpretation of carnival, has been overplayed and that, 'Confronted with a crowd temporarily freed from work and engaged in the pursuit of pleasure, it seems that many writers cannot resist the temptation to turn to Bakhtin' (Webb, 2005: 121):

> There is now a large and increasing body of writing which sees carnival not simply as a ritual feature of European culture but as a mode of understanding, a positivity, a cultural analytic. How is it that a festive ritual now virtually elimin-ated from most of the popular culture of Europe has gained such prominence as an epistemological category? (Stallybrass and White, 1986: 6)

However, although Bakhtin's version of carnival has been criticised in some quarters as being 'nostalgic and over-optimistic' (*ibid.*: 18), I found it a highly useful ethnographic tool.

Carnival was the people's 'second life', a highly distorted mirror image of their 'official' life based upon want, hard labour, a shorter average lifespan and often lived under an oppressive hierarchical regime. And, for Bakhtin, carnival was *lived*, not merely watched. 'Carnival is not a spectacle seen by the people; they live in it, and everyone participates because its very idea embraces all the people. While carnival lasts, there is no other life outside it. During carnival time, life is subject only to its laws, that is, the laws of its own freedom' (1984: 7). At the time carnival was described as the world turned 'upside down' (Curtuis, 1953: 94–8; Burke, 2002: 185) or 'inside out' (Bakhtin, 1984: 11), in which the normal rules of hierarchical rank were suspended (*ibid.*: 10); social roles were redistributed (Stam, 1988: 134) and folk would be free to insult each other and criticise the authorities (Burke, 2002: 187). It was also a time where violence and disorder were commonplace, a point Burke illustrates with reference to an incident at the Shrove Tuesday festival where youths with cudgels, hammers and hacksaws went on the rampage and then attacked the constable and his men with stones when they arrived to quell the disturbance (*ibid.*: 188). But most importantly of all carnival was fun; a time that people anticipated and then reminisced about when the world returned to normal. 'Carnival was a holiday, a game, an end in itself, needing no explanation or justification. It was a time of ecstasy, of liberation' (*ibid.*: 185–6). The French philosopher Roger Caillois wrote of the human need for carnival that man lives, 'in remembrance of one festival and in expectation of the next' (1950: 125; translation in Burke, 2002: 179).[3]

The construction of football fandom as carnival is not new, but it is one that demands further elucidation and development. It was most prominently used by Giulianotti, who carried out ethnographic research with fans of the Scottish national team at the 1990 World Cup and the 1992 European Championships. He noted 'the potential of soccer matches as sites for expressions of the carnivalesque' (1991: 508) and later contended that, 'an appropriate way of depicting the culture of these international fans overseas is through the metaphor of "carnival"' (1995: 194). The view is also shared by Brown, who in his descrip-tion of ticketless Manchester United fans in Montpellier in 1991 refers to an unofficial '"carnivalesque" fans' celebration of "just being there"' (1993: 35). Giulianotti also argues that while fan carnival 'harbours the potentialities of socially and politically disruptive activity' (1995: 214), it can also 'facilitate internal monitoring of behaviour and self-policing' (*ibid.*: 194). This latter argument is a contentious one, particularly for those who believe that alcohol consumption, ticketless fans and 'maverick' travellers lead to an increased chance of crowd disorder. However, as we will see, Giulianotti's findings with fans of the Scottish team hold weight when tested against my own findings with fans of England and Manchester United abroad, particularly on the issue of the availability of alcohol.

Giulianotti, however, takes a rather restrictive view of what constitutes carnival. At one stage he argues that that carnival exists at football tournaments because the authorities carve out spaces for it to take place (*ibid.*: 194) and that impression management by the Scottish fans restricted the 'carnivalesque of *spontaneous* activity' (1991: 511). He also observed instances where Scottish fans did not engage in 'full-blown carnival' (*ibid.*), that Irish fans did not create a 'carnival atmosphere' by not gathering in large enough groups to march as one to the stadium (*ibid.*: 518) and noted that by exerting too much control on a designated fan zone, 'the authorities had at a stroke subverted and neutralised the very essence of carnival' because there could be no inversion of the rules of social control (*ibid.*: 520). However, the essence of traditional carnival is useful in describing, and explaining, football fandom not only when spaces are 'carved out' for fans or when the fans remain peaceful. From my observations, carnival, or at least the attempt to recreate the carnivalesque, occurred even when only a handful of fans gathered together for a match, where alcohol bans and restrictive social control measures were enforced, or where 'hooligan' fans were present. Indeed, violence, or at least the threat or presence of violence (including on occasion overreaction by the authorities) was for many of the research participants an important aspect of a memorable football experience. Hughson also argues that Giulianotti's differentiation between hooliganism and the carnivalesque fails to recognise that 'hooligan fans are those who take the liberties of the carnivalesque to extremes and, accordingly, unsettle social authority' (2002: 45). Disorder and occasionally violence could be part of a football carnival in the same way they were important to the traditional carnivals. Indeed, Presdee (2002) argues the case for many acts of violence, disorder or crime in modern society to be viewed in themselves as expressions of the 'fragments' or 'debris' of carnival.

My observations suggested the primary motivation for the hardcore of travelling football fan groups was a recreation of the type of behaviour and release that is described by Bakhtin and others in their (admittedly nostalgic) accounts of the carnivals and festivals of early-modern Europe. For the creation of a successful football carnival, one that was enjoyed at the time and frequently recounted, it was not necessary for authorities to 'carve out' spaces, for marches to take place, for displays of colour to be shown, or even for large numbers of fans to gather together. For the carnival fan, the most important aspect of a successful carnival was the ability to escape into a 'second life'. The bigger the social group and the lesser the suppression by the authorities, the better this carnival was usually considered to be. But the carnivalesque in Bakhtin's terms could be expressed inside a pub in which police had barricaded fans, or in an escort surrounded by police horses and riot vans. Small groups of fans travelling to relatively meaning-less matches would also attempt to recreate football carnivals of the past, particularly abroad, through attending similar social establishments and repeating similar behaviour. We should be careful not to fall into the trap of seeing carnival everywhere, or of interpreting fairly standard human behaviour on nights out as being 'the world turned upside down'. But the creation of a carnival around a match was typically the endgame for the research participants in the present study. For them, Roger Caillois's simple summary of what carnival means was entirely appropriate.

Locating carnival – Blackpool FC, 1995–98

The rowdiest part of Blackpool's Bloomfield Road stadium was perceived to be the South Paddock, a 1,500-capacity terrace behind one goal that formed the lower tier of the South Stand. Even for smaller games where Bloomfield Road was less than half full, the section directly behind the goal would still be busy as fans deliberately gathered there for the atmosphere and camaraderie. During my research, the Paddock had no crush barriers (waist-high metal bars secured inter-mittently onto the steps to prevent significant crowd movement), meaning that crowd surges all the way down the terrace were a common occurrence. When the perimeter fences at the front of the Paddock were removed in the 1995–96 season, these surges frequently led to pitch invasions for important goals. The presence of terracing at Blackpool assisted my access to the research field as I could decide where to stand and with whom on a game-by-game basis. Typically I stood in the area that I identified as being the most rowdy which (in contrast to my experi-ences in all-seater stands) required taking up my position fifteen to twenty minutes before kick-off. One of the first observations of the culture of the South Paddock was that regular fans would have their favourite area of the terrace and would return to the spot with regularity.

The South Paddock terrace, and other terraces on which I watched Blackpool, were complex social spaces and for regular match-goers a decision on where to stand usually indicated the type of activity in which they wished to engage during the match. Sometimes new match-goers who arrived early found themselves standing in the middle of a crowd crush they were not expecting, or fans who wished to participate in crowd surges and crushes would arrive late and find the terrace too crowded to reach their preferred location. However in the main, fans on the South Paddock chose their location on the terrace depending on how much participation they wished to have in the active fan culture exhibited there. Even choosing to stand on the South Paddock usually demonstrated that a decision had already been made, because of the Paddock's reputation as being noisy and rowdy. This was not the case for every fan on that terrace; the Paddock was the only area in the ground where home fans could both (a) stand; and (b) watch the match from behind a goal. While the overall view of the match was poorer from behind the goal (it was difficult to judge offside decisions or see the activity in the opposite goal mouth), many fans wanted to watch from that location. Chants almost always started in the South Stand, Blackpool would normally attack that goal in the second half and Blackpool players who scored would usually celebrate in front of, or even with, fans in the Paddock. Standing on the terrace was also cheaper than sitting in the seats above.

This meant that the South Paddock had a rich mix of football fans, both men and women of all ages, and these fans located themselves on the terrace with a view to the experience they wanted from the match. In one sense, the social structure of the Paddock reflected the findings of research on the London Road End terrace at Oxford United in the 1970s. Peter Marsh's research team noted how different zones of the terraces were taken up by different types of fan, from part-timers at the edges, children at the front, the 'rowdies' in the middle and the 'Town Boys' nearer the back (Marsh *et al.*, 1978). This research highlighted the social structure of the rowdier elements of the Oxford United crowd and how this structure meant that disorder which occurred was actually highly ordered and less serious in terms of actual violence, damage and injury than was claimed by the media at the time. While many of Marsh's findings are still valid for today's football crowd, the rigidity of the structure on the terrace was not replicated on the South Paddock. Instead, the social structure of the Paddock bore more similarities with the findings of Wendy Fonarow's ethnography of 'indie' music gigs. Fonarow identified various 'zones of participation' 'based on the distinct type of activities exhibited in these areas' by those attending the gigs (2006: 82). These activities would make the attendance at the gig not only more pleasurable for the audience, but would also allow them to construct the social meaning of the event and communicate these values: 'Space is culturally organised, and therefore the use of body in space is a meaning-making process' (*ibid.*: 80). Fonarow concluded that indie gigs were split into three of these 'zones of participation'. Zone one, at the front of the crowd comprised the most physically active, either through the constant struggle to avoid being crushed at the front or through jumping up and down and engaging in 'mosh pit' activity: 'the mosh pit is still characterised by circular movement and pushing and running into others' (*ibid.*: 87). Zone two, further back, although further from the stage, allowed the less active audience to watch the performance without being crushed or jostled.

Observations at Blackpool revealed similarly structured 'zones of participation' on terraces such as the South Paddock; fans would choose their location depending on how physical they wanted their participation in supporting the team to be. Furthermore, several 'types' of participant bore close similarities to those identified in Fonarow's research at indie gigs – fans who would gather at the front of the terrace to be as close to their heroes as possible (and maybe get an autograph or a quick conversation), fans who wanted an absence of jostling and movement so that they could watch the match undisturbed, and finally those for whom crushing, jostling and surging was an essential part of the experience. There were, however, key differences in how these 'zones of participation' were set out on the terrace compared with Fonarow's study. One significant factor was that from the South Paddock the view of the match improved the further back one stood, but only if you were tall enough to see over the heads of the people in front. Second, the terrace equivalent of 'moshing' – the crowd surge – worked best from the back of the terrace. Third, fans believed that more noise could be generated from the back of the stand than the front due to the overhanging roof. And, finally, cover from the elements was best at the back of the terrace. This meant that, in contrast to the indie gig, the more rowdy elements gathered towards the back of terrace, with younger fans and females typically gathered nearer the front of the terrace (particularly near to the tunnel to the dressing rooms). Those who wanted a good view of the match without being jostled (but still wanted to stand behind the goal), typically gathered at the back, but at the edges of the terrace nearer the corner flags.

As a result of the existence of these 'zones of participation' at home matches I found myself standing with the same group of fans, week in week out. For more important games, a regular fan's favourite place on the terrace could not be guaranteed due to irregular fans arriving early and seeking out the best view. Even arriving early for matches would not guarantee you your favourite position on the terrace, as a terrace filled to capacity would move around, particularly at moments of high excitement. For popular matches such as derbies, irregular fans who unwittingly positioned themselves in areas of the terrace usually occupied by groups of regular fans would be faced by ninety minutes of jostling and shoving as the regular fans attempted to squeeze their way into their normal position on an already full area of the terrace. Occasionally these regular fans would make comments about 'part-timers', but it was rare for these fans to ask or demand that others should move. Instead the regular fans (particularly if they arrived in a group) would quite simply make it physically uncomfortable for those in their place. Goal celebrations were often used by regular fans to regain their 'rightful' place on the terrace; they would surge down on to the imposters, jump into them, or (using their superior knowledge of the movement of the terrace), ensure that they avoided the crowd surge that would take the irregular fans tumbling down the terrace. When the irregular fans returned after the crowd surge they would often find that their position on the terrace was retaken. When I first arrived on the South Paddock, I perceived this unspoken animosity after unwittingly choosing to stand on part of the terrace usually occupied by a group of regular match-goers. It was only through continually standing in the same place that my presence appeared to be first tolerated, and then accepted by those around me.

Crowd surges were a theme of many popular terraced ends including the South Paddock, and a part of football fan culture that cannot be replicated in all-seater stands, even when everyone is standing. A surge would occur when fans near the back of the stand pushed down on those in front of them, creating a domino effect and forcing the fans below down several steps. Where a terrace was full to capacity, the crowd would then surge back up the steps as a crush developed either at the front or against any crush barriers. Where a terrace was only partially full, those in the crowd surge would sometimes fall over each other as they lost their balance. Crowd surges on the Paddock usually occurred at moments of high excitement – normally for goals – but sometimes those at the back would start a crowd surge purely for the enjoyment of watching those nearer the front being pushed down the terrace. I found the sheer force of a crowd surge to be exhilarating rather than intimidating and gradually managed to establish my position – both physically and socially – on the terrace for the duration of my research.

An important goal for Blackpool, particularly if it was scored at the south end of the ground, would see the centre section of the Paddock surge down the terrace for as many as ten steps. One knock-on effect of the crowd surge in games where the Paddock was full would be to send those at the front of the terrace onto the pitch (although many of those who invaded the pitch merely used the surge behind them as an excuse to celebrate the goal on the pitch). The safest way to 'ride' the crowd surge was to join in, bouncing down the terrace as you celebrated the goal, both pushing and hanging on to the person in front of you as you went. On numerous occasions someone nearer the front would fall, leaving those of us behind them tumbling over them onto other bodies or the concrete steps. For bigger games where the Paddock was full, keeping your balance in the crowd surge and then regaining your position on the terrace (or stealing someone else's position) was a feat of strength, balance, nous and cardio-vascular endurance. As a result, standing in areas where crowd surges took place, while being popular with the more rowdy fans, was deliberately avoided by others; some fans explained how they deliberately stood in other areas of the terrace to avoid the 'nobheads' who would push from the back.

The carnival on the terraces (both home and away) by Blackpool fans also involved regular committal of criminal offences. Following the legislative programme of the Thatcher and Major governments to reduce 'hooliganism', between 1985 and 1994 it became illegal to be drunk at a match, to sell tickets in a public place, and – under the Football Offences Act 1991 – to throw any object inside a stadium, invade the pitch or engage in racist or 'indecent' chanting. My observations suggested that none of these laws were effective and that offences under the 1991 legislation were particularly prevalent among Blackpool fans (the alcohol legislation is discussed in Chapter 6). The new offence of running on the pitch[4] was advertised to fans by signs on the reverse side of advertising hoardings and on occasion the public address system would also warn fans to 'keep off the pitch'. However, in eleven of the seventeen matches observed at Blackpool following the removal of perimeter fencing at the start of the 1995–96 season, pitch invasions occurred. At some matches, there was more than one pitch invasion, sometimes by fans of both teams; at the 1996 play-off semi-final, the final whistle saw rival fans spill onto the pitch from both ends of the ground and run towards each other, forcing intervention by mounted police. At the end of the final home match of the 1997–98 season, both Blackpool and Bristol Rovers fans invaded the pitch, but this time met on the halfway line to swap shirts and scarves and wish each other good luck for next season.

Goals were regularly greeted by minor pitch invasions from fans in the South Paddock, often as a direct result of a crowd surge from the back of the terrace.

However, most pitch invaders did so intentionally, and, on one occasion, I witnessed two fans making 'sportsman's bets' with stewards on the gate that they would 'get past them' for the next goal. The stewards' response was simply to try to catch the pitch invaders and push them back to the terrace and very few ejections or arrests were made for this offence during my observations. Away from home, the Blackpool carnival fans invaded the pitch less frequently. However, for the final game of the 1995–96 season at York, hundreds of Blackpool fans climbed over the perimeter fencing before the final whistle and stood on the cinder-track surrounding the pitch as the final moments of the game were played out. When the match finished, the fans (and hundreds behind them climbing over the fences) ran onto the pitch and charged the York fans at the opposite end (who also invaded the pitch from the other side of the ground), chasing them back into their section. Most of the fans invading the pitch did not do so with the intention of confronting the York fans and when it became clear that a confrontation was likely, many fans turned back. However, once the home fans were back behind their fences, the Blackpool fans celebrated having 'taken' their pitch. Although the team missed out on promotion that day, fans reminisced long after about their carnivalesque rule-breaking.

From the outside, the terraces holding Blackpool fans were very unruly places. Crowd surges and pitch invasions were common place and missiles were thrown. To be hosting Blackpool at your stadium on the final game of the season – particularly if the game was of importance – was to invite thousands of garishly dressed fans to take over your town, infiltrate the home sections of your ground and invade your pitch in huge numbers, sometimes before the final whistle. However, in reality there was a complex social code to which the carnival fans adhered. Pitch invasions were only accepted at certain times and at certain – relatively non-threatening – venues (Blackpool fans did not invade the pitch at Preston or Burnley for example). The missiles thrown tended to be non-dangerous and crowd surges could be avoided by simply moving a dozen steps to the right or left. There were clear boundaries about what behaviour was acceptable and what was not; following Blackpool gave the fans an opportunity to break down the usual social norms that they adhered to in everyday life, but this disorder and carnival was performed within another set of unspoken parameters. The terraces were not a free-for-all. Indeed, the ability of fans on terraces to choose where to stand, and who with, meant that the Paddock was probably a safer area for non-rowdy fans to watch football than, for example, all seated away stands (or the back of the Stretford End) for Manchester United games in 2011. On the Paddock a fan could avoid having someone tumbling down on them when a goal was scored, something which is not the case in all-seated grounds.

Locating the carnival – Manchester United FC, 2001–11

The rowdy and noisy section at Manchester United's Old Trafford stadium was the Stretford End Tier Two (ST2), although sections such as the J and K-Stands of the East Stand (or 'Scoreboard End') also shared some of the characteristics. For many of United's carnival fans, ST2 remained the last place in the ground where the old style of supporting the team remained, albeit in a watered-down form. Although this was an all-seater stand, with the exception of the front few rows, fans here stood for the duration of the match, grouped together with their friends (even where their seats were separated), smuggled alcohol into the ground, and occasionally had half-time 'concourse parties' which consisted of the fans gathering under the stand, jumping up and down, chanting and throwing beer over each other (King also refers to this type of concourse activity in the Scoreboard End, 2003: 161). As with many South Paddock regulars at Blackpool, expressions of rowdy fandom in ST2 were considered as important as watching the game.

However, in contrast to the Paddock, fans in ST2 who did not want to participate in this rowdy fandom did not have the same freedom to avoid it. For those (non-carnival) fans with tickets towards the back and centre of ST2 who did not want to stand all match, the match-day experience appeared to be a frustrating one. Children who found themselves there were often unable to see the action and ended up standing on seats or being picked up by parents, while senior supporters who found it physically taxing to stand for ninety minutes were observed sitting down and missing much of the match. Some casual supporters were surprised to find that they were unable to actually 'use' their seat, although others deliberately chose to buy a ticket in this area of the ground for the 'atmosphere'. For carnival fans, however, ST2 provided what was perceived to be a sterile and overly regulated environment that paled in comparison to the old terraces and the more rowdy setting of a United away match. During a match against Everton in 2009, an elderly female supporter objected that she could not see due to fans standing in front and complained that one of the research participants was swaying back and forth as he tried to watch the game over the heads of the supporters. His view on the complaint was one of anger: 'I never thought I'd see the day when I was asked to sit down on the Stretty. I'm seething mate, I tell you'.

For the carnival fans, watching United away from home was a far more pleasurable experience because it was less routine, less regulated and provided for greater 'incident'. The scarcity of tickets for the United section at away matches also meant that the proportion of carnival fans was significantly higher than at Old Trafford. United fans were usually allocated between 1,000 and 7,000 tickets for away matches, with average allocations around 2,800, and the number of applications for matches around 20,000. Although casual fans and 'tourists' did attend away matches, their numbers were not usually perceived to be significant enough to dilute the atmosphere and opportunity for rowdy support of the team. One of the most significant reasons why carnival fans enjoyed away matches more than home ones was because the atmosphere was perceived to be better. Although United's carnival fans complained about the atmosphere at Old Trafford, they considered their away support second to none in terms of generating noise and possessing a 'varied songbook'. The rowdiness that accompanied United's away following was also viewed with pride by the carnival fans, although it caused complaints by host clubs and police and often led to reduced allocations. A senior British Transport Police officer identified United fans as the worst in the country for low-level disorderly behaviour inside stadiums (interview, 15/09/04) and following a match at Southampton in 2011, the Football Licensing Authority Inspector present reported:

> The whole of the away end had stood and there had been problems of ingress and egress. 20 minutes before kick-off there had been a problem with the away turnstiles, queues had surged forward and searching had been suspended as stewards were forced back against the stadium walls and had to be rescued by police. The pressure of the crowds had forced barriers open and a general melee had developed. While that was happening the police had been called to support stewards in the away concourse as a flare and smoke bomb had been discharged. Throughout the match away fans had stood en masse continually chanting 'We're United, we do what we want'. The Inspector commented 'and they certainly did'. The Inspector said that man u [*sic*] fans had continually abused stewards, filled gangways, smoked, crowded perimeter fences and were generally aggressive. Further flares had been discharged in the crowd and smoke bombs thrown. At the end of the match man u [*sic*] fans had refused to clear the away concourse until forced out by police, and threw waste bins at stewards, police and home fans. Outside the ground they were overturning bins and generally being a nuisance. There were 19 ejections and 7 arrests, including for pitch incursions. (IFO Report; complaint ref.: 11/02)

The contrast with the highly regulated and sterile atmosphere of most sections of Old Trafford was striking (see Williams, 2001: 42).

A number of factors contributed to the ability of United's away following to exhibit its fandom in a rowdy way. As we have seen, the demographic of the away following was significantly different from home games. Tickets were difficult to obtain, being officially allocated only to season ticket holders or executive facility holders. Applications from season ticket holders not in the loyalty pot (around 700 fans who had applied for every away match since 2002) were unlikely to be successful and some season ticket holders went an entire season being 'chubbed' for every match they applied for. However, there existed a network – largely but not exclusively Manchester based – of regular away match-goers around which unused tickets would circulate (usually for the face value on the ticket: touting between the United carnival fans was generally frowned upon). As a result of this network, a 'chubbing' did not necessarily mean a carnival fan would not get a ticket; fans without tickets would ask friends for 'spares' and as match day approached, more spares would become available as ticket holders dropped out (usually for work reasons or lack of money). The tickets would be passed on through this network to friends and then 'friends of friends'. For example, while drafting this chapter, I was simultaneously involved in a transaction by both message board and text message to 'shift a spare' for a cup tie at Barnsley. The spare ticket belonged to a friend of one of the peripheral members of the Red Brigade and, through me, ended up being taken by another fan I knew, whose friend needed a ticket. In other words, there were five 'degrees of separation' between the holder of the spare and the previously ticketless fan.

If on the match day, a carnival fan was still ticketless, he or she might travel to the game in the hope of picking up a spare in one of the pubs frequented by the United away following. The group would listen out for conversations about spare tickets, ask other carnival fans about them and generally just 'hang around' in the hope that one might materialise. For the more popular games this strategy often led to disappointment, and could result in the fan having to watch the match in a pub, often surrounded by fans of the home team. In order to avoid this fate, some bolder fans would attempt to 'jib' into the match without a ticket or with a 'snide' ticket. The most successful way of achieving this was to 'double up' with another ticket-holding fan and try to sneak through with them on one click of the turnstile. Other methods included sneaking under or over turnstiles or a ticket being passed back once the holder had gone through the turnstiles. Some fans, particularly younger ones, were extremely persistent in attempts to jib into grounds, and during my research many successful attempts were made (around ten of the Brigade successfully jibbed in to the Champions League Final at Wembley in 2011). At certain grounds, fans would jib each season and some were so confident of their ability they would sell on their ticket at the last minute. Tales of other more daring jibs (involving bribes, false press passes, flashing student ID cards or wearing luminous jackets) were also recounted and I was also sworn to secrecy about one particular scheme. It was also possible for a jibber to buy a ticket for the home section of the ground and then attempt to get into the United section through finding unlocked dividing doors (or persuading stewards to open them) or jumping over the barrier separating the rival supporters.

Alternatively, the ticketless fan could sit in the home section of the stadium but this meant that he or she could not join in with the carnival in the United end and might not even be able to celebrate United goals for fear of being attacked by home fans or ejected by stewards. As a result, this strategy was usually reserved for only the most important matches, where United would be lifting a trophy or for European away matches where it was deemed safe to sit in the home sections. When Manchester United travelled to Wigan Athletic for the final game of the 2006–7 season needing a victory to secure the championship, large numbers of carnival fans travelled without tickets. Many of these sat in the home sections, but others watched the match in a nearby pub. When United went 2–0 up late in the match, the fans ran to the stadium and hundreds entered through exit doors left open for exiting Wigan fans, streaming into the home sections for the final moments of the game and the trophy celebrations.

For those fans who obtained away match tickets the typical away trip started with the journey to the match. The favourite mode of transport appeared to be train, but this was often expensive or unfeasible for evening matches and fans would hire minibuses or coaches, or simply travel by car. Carnival fans normally aimed to arrive by the stadium in time to drink at a pub beforehand, which often necessitated an early start. However, this early start did not stop supporters taking cans of lager or other alcoholic drinks onto the transport and consuming them on the journey. It was rare for the carnival fans to consider travelling on transport put on by the club because official travel was perceived as overly restrictive (alcohol consumption was prohibited) and the travel option of choice for the 'tourist'. Since the lure of away matches for carnival fans was the chance to be together with like-minded individuals (in contrast to the Old Trafford experience) this was something they wished to avoid.

Once in the host city, carnival fans would identify a pub near the ground. Without previous knowledge of the city, this could be a frustrating and even dangerous task, with many pubs closed to away supporters or dangerous for those who entered. Some of the carnival fans looked for quiet, 'safe' pubs, often that they had experienced an enjoyable time in at previous matches but most gathered in the pub that the United fans had in the past 'taken over'. The large number of United fans travelling to away matches meant that they would usually take over a pub near the ground, simply by arriving in numbers earlier than large numbers of home supporters. Sometimes, this pub would be designated an 'away pub' by the local police, but this designation did not always mean that this pub would be chosen – due to the resistance towards doing what they were told by the police, and the perceived over-regulation of these establishments. This resistance to authority was a key feature of United's carnival support, and requests by police or tannoy announcements for fans to act in a particular way were typically greeted in the 2010–11 season by the chant: 'We're Man United, we'll do what we want'.

For matches against regular opposition, the same pub would usually be revisited, with hundreds of United carnival fans packed inside and hundreds more outside, often drinking cans purchased from nearby off-licences. As the match approached, many of the fans would chant and jump up and down, to create a carnival atmosphere. Externally this looked like a single cohesive group of United supporters, but it actually comprised many different sub-groups (such as the Red Brigade), who used the location as a meeting point before the match. These groups could range from two or three fans through to an entire coach load. Although these groups had much in common, and members of different groups knew each other and would mingle, the sub-groups usually maintained cohesion through a core of members standing together. These would on occasion start chants which would sometimes be joined in with by fans from other sub-groups. Occasionally these sub-groups would chant against each other, particularly if they did not approve of a particular song or if they were made up of members from different locations. On a few occasions arguments broke out between groups and even escalated into minor incidents of violence.

Shortly before kick-off the fans would usually leave for the ground in these cohesive sub-groups, but, at higher-risk venues, police would corral the occupants of the pub as a whole and then escort them to the ground, surrounded by police vans and officers, some on horseback (the police escort is explained in Chapter 5). Gaining access to the stadium was usually highly disorganised due to the large numbers of fans and little time available before kick-off. Arguments would often break out between supporters and police/stewards which were exacerbated by a perceived lack of communication about the reason for delays or by what was viewed as poor crowd management, for example not all the turnstiles being opened (similar patterns of behaviour were observed with Blackpool and England fans). Police and steward responses to the crowd at this point were highly influential in whether arguments would escalate or be contained, and whether the crowd would respond en masse or whether the sub-groups would remain identifiable. Tensions were also increased by presence within the crowd of jibbers who were assisted by the crush and disorganisation, but were typically tolerated and even encouraged by carnival fans with tickets. I witnessed many incidents where ticket holders would help jibbers to gain access to the ground, either by 'doubling up' or by creating a diversion. Where crushes developed at turnstiles, the social identity of the supporters changed; sub-groups would be split up and fans would find themselves pressed against other United fans whom they did not know. This appeared to create an increased 'us and them' mentality between the supporters as a whole on one side, and the police and stewards on the other.

Once inside the ground, fan attitudes to the seat identified on their ticket varied widely. Most would locate their seat and stand in front of it but many carnival fans ignored their seat number and, with other members of their group, simply chose a suitable location to stand as if they were on a terrace. Those arriving late often found their seats taken and looked for another location to stand (asking a steward to force other fans to move was unconventional among carnival fans and could cause antagonism), which would have a knock-on effect. Often, the late rush of fans (at kick-off or the start of the second half) would cause congestion at the entrance to the seated area and on the steps leading down to the front, and watching the match from the steps was popular in carnival fan groups, reminding older fans of the terraces. However, unlike the terraces, the lack of crush barriers on the steps made these areas unsafe in the event of a crowd surge. Without observed exception, United fans away from home stood for the duration of the match, and attempted to create as much noise as possible to support the team and insult or antagonise the home supporters. At half-time, many of the research participants would return to the concourse to purchase and drink beer, smoke in the toilets and meet up with those located in other areas of the away section. Concourses at half-time were typically crowded and noisy places, with fans chanting and occasionally throwing beer in the air. On occasion scuffles and fights between different groups broke out, some resulting from pushing or beer spillage, others from longer-running feuds.

The second half of United away matches was typically rowdier than the first. Many of the groups who had reunited in the concourse at half-time would watch the match together for the second half, often from where they perceived the atmosphere to be the best. Additionally, it was typical for United to attack the away end in the second half, usually leading to more excitement and crowd movement than when attacking the other goal, particularly late in the match where a goal was more likely to be decisive. There was therefore an increased tendency to crowd together near the front of the stand as the match progressed. If United were pressing for a last-minute winner or equaliser, fans would push forward, or stand on seats in the excitement. When such a vital goal was scored, this often led to fans tumbling down steps and over rows of seats. The day after such a game, it was not uncommon for fans to complain of cuts and bruises gained in the celebration, and to relive the bedlam that followed in the immediate aftermath of the goal.

While the United away experience was relished by their carnival fans, trips to see the club abroad were anticipated even more. A number of authors have noted that 'Euro aways' provide the best experiences for the traditional (as opposed to 'new consumerist') fan because they provide the most hedonistic experiences (Brown, 1993; King, 2000; Millward, 2006). For the research participants, the European away experience was not purely centred around the match itself; instead it was an opportunity for groups of friends and acquaintances with shared interests and views to spend time together. A typical Euro away for these groups would last for three days with the match being played on the second evening (although fans under pressure of work might fly out on 'day trips' to the match). Reflecting the findings of Sugden (2002: 74), I found that for carnival fans, the Euro away provided a break from work, a chance to see a new place, gain new experiences and overindulge in drink, food, drugs and occasionally sex. As such, the Euro away tied closely with Bakhtin's view of carnival, with no other life outside the event for its duration, and the fans 'subject only to its laws, that is, the laws of its own freedom' (1984: 7). During a Euro away, fans had the freedom to adopt completely different attitudes and personalities from their everyday life under no pressure from family members or work colleagues. Afterwards, they could return to normality often without speaking truthfully (or at all) about the experiences they had encountered. Sometimes this was because they did not think their family or colleagues would understand the 'meaning' of a Euro away, sometimes because they did not want to reveal some of their experiences (especially if these involved drugs, sex or violence). It was expected that those they travelled with would also keep secrecy where necessary; as with stag parties or sports team outings, 'what goes on tour, stays on tour.'

Caillois's claim that we live 'in remembrance of one festival and in expectation of the next' was particularly apt for the attitude of United carnival fans on Euro aways. On return from a trip, members of the Red Brigade would usually upload photos taken on the trip on to their message board and write down their experiences in a 'match report' (which barely mentioned the match at all). This served both to tell the tale of the trip to those who were not fortunate enough to attend, but to also allow those who did go to relive their experiences as a group. The expectation and preparation for the next Euro away started well in advance of the fixture, usually when the draw was made. For an attractive fixture in Wolfsburg, Germany in December 2009, only a matter of minutes after the draw in August, a 'thread' had been started on RedBrigade.net entitled 'Germany': 'Who fancies this one?' asked one poster. By 2 October, after much discussion of flights and accommodation, over twenty-five of the group had taken the time off work and booked cheap flights and accommodation, most deciding to fly to Hamburg and spend an evening there before moving onto Wolfsburg. Johnny recounted a conversation with his pregnant wife when he attempted to talk about the trip with her: 'I said to the missus earlier, "Can't fucking wait til December". She said, "Yes, only a month to the baby then". I didn't have the heart to tell her, I just said, "Exactly chicken"'. The lengths that fans would go to in order to attend Euro aways were also extreme. In order to get permission from his parents to be out of the country for this match, one of the youngest fans, Moston, claimed he was going on a school skiing trip. This elaborate lie started to unravel when his mother bought him skiing clothes, which made him feel guilty and also meant he would need to carry these around with him in Germany. The Hamburg leg of the trip, the group agreed, was going to be the highlight. The actual match itself was barely mentioned in the early discussion and planning, other than discussing whether it would be finished in time to catch the last train out of Wolfsburg. The problem of actually obtaining tickets for the match was barely discussed, with a number of the group simply noting that they didn't expect to 'get near' the stadium. In reality, nearly all the members of the Red Brigade got tickets, although a number of carnival fans from other groups were left outside (and some did not even leave Hamburg).

Fans who could not take much time off work, or those travelling alone, sometimes purchased the official travel package from the club, but this option was generally considered to be expensive, sedate and overly restrictive. Both Sugden (2002) and Giulianotti (1995) note that large numbers of football fans travel independently from the official tours, due to flexibility, cost and – for some – also out of protest again the commercialisation of their club (Sugden, 2002: 51–2). As a result, the vast majority of fans travelling for more than one day travelled on unofficial package tours catering for the 'non-tourist' fan or made their own travel arrangements, usually in small groups. For United carnival fans, arranging the cheapest trip was a matter of pride, especially as the rush for direct routes pushed the prices of plane tickets up dramatically. This required early planning, imagination, ingenuity, experience and often time. My first meeting with the Red Brigade group, for example, was in an Irish bar in Warsaw two days before United were due to play in Kiev. Flights to Kiev were expensive, and internet 'chatter' on the United forums suggested a cheap route was to fly on a budget airline to Warsaw and then catch a nineteen-hour sleeper train. Around forty United fans, from various different carnival sub-groups, were present on this one train. Coaches, hire cars, boats and even long-distance taxis were also used on occasion. My journey to Moscow for the 2008 Champions League Final involved an overnight stay in Milan, and another fan's journey to the 2009 Final in Rome involved a train from Milan followed by an overnight stay on the floor of an airport terminal in Frankfurt on his return. The 2007 Kiev trip was relived three years later when the same group of fans travelled to a match in Bursa; involving flying to Sofia (Bulgaria), taking the overnight train to Istanbul, and then a series of trams, trains, boats, ferries and finally a minibus to the stadium in Asian Turkey. Once a cheap option was booked, it was common for the supporter to immediately boast about this to everyone else which in turn would lead to more fans taking that route. For groups of fans, the longer and more convoluted a journey, the more opportunity for 'incident' (and subsequent reliving of this after the trip); the journey was therefore part of the excitement. Stories of bartering with peasant women through sleeper train carriage windows on the Ukrainian steppes and exchanging copies of *Red Issue* fanzine for local beer became legendary. An incident where a fan fell into the Sea of Marmara when attempting to get off a ferry en route to the match in Bursa became the defining point of that season for the Red Brigade. Tales like this were recounted at matches, in pubs and over the internet for years after the event, and almost always long after any discussion of the game had died away. Opportunity for excitement, incident and comedy was therefore an important influence when fans planned their trips, and for many carnival fans was put ahead of comfort and ease (although not usually price).

Once the carnival fans had landed at their destination (or stop-off), their first port of call was inevitably a bar, usually determined by location, price of beer and whether other fans had gathered there. Many fans wanted the experience of singing and chanting with large groups of United fans, demonstrating their support and passion for the club to the locals (this was also true for both England and Blackpool), so the bigger and more rowdy the group, the more flags on display and the louder the singing, the better. For some, this gathering together was unintentional and a mere consequence of meeting friends, or fans they needed to collect tickets from. Fans would use mobile phones to arrange meeting and inevitably where small groups gathered and intermingled, this would bring other groups to them. Fans would then often return to the same bar later in the trip because they enjoyed the experience and hoped to meet other friends, and this often resulted in large groups of United fans gathering. In cities where alcohol bans were in place, these gatherings would inevitably be more concentrated around bars or cafés which were selling beer. A third factor came into play when selecting bars in cities where United fans felt threatened by the locals. On trips to cities such as Rome, Moscow, Kiev and Istanbul, drinking in large groups was seen as safer than in small groups, which could become the target for local hooligan or Ultra gangs. Late at night, some groups of usually all-male United fans would seek out 'titty-bars', which would often be open later than normal bars. Some fans would also seek out brothels, especially in the Netherlands and Germany. Most, however, were content drinking or, in red-light districts, simply 'window-shopping'. The trip to Hamburg in 2009 for example saw the entire group gathering in the main red-light district, with a number excited at the prospect of finding, and 'nailing', 'a brass'. However, although a few entered into negotiations with prostitutes, and some entered one of the brothels, only one or two actually paid for sex.

While drinking remained the primary objective for most of the carnival fans on a Euro away, some also took the opportunity for tourism. On the morning of the game, it was common to see United fans, many hung-over from the night before, doing a quick tour of the sights – in Athens this consisted of a trip to the Acropolis, in Rome a tour of the Coliseum, and in Milan, the Duomo. However, by early afternoon the fans typically drifted back towards the bars, often the setting for the previous evening's festivities. As the afternoon before the match progressed, these groups would often attract the attention of the locals, who would observe and take photographs of the fans and their flags. Almost always the relations between the locals and the fans would be good, and it was common for photographs to be taken together and badges and scarves to be swapped. These gatherings typically also attracted the attention of the police, who would often watch from a distance in riot vans. If small numbers of police entered bars, they would normally be welcomed and sometimes ask to pose for photographs. The reputation of English supporters as being hooligans, was something that United fans at Euro aways constantly had to deal with. Alcohol bans were occasionally invoked, and United fans would sometimes be the victims of attacks by local gangs wanting to establish a reputation, or by police overreacting to rowdy but almost always non-violent expressions of English fandom. As we will see, normally the victims of these ill-judged responses were normal supporters rather than hooligans looking for confrontation.

Most European matches kicked off at 8.45 p.m. local time, and supporters would attempt to gain access to the stadium earlier than for domestic matches. For matches where it was perceived there was a high risk of attacks by local hooligans, fans would take bus escorts arranged by the local police, or on a few rare occasions, walk up to the ground in a large group for protection. Normally, however, carnival fans used existing public transport, walked or took taxis to the stadium. Gaining access to the away section for important Euro away matches was often more chaotic even than a domestic away match; in many stadiums a single entrance gate (rather than multiple turnstiles) and body searches by police or stewards would exacerbate crushes and delay entrance. On occasion, fans queued for over an hour to gain entrance to the ground, and as kick-off approached this would lead to fans becoming frustrated and pushing to get into the ground.[5] Occasionally fans without tickets would try to take advantage of this confusion to create crowd surges to enable them to break through temporary metal-fence barriers or police cordons. In these moments of chaos, disorder and – for fans unused to the Euro away experience – panic, there was the risk that police would use batons or even tear gas against the crowd. On several occasions I witnessed fans at the front of a queue being pushed from behind in this way being struck with batons by police officers. Such overreactions often escalated disorder and further delayed access to the stadium. On a number of occasions fans did not gain entrance until half-time, and where fans were late entering the ground, this would lead to overcrowding in areas of the away section nearest the entrance. It was exceptionally rare for carnival fans at Euro aways to find their allocated seat; fans would simply pick an area where they wished to stand (sometimes a decision made on the basis of which areas looked less vulnerable to missile-throwing by home supporters), leading to overcrowding in some areas of the section, while other areas remained empty.

As with a domestic away, fans stood for the duration and judged their own performance on their noise levels and the originality of their chants. Following the match, the local authorities typically kept the United fans locked in the away section while they cleared the surrounding area of home fans to prevent potential confrontation. This detention usually lasted for around forty-five minutes, although in some cases as long as an hour and a half. Normally this was tolerated as part and parcel of a Euro away, and the fans often entertained themselves by chanting at each other or ridiculing any locals remaining in the stadium or were entertained by the United players as they did warming-down exercises, or a big screen showing United goals. However, the longer the detention lasted, the more tensions rose and when police looked likely to release the fans but then appeared to change their minds, fans often started shouting abuse and sometimes surged towards the exit gates in the hope of pressurising the authorities to let them exit. Serious disorder resulting from United fans being detained after the match was rare but following United's elimination from the 2001–2 Champions League at the semi-final stage at Bayer Leverkusen, the frustration of the fans at losing and being held back afterwards boiled over as the tannoy started playing the anthem of United's main rivals, Liverpool, while the home players and fans celebrated. United fans attacked the locked gates holding them in place, pushing and pulling them violently until they gave way and then spilling out of the stadium. In Marseilles in 2011, fans again broke through a locked exit gate, this time after a dangerous crush had developed as they left the stadium. Normally, however, the excitement of the trip would appear to be dissipating and, with the exception of a hugely important victory, fans would return to the city centre to try to find bars that were still open, or just return to their hotels. Large gatherings of fans following the match was rare; by the time they were released it was late, many of the bars had closed and some fans were travelling back that night or early next morning. For most carnival groups, finding any bar for a few quiet drinks and to discuss the match was of primary concern, particularly as they had been standing and singing for the previous three hours with no access to beer.

For the carnival fan, the Euro away therefore usually involved a great deal of planning and anticipation, followed by a burst of excitement and hedonistic activity over the two days building up to the match itself. During this period there was indeed no life outside of the Euro away, and the fans' experiences during this time were a kind of 'second life' (Bakhtin, 1984). Work and family were rarely discussed, and all attention was focused on the camaraderie of being with 'mates' in a different country following the same football team. However, until several hours before kick-off, the actual match was rarely discussed, and topics of conversation focused on planning the activities of the trip and participating in foolery and mockery within the group. Fans would often deliberately engage in activity that would lead to incident, and some certainly chose to adopt the carnivalesque role of the fool for the entertainment and amusement of themselves and others; in Hamburg in 2009 for example, Jay spent much of one evening wearing women's make-up (on warmer trips he would often wear tennis whites and oversized sunglasses). Towards the end of the trip to the Wolfsburg match in 2009 (a relatively meaningless group-stage match), I asked the Brigade whether they considered it a successful trip:

Denis: From my point of view the company we keep always makes every Euro
          away good … It's funny, we were talking about this the other day, me
          and Dougal, right? And we said one of the best Euro aways we'd ever

had was Rome last year, right? And we lost the European Cup Final.
And yet 'cos of the company and the craic it was one of the best.

Freddy: I reckon sometimes they can be better when the game's not ... that
important.

Denis: I don't like to admit it but for me it's the support and the craic ...

Freddy: I mean when you've not got to worry about the result, it's a bit like,
you know, when we were celebrating them scoring their goal last night,
right? When the result's not that important sometimes it can be an
even better craic.

Jay: That's why I always like to book pre-season friendlies ...

Denis: When you reflect on the trip though, and you think there's Moston
asking moustachioed men to buy him drinks at gay bars right? You've
got Jay wearing make-up and walking around asking where 'the dirty
sex' is on the fourth floor [of a brothel]. You've got CK – imagine him
in the nude for a start – having his pocket picked for 500 notes from
the brasses. You've got people snorting plant food and falling over. It's
a typical Euro away.

Freddy: That's what it's all about isn't it, the stories? You've got to have three or
four good stories come out.

Denis: Oh yeah, it's never any other way is it?

It was the camaraderie, the comedy and the feeling of belonging that made Euro
aways so special for the carnival fans. In Hamburg I found myself looking around
the pub at the assembled group of around thirty fans, most of whom I now knew,
and feeling proud to be part of it. I found myself recounting stories from the trip
to others, and already looking forward to recreating the same type of experiences
at the next match. By the final whistle of the match itself, fans were left considering their journey, both physically and psychologically, 'back to reality', while
replaying and recounting recent events with their friends.

The Euro away – and to a lesser extent, United matches as a whole – did appear
to form an important part of their life, and, it could be argued, played a cathartic
function in allowing fans to 'let off steam'. Presdee contends that, 'under the
"unbearable" rationality of modern life, acts of carnival become a daily need for
social survival' (2002: 33). In this sense these football trips can be assessed against
the 'safety-valve' theory of the value of traditional carnival. As the French clerics
noted of the 1444 'Feast of Fools', 'Don't wine skins and barrels burst very often if
the air-hole is not opened from time to time?' (Burke, 2002: 202). As a result, it
could be argued that in contrast to outward appearances, carnival did not
undermine authority because it was licensed (in a very similar way to contemporary football events) and that in the long run, carnival made people 'easier to
police' (Sales, 1983: 169). Whether this is correct in relation to the carnival fans is
beyond the scope of this book, but it was clear that many of the fans believed it to
be true:

Author: So where do those games sit in your lives? So how important are they
for your working week, before and after, for example?

Freddy: They're massively important to me, domestic or European. I think

European ones are the ones I look forward to a bit more because it's ...

Dave: It's a jolly isn't?

Freddy: It's a bit more of an event, a bit more of a jolly. Even a big away game in the cup is something I would really look forward to because it's a real full day event, you know, get up at half six, seven, in the morning, get the train to where ever we're going to, it's a day on the beer and it's a really good laugh.

Author: Does it make the working week before and after more easy to deal with?

Freddy: I'd say the working week before, maybe not after! [laughs]

Dave: I've looked forward to Euro aways for weeks and weeks, to the extent that you're a kid again – you can't sleep, you're buzzing ...

Freddy: Even after, even though you feel rough those days after, you're still buzzing off the events that happened while you were away.

Moston: Just the things that happen, you've got stories, like, for your life ...

Freddy: What, like you being caught on telly [at Wolfsburg away] when you're supposed to be on a fucking school trip? [laughs]

Author: I'm wondering if football – well, going to football – is a bit of a carnival, that's the metaphor I'm using ...

Freddy: It's escapism isn't it? You know? Escapism that's what it's about. It doesn't even matter about the result ...

Moston: Sorry, but, literally, it plays a part in it, but I really don't care if we've won or lost. I mean I care but it doesn't change my mood at all, like ...

Dave: That's it ...

Freddy: Yeah, football is almost, **almost** [his emphasis] secondary but it is actually the reason you're there.

Dave: Yeah.

Moston: Yeah it is the reason you're there, to, like support them, but win, lose or draw ...

Freddy: It gives you a purpose. The reason to go on the piss.

Dave: I've found I've been worse watching on the telly when we've got beaten. At that point that's all that matters, we've got beat, you're in a mood. When you actually go out there and experience it, in fact the more often you go, actually it's not that the result's not important, but it doesn't ... if you get hammered and you hold your hands up and say, 'well, I've been on the beer for four days then ...'

Freddy: I know more casual United fans than me. And they get more worked up, disappointed, when we lose. And I think that's actually because the result for them is everything. And the result for me isn't every-thing, this [the craic] is ...

Moston: I can't watch football with my Dad anymore ... the result is every-thing to him. His United is like, the team, wanting them to win. Whereas mine is being with my mates, meeting everyone, like organ-ising everything ... like last night when we were all out ... it's a social thing.

Author: What would your lives be like if football didn't exist?

Dave: Hell.

Moston:	Dull.
Freddy:	Hell, er. I think that football's the release really, like. Monday to Friday I have to be reasonably serious, hold down a reasonably decent job …
Author:	[Explains carnival and theories about its cathartic nature]
Freddy:	I think that's right. If you don't let people let the pressure off … you know, you can't lead a normal life.
Moston:	I like to completely separate one from the other … No one [at work] had an idea that I supported United …
Dave:	I don't know about anyone else but summer's [close season] long for me. I hate it … And you get to that stage … you haven't got it … and you wake up and you look forward to Saturday and go, 'oh look, there's nothing happening …'

Locating the carnival – the England national team

A larger scale re-enactment of carnival could be found when travelling with fans of the English national team abroad, particularly at international tournaments. My first observation of England fans abroad came from their visit to Marseilles during the 1998 FIFA World Cup. As we will see, the visit resulted in serious rioting, but the behaviour of England fans prior to this (and to a certain extent afterwards) displayed much of the hedonistic, rule-breaking and collective escapism found among United fans. When I arrived at the Old Port at around 3 p.m., two days before the match, England fans were already in full party mood, filling every bar in the vicinity and spilling out onto the pavements. Due to excessive alcohol consumption some fans were barely able to walk, while others were unconscious on benches and pavements. Flags were displayed from hotel windows and outside bars and some fans were engaging in pro-England and anti-IRA chants, while some serenaded the French public with the chant of 'If it wasn't for the English you'd be Krauts'. Aware of the reputation for England fans for hooliganism, I initially saw threat in this behaviour, but after spending time in this subculture of English supporters, I started to recognise the same carnivalesque behaviour I had seen elsewhere. At the second match in Toulouse, when the local campsite was full, England supporters simply pitched tents and parked camper vans on the fields next to it and in the evening England fans climbed on to the roof of the campsite bar, drinking and chanting long into the night. In the town on the day of the match, thousands congregated in the square outside the town hall, drinking heavily and displaying the flag of St George from every available building and statue. One England fan climbed up the town hall to display his flag, before finding himself stuck on a balcony to the amusement of the crowd below who laughed and chanted at him. Very few of the supporters had tickets for the match, and although some tried to purchase tickets from touts, it was clear that many had come purely for the 'craic' rather than to get into the stadium. This same pattern of behaviour was to be repeated at every international tournament I attended with the England team.

Despite the reputation for England fans becoming involved in 'hooliganism', my observations indicated that it was quite possible for large numbers of ticket-less English supporters to gather together to drink heavily, chant and act raucously without crowd disorder taking place. At the 2004 European Championships in Portugal and the 2006 World Cup in Germany up to 70,000 England fans attended host cities on match days; bars remained open, giant screens showed the match and ticketless fans were not only tolerated, but made to feel welcome participants at the football party. At these tournaments, the main squares of the host cities became the scene of hedonistic mayhem for England supporters. Buildings, statues and fountains were dressed up in England flags, England supporters stood on tables chanting abusive songs denigrating their hosts, or lay unconscious due to excessive alcohol consumption. Some fans wore fancy dress (a Crusader version of St George was particularly popular) or had their faces painted, and some female fans exposed their breasts on demand to groups of lads chanting 'Get your tits out for the lads'. Mass games of football took place, with balls landing on bar tables, sending food and beer flying, hitting bewildered passers-by and smashing the occasional window. Every now and again groups of England fans would break out into a chant of 'Let's all have a disco' and jump up and down, throwing plastic glasses full of beer into the air and soaking themselves and all around. Some fans took drugs (particularly cocaine and cannabis) and others visited brothels. As with the fans of Blackpool and Manchester United, it would be misleading to claim that all fans of the team were interested in recreating the carnivalesque. However from my observations with fans of England abroad, the carnival fans dominated the overall support to a far greater extent than with either of the other teams.

Conclusion

The metaphor of carnival, drawn from accounts of the feasts and festivals of early-modern Europe, is apt to describe a significant proportion of fans who attend matches, particularly away. For these carnival fans, having 'good craic' was as, if not more, important than events that transpired on the pitch. A consistent finding across my research with fans of Blackpool, Manchester United and England was the importance of using the match and the time around it to 'get away from' the norms of everyday working and family life. The fans observed would use a number of different methods to achieve this break from normality and the mundane. Fans would often change their dress (ranging from wearing a particular coat, through to face painting and fancy dress) and would engage in hedonistic activity, especially the consumption of large amounts of alcohol. Being part of a like-minded crowd was also central to the motivations of these fans and once in this crowd, they could adapt their behaviour to further depart from the norm, engaging in singing, banter, jostling and general tomfoolery. An important goal in the match could form the peak of this experience for fans both inside and outside matches (for many fans travelled without tickets), with carnival fans reflecting positively on rowdy celebrations which were as likely – if not more – to result in minor injury in modern all-seated ends as the traditional terraces. However, research participants also reflected favourably upon trips where the team had lost or not scored a goal, highlighting incidents of humour or camaraderie. Engaging in low-level rowdiness and disorder often also formed part of this experience and carnival fans felt empowered within a crowd to push at the edges of the law. However, there were unwritten rules of what was acceptable and those perceived to be going too far risked censure and embarrassment in front of their peers.

Notes

1 Court observations, *Chief Constable of West Yorkshire* v. *Nye and others*, Leeds Magistrates' Court, 21/06/10; *Chief Constable of West Yorkshire* v. *Etherington and Punter*, Leeds Crown Court, 06/10/10.

2 Carnival literally means 'farewell to the flesh', referring to the feasting of meat immediately prior to the fasting of Lent. Shrove Tuesday or 'Pancake Day' marks the end of the traditional carnival season.

3 'Il [*l'homme*] vit dans le souvenir d'une fête et dans l'attente d'une autre, car la fête figure pour lui, pour sa mémoire et pour son désir, le temps des émotions intense set de la métamorphose de son être'.

4 This offence was introduced following the Taylor Report's recommendation that perimeter fencing should be removed following the Hillsborough disaster (1990: para. 299).

5 In many European countries (especially Italy), fans arrive earlier and so the 'flow' of fans through these entrances is slower. As a result, the late rush of English fans cannot be dealt with by either the infrastructure or the personnel at the stadium (see Pearson and Sale, 2011).

3

Identity and expression

The off-pitch performance

Creating an 'impression' for the opposition fans, locals and viewers on the television was a fundamental part of being a carnival fan. This 'cultural performance' of fandom (Armstrong and Young, 2000: 184) was engaged in by fans at various levels and could change from season to season or match to match. Furthermore, engagement in this performance was not limited to carnival fan groups, although it was not the driving force behind all match-going supporters, many of whom attend purely to watch the game (although they may also appreciate the colour and atmosphere created by the more active fans). For the carnival fans, creating an 'atmosphere' of noise, colour and imagination was seen as a vital part of the match-day experience. In a sense, there were two contests taking place: the one on the pitch between the two teams but also the one in the stands between the sets of supporters. Victory for the team on the pitch was not the be all and end all, and a good performance by the fans could go a long way to making up for a disappointing one from the team.

However, while 'impression management' (Goffman, 1984) was important to carnival fans, it was secondary to having a good time. Here, it would seem that the English carnival supporter differs significantly from the likes of the Italian Ultras, who often sacrifice their own hedonism in order to create a spectacle for their club. Chanting, swaying, surging and showing colours were, to varying extents, all important activities for the carnival fans inside stadiums, but these were seen as enjoyable activities in their own right and part of the 'craic' of going to matches. Significantly, they did not interfere with the fans' other activities – primarily drinking (which is illegal in sight of the pitch). Since the removal of terracing from English grounds, fans typically enter the stadium later because there is no need to arrive early to get a good position. Any attempts to persuade carnival fans to arrive half an hour before kick-off to create an Italian Ultra-type 'spectacle' would be likely to fail as research participants would prefer to drink in the pub. That said, in exceptional circumstances carnival fans would reluctantly muster themselves to arrive early – normally this was for reasons considered very serious rather than the relative frivolity of creating a spectacle. For example, in 2005, many of the United fans left the pubs early on a number of occasions to take part in mass protests and marches against the incoming owners, and in 2008, fans arrived at the ground early in order to take part in a minute's silence in honour of the fiftieth anniversary of the Munich air disaster. At England games, fans also typically arrived slightly earlier to sing the national anthem, although this was in itself seen as a pleasurable activity.

'Piss-taking'

On the whole, however, 'the craic' governed what activities the fans would become involved in and an important aspect of this was the role of humour. Ironically, although English fans abroad have a reputation for being involved in hooliganism, the carnival fans were driven by a desire to have a good time and engage in humorous interaction and activity. They did not take themselves seriously all the time, and banter within the groups and between the groups and outsiders was a fundamental part of being an English football fan. Kate Fox contends that, 'the most noticeable and important "rule" about humour in English conversation is its dominance and pervasiveness. Humour rules. Humour governs. Humour is omnipresent and omnipotent'. In essence, it is the 'default mode' for the English (2005: 61); light-hearted banter, jokes at the expense of others, and fooling and clowning around have been noted to play a vital role in English life, in the pub (Fox, 2005), the workplace (Ackroyd and Thompson, 2003) and the schoolyard (Willis, 1977). As Collinson (1992) argues, an essential part of culturally 'being a man' is the ability to engage in humour and laugh at oneself. Making jokes at the expense of others was also an important part of the football carnival (Giulianotti, 1995; Jones, 2006) at it was in Bakhtin's. In the stands, in pubs before and after the match, on journeys to and from games and on internet message boards and text message conversations, humour and banter were omnipresent. While fans are frequently accused of taking themselves and their sport too seriously (and often object to being told 'it's only a game'), within the subculture of their own support, the carnival of fandom relied heavily upon supporters' ability to use humour and to laugh at themselves and others. Even when fans were put under pressure of aggressive policing, attacks by rival fans or a disastrous football result for their team, humour was often used to alleviate the situation. As Bakhtin (1984) argues, a carnival needs both fools and humour in order to survive, and football trips often demanded that one fan delivered himself (either intentionally or not) as the trip's fool. For the Brigade's trip to Bursa in Turkey, it was Parkey who found himself in this role, having fallen off a ferry en route to the match and then missed his flight home.

'Banter', 'piss taking' and 'winding up' ruled, with fans constantly coming up with new ways to make fun of others and making football 'a place where societal norms about politeness are suspended' (Jones, 2006: 4). Fans were given nicknames, accused of homosexuality, and had fun made of their hair, dress sense and choice of drink. Some of these responded in kind, others played along with stereotypes given to them. The fans also swore at each other constantly – friends were frequently referred to as 'fuckers', 'cunts' and 'twats', although usually with a smile on the speaker's face to indicate they are not being serious. However, the atmosphere remained convivial, and no one suggested to me they felt any sense of bullying or being bullied (although undoubtedly some fans were the butt of more jokes than others). At the same time, the fans within the carnival groups would show each other signs of affection – fans often greeted each other with hand-shakes, hugs and even kisses on the cheek or forehead and as alcohol was consumed, fans would put their arms round each other, ruffle each other's hair or pat each other on the back. Bakhtin's summary of interaction between people at carnival is appropriate here:

> When two persons establish friendly relations, the form of their verbal inter-course also changes abruptly; they address each other informally, abusive words are used affectionately, and mutual mockery is permitted ... The two friends may pat each other on the shoulder and even on the belly (a typical carnival-esque gesture). Verbal etiquette and discipline are relaxed and indecent words and expressions may be used. (1984: 16)

At carnival, profanities which were normally taken seriously, became humorous (*ibid.*: 17). For Bakhtin, writing in the Soviet Union, this mode of interaction appears to have been a stark contrast between the more formal communication of everyday life, and indicated a suspension of the norms of speech and interac-tion during the time of carnival.

However, for the carnival fans, the difference between how they acted around football and how they acted in everyday life was less pronounced. Most admitted to acting this way with friends who did not attend football and for some, this type of interaction was also part of their work relationship with colleagues (as Ackroyd and Thompson suggest). However, most admitted that in the context of football, the informality, physical contact and use of profanities increased signif-icantly. Indeed, aside from Bakhtin's depiction of carnival, the most striking comparison for the behaviour of the carnival fans was that of Paul Willis's (1977) working-class lads 'having a laff' during their time at school, often with a fine line between this, misbehaviour, vandalism and even violence.

Football chants

Another fundamental part of a 'good' fan experience for the research participants was the ability to congregate in a group. Whether these groups were made up of friends who met regularly and travelled together, or whether individuals located like-minded fans in order to drink and chant, the carnivalesque activity that drove the fans could only be achieved in a group. The nature of these groups made them at times unruly and posed crowd management challenges and they could also lead to the reinforcement of sexist and occasionally racist norms of behaviour. As a result, they were often stigmatised, criticised and contrasted unfavourably with the 'new consumer' fan (King, 2003). However, these groups of carnival fans – once formed – provided a key function in the creation of 'atmosphere' at matches. While these fans provided only a small proportion of the overall fan base at their team's home matches, their influence on crowd noise and chanting was vastly disproportionate to their numbers. This is because, through their activity at away matches in particular, the carnival fan groups were the driving force behind the creation of demonstrations of fandom (usually audible, occasionally visual). They also tended to perform the function of orchestrating these demonstrations inside the home stadium, usually by starting chants and by keeping new chants going when non-carnival fans were still learning the words.

Observations with fans of all three clubs revealed that it was the carnival fans, normally at away matches, who were responsible for creating new chants and getting them sung at home matches by the wider fan base. My research suggested that for a wholly original chant (as opposed to a reworking of an existing one) to become popular with the home support, the number of fans able to join in needed to be gradually increased over a long period. Fans in the immediate proximity to chanters would then pick up the tune and lyrics and over time the number of supporters who were fluent in the new chant would grow, increasing participation, noise and the likelihood of the chant becoming a regular one. Interestingly, watching the process at United, it seemed that despite the popularity of online message boards, the internet was not a good way of launching a new chant. Attempts at starting new chants by posting lyrics on message boards or even by posting links to YouTube videos of fans singing the new chant were not successful during my observations (this may be different for clubs with smaller fan bases), despite positive responses on the forums at the time.

Most chants failed to gain popularity among the wider fan base altogether. At both Blackpool and United, carnival fans were constantly making up or trying out new chants, on journeys to and from matches and in pubs before the game. Many of these chants were not for consumption outside the immediate group. Often the chants were spontaneous and humorous commentaries on recent or ongoing incidents involving the group at the time; in one incident on a tram heading back from a United match, Ruby took offence at another supporter singing, 'Hillsborough, '89' (a song celebrating the deaths of Liverpool fans in a stadium disaster) and started a chant of 'Nobhead, 2009', to the same tune, pointing at the other fan. The song drew much support and laughter from the tram, but was meaningless beyond that particular context. Many chants were created purely for entertainment and the amusement of the creator and those around, with no intention of them receiving a wider audience or catching on in the stands. Others that become popular at particular away matches (especially Euro aways), were sung occasionally by those that were present, but never become popular due to references which were meaningless to those not at that match. For these chants, it may have been that the fans did not *want* them to catch on, preferring the exclusivity and the ability to use the chant to say to other fans: '*I* was there'. For example, a chant in honour of the Portuguese beer 'Superbok', was sung by United fans on Euro aways to Portugal:

Superbok, Super Star,
Gets you more pissed than Stella Artois!

However, for the new chants that were intended to become terrace anthems, the process could be a long one. This was especially the case at United where carnival fans prided themselves on the originality of their songs and often objected to chants borrowed or mimicked from other teams or more generic football chants sung by a number of other clubs. It took nearly four years from its creation for the 'Viva Ronaldo' chant to become widely sung at Old Trafford. Usually, however, the process was one that took place over a number of weeks or months, depending on the complexity of the chant. In 2008, a chant about United's Brazilian midfielder, Anderson, started to be sung in pubs by carnival fans before United away matches. Marsh *et al.* noted that during the 1970s new chants typically started on 'football specials', when 'chant leaders' were encouraged to invent or rework chants (1978: 67–8), but although trains to and from matches were still sometimes used to spread new songs, in the 1990s and 2000s, it was the pub that became the real factory for new chants – and a 'chant leader' could be anyone inventive and bold enough to try to get a new song to catch on. The Anderson chant was a complex one, with the lyrics in the middle sung quickly (to the tune of 'Agadoo'), making it difficult to pick up:

> Anderson, son, son, he's better than Kleberson,
> Anderson, son, son, he's our midfield magician,
> To the left, to the right, to the Samba beat tonight,
> He is class with a brass, and he shits on Fabregas!

For a number of weeks the song was sung in pubs away from home, then sporadically in pubs around Old Trafford and increasingly in the stadium at away matches as more and more carnival fans and then other regular away matchgoers started to pick up the lyrics. Upon United's visit to Fulham that season, the chant was one of the loudest sung by the away end of around 4,000 and the tune and final line was clearly audible on television coverage. The following week, the chant was being sung in pubs around Old Trafford and the final stage was its introduction to the Stretford End. Despite several weeks of the chant in pubs and at away matches, very few in ST2 knew the lyrics other than the final line. However, there were enough pockets of fans who knew the chant and wanted it to catch on to get it going. After another couple of home matches, with these pockets starting the chant several times a match, it finally became one of the terrace anthems of that and the following season. However, considering the efforts that went into getting it to become popular, it is not surprising that so many chants fell by the wayside.

At Blackpool, starting chants was a considerably easier task due to smaller crowds. Songs which caught on at big away matches would inevitably catch on inside Bloomfield Road due to the proportion of fans who had attended (sometimes as high as half the home capacity). The birth of one chant at Blackpool demonstrated a stark contrast with the complications at United. Here, a fan sitting in the seats directly above the South Paddock was challenged to invent a chant for one of the Blackpool players. Apparently off the top of his head (it may have been that this chant had already been made up in a pub prior to the

game), the fan then created a song (to the tune of 'Hava Nagila') as the fans at the
back of the Paddock, turned and listened:

> Andy, oh Andy Andy,
> Oh Andy Andy,
> It's Andy Watson – superstar!

When he had finished, they started repeatedly singing the chant, with it gradually
picking up volume as more and more fans picked up the tune and lyrics. The
chant quickly became the anthem for the player, and was sung home and away for
the duration of his career with Blackpool. I was not aware of the individual
creating another chant before or after.

Most chants were designed to provide support to the players on the pitch,
either collectively or individually. They focused on positive aspects relating to the
team and its history, players, management, fans, and the city, town or country
from where the team originated. Most of the fans believed that in creating vocal
support of this kind, they were assisting the players on the pitch; this belief
was often encouraged by players, managers and club officials (in the 1995–96
season, Blackpool FC launched a 'carnival atmosphere' initiative to try and
support their promotion push). Popular and simple chants such as 'Come On
You 'Pool', 'U-ni-ted!' or 'In-ger-lund' would reverberate from all around the
ground at times, giving the impression that every person inside the stadium was
singing at once. It was impossible to ascertain how many fans were singing, but in
'rowdy' areas of the ground such as the South Paddock or ST2, the number of
fans involved in *popular* chants appeared to be much more than half.
Additionally, fans would aim abusive or insulting chants at rival teams and
players, and sometimes boo or whistle. Here, the fans were intending to intimidate and distract the opposition. When the atmosphere in the stand died, it was
typical for some fans to shout to those around them that they need to 'get behind'
and 'support' the players. 'Sing your hearts out for the lads' was a chant heard at
all three clubs when the team were struggling and the atmosphere was perceived
to need boosting. However, the creation of noise was not always to enhance the
chance of success on the pitch. Some of the noisiest atmospheres were unexpected, when the team was winning convincingly or losing badly, or in
competitions or matches that were not important. In fact it seemed that at some
of the tighter and more important matches, the crowd were too nervous to create
noise, even though those were the times that the team needed the most encouragement. Other chants were designed to encourage participation from different
sections of the crowd. The South Paddock and ST2 would on occasion demand
that the rest of the crowd join them in standing with a chant of 'Stand up for the
Champions' (United) or 'Stand up if you hate Preston' (Blackpool). This would
usually result in many fans from other parts of the ground standing and the chant
spreading to other stands (it was also on occasion used as a strategy to confound
stewards who were trying to get fans to desist in persistent standing). At
Blackpool, following this chant, it became common for the seated area of the
South Stand to then chant 'Sit down if you hate Preston', which resulted in the

fans on the Paddock crouching or sitting down on the terrace – the world turned upside-down indeed.

Chants performed a second important function, which was to establish internal coherence among a group of fans, reaffirm identity and, often through doing so, insult the opposition supporters. 'Winding up' opposition supporters was a key aim of vocal fans (not just carnival fans) inside grounds and supporters would go to great lengths to find new and novel ways of insulting clubs, players and localities. As Armstrong and Young write, 'The ability to manoeuvre any material into a suitable framework is part of the skill of the creativity of support or denigration' (2000: 184). Supporters from areas perceived to be rural were invariably inbred 'sheep shaggers'. Visits to towns such as Burnley would lead to fans chanting:

> Your mum's your dad, your dad's your mum,
> You're interbred, you're Burnley scum!

Fans would give the opposition supporters the six-fingered salute (placing the second hand behind the first to give the impression of having six fingers) to suggest they were the result of inbreeding, and fans leaving early were serenaded with 'You're going home to shag your sister'. Both United and Blackpool insulted supporters from Merseyside as being slum-dwelling, jobless thieves, while fans from Yorkshire were alcoholic wife-beaters. Fans would also attempt to wind up the opposition fans by praising their rivals. At a Manchester City vs. Blackpool match, when City fans chanted 'We're the Pride of Manchester', Blackpool fans responded by chanting 'United' (had they been playing United, they would have probably chanted 'City come from Manchester') and Nottingham Forest fans were told their city was 'Just a small town in Derby'. When United played Glasgow Rangers, United fans chanted 'Ian Paisley, what a wanker, what a wanker' in order to try and wind up their fans (who were perceived to be loyalist protestants), but when they played Glasgow Celtic (whose fans are perceived to have Catholic and pro-Irish Republican leanings) a few years later, the same fans chanted 'Fuck the Pope and the IRA'.

In the course of winding up opposition supporters, chants were created that some carnival fans – and other supporters generally – considered to be morally unacceptable. It is worth noting here that it was not always the case that carnival fans would be more tolerant of abusive and 'edgy' songs: on many occasions they objected to chants that were sung by a large proportion of non-carnival match-going fans (see Chapter 7). Usually, however, it was carnival fans who created and sang the 'edgier' chants, although not all would necessarily agree with them or join in. Songs revelling in the deaths of opposition fans, players or officials in particular drew mixed responses from carnival fans. Some of these chants would not be sung inside the stadium, possibly due to the negative response they would receive from non-carnival fans. At Blackpool, some fans would chant 'Always look on the rooftops for ice' at games against Burnley, referring to the death of a club employee killed falling off a stand roof. This chant was sung by many fans on the

South Paddock, and also at away matches. At England matches, some fans would chant about Bobby Sands, the Irish republican prisoner who died on hunger strike in 1981.

United fans had a great array of contentious chants. Leeds United supporters were regaled with 'Always look out for Turks carrying knives' in reference to two Leeds fans murdered in Istanbul. The chant was relatively popular in the stands at United, and many fans justified it on the grounds that Leeds fans had been chanting about the Munich air disaster (to the same tune) for decades. The fact that many clubs' supporters had chanted about the Munich disaster was used by many United fans to justify chants of this nature and chants against Liverpool in particular resulted in considerable disagreement. For the United support there was a sliding scale of acceptability regarding chants about the Heysel disaster (where thirty-nine Juventus fans were killed after disorder involving Liverpool fans in 1985) and the Hillsborough tragedy. One of the most popular chants when United played Liverpool was, with reference to Heysel, 'Without killing anyone, we won it [the European Cup] three times'. This chant was generally seen as acceptable as it lauded the behaviour of United fans in their European Cup campaigns in contrast to Liverpool. Marginally less acceptable, but still popular in the stands both home and away, was the chant of 'Murderers' in reference to this disaster. However, other chants such as 'We want justice for Heysel' were generally limited to pubs before and after matches.

Chanting about the Hillsborough disaster was considered significantly less acceptable among the fan base due to the fact that the fans who died included children and that, as most of the United carnival fans agreed, they themselves could have easily been the victims of the disaster instead. However, the intense hatred of Liverpool by most United fans, combined with the fact that Liverpool fans had sung about Munich (and occasionally still did so), meant that some fans were happy to use the Hillsborough disaster to goad Liverpool fans. The most acceptable of the Hillsborough chants appeared to be 'You killed your own fans', referring to the initial belief (since disproved by the inquest into the disaster) that it was ticketless Liverpool fans gaining access to the stadium that caused the over-crowding and subsequent fatalities. However, even this chant was rarely heard inside grounds, usually only at Anfield on occasion of a United defeat, and even then by only a small proportion of the away section. Other chants, such as 'Hillsborough '89' and 'Ninety-six was not enough' were usually only heard by certain carnival fans on journeys to or from matches, or in pubs. Even here, chanters would sometimes be challenged by other carnival fans, as evidenced by Ruby's response to a Hillsborough chant above. Another controversial (and slanderous) chant was 'Sit down you paedophile', chanted at Arsenal's manager, Arsene Wenger by large numbers of United fans at Old Trafford (although this was not a serious accusation). Other chants of this nature about Wenger were also sung by carnival fans including one suggesting that he was responsible for the disappearance of the missing child Madeleine McCann; this was considered objectionable by many carnival fans and as a result was limited to small groups in pubs or on journeys to or from matches.

Since 1991, the chanting of 'indecent or racialist' songs in football stadiums has been unlawful, but this has had little impact upon the behaviour of fans. The majority of United chants, and a substantial number of Blackpool and England chants, contained indecent language but during my research I did not witness a single arrest or ejection from the ground on these grounds. At a single match between Blackpool and Burnley in 1996, seven specific 'indecent' chants were heard aimed at the Burnley fans/players *in addition* to racist chanting:

> He's shit, he's scouse, he'll rob your fucking house, David Eyres, David Eyres.
> Always look on the Turf Moor for shite.
> Chim-chiminee, chim-chiminee, chim-chim-cheroo. We hate those bastards in claret and blue.
> Cheer up Adrian Heath! Oh what can it mean? To a sad Burnley bastard and a shite football team.
> Shit on the Burnley, shit on the Burnley tonight.
> Fuck off Burnley, fuck off Burnley.
> You scouse bastard, you scouse bastard [to David Eyres].

In addition to this, other more general chants which contained 'indecent' language were heard at the vast majority of Blackpool's home games:

> If I had the wings of a sparrow, the dirty black arse of a crow, I'd fly over Deepdale tomorrow, and shit on the bastards below.
> You're just a bunch of wankers.
> Fuck off [team name].
> You're gonna get your fucking heads kicked in.
> Who ate all the pies? You fat bastard, you fat bastard, you ate all the pies.
> The referee's a wanker.
> Where's your father referee? You haven't got one, you never had one, you're a bastard referee.
> You're shit and you know you are.
> [Player name] is a wanker, is a wanker.
> You're just a soft/dirty southern/Yorkshire bastard.
> Oh, Lancashire, is wonderful. It's full of tits, fanny and Blackpool.
> You're the shit of Lancashire.
> Can you hear the [team name] sing? I can't hear a fucking thing.

I attended no match with Blackpool where their fans failed to sing an indecent chant. At a low-key league match with Millwall in 1997, I attempted to count the number of chants containing 'indecent' language. After the first ten minutes there had been six different indecent chants within earshot, and twelve indecent chants in total. Matches at United, and to a lesser extent England, followed a similar pattern of using indecent language in chants to both support the team and denigrate the opposition.

The carnival in the stands

Chanting was not the only way in which carnival fans attempted to create an impression, inspire the team and express identity. Colour also formed a major part of the carnival in the stands. At Blackpool, the colour tangerine performed a major role in promoting the identity of the club and its supporters. Many supporters, including carnival fans, would wear replica shirts, and for important matches – e.g. play-off games, crunch promotion or relegation matches or local derbies at home (away from home wearing colours was often perceived as too dangerous for those travelling independently) – fans would attempt to make the Blackpool stands a 'sea of tangerine', often involving flags, balloons, boiler suits and wigs. The importance of colour in the display of fandom was less important to fans of England or United, but here, flags performed the visual role of express-ing identity. England fans would cover the stadium with the Cross of St George, usually bearing the name of the town, city or club that the fans supported. United fans would cover the away section with flags proclaiming localities from where the fans heralded, or other messages of support, for example: 'United, Kids, Wife – In That Order'. In contrast to most other English clubs, United fans did not typically use the Cross of St George or the Union Flag, but instead preferred to use red, white and black. ST2 at United also had a number of banners across the hoardings at the front with messages such as 'MUFC – The Religion', 'Republik of Mancunia – Red Army', and 'One Love – Stretford End –MUFC'. 'One Love' was a reference to a song by Manchester band the Stone Roses, and at United in partic-ular, local popular music played a significant role in defining the identity of the fans and the club.

On occasion, particular matches (usually away from home) would be desig-nated special occasions for expressions of fandom. At Blackpool, the last game of the season for some of the carnival fans was seen as an opportunity for fancy dress (and, if possible, invading the pitch), and various outfits were worn in the stands, ranging from orange boiler-suits, to nuns' habits. For England matches in international tournaments, fancy dress was also popular, with some fans dressed as St George, and others painting their faces. However, this was generally more popular with non-carnival fans (although carnival fans occasionally decorated cars or campervans they were travelling in). United's carnival fans generally considered themselves 'above' this type of activity, and many wore no colours to matches whatsoever. However, even United fans on occasion designated a match as an opportunity to dress up. At Anfield in 2009 some fans wore Eric Cantona masks, and at Blackburn in 2004, the fans designated the match '70s Day'; large numbers wore 1970s-style bar scarves around their wrists and old football shirts and hats, some were dressed in decorated butcher's coats and during the match they chanted old football songs. The '70s Day' was considered a great success, and the fact that United lost 1–0 barely registered for many fans, who were more concerned with what was happening in the stands than on the pitch. The 2009–11 seasons at United also saw an extraordinary use of colour, when United fans (both carnival and the wider support) started wearing green and gold scarves and other clothing to matches in protest at the club's ownership. Green and gold were chosen because they were the original colours of Newton Heath (United's previous incarnation), and large numbers of United's carnival fans wore those colours, including carnival fans who did not normally wear football scarves. The culmination of the protest came during a match against AC Milan where the Stretford End displayed three giant anti-Glazer banners and thousands of fans lifted their green and gold scarves above their heads as they chanted 'We'll never die'. It was the most impressive show of colour and coordination I witnessed at Old Trafford and demonstrated that the accepted norms of how different groups dressed or acted could be altered in exceptional circumstances.

Other visual acts of carnival inside stadiums were carried out during the course of the research even though they broke various criminal laws. Blackpool fans would often throw ticker tape into the air when the team entered the pitch, which while harmless, was technically an offence of missile throwing under the Football Offences Act 1991. The throwing of toilet rolls (as streamers) or inflatables (often a blow-up sex doll) was also acceptable among fans of Blackpool and United, as indeed was anything 'harmless'. The most bizarre incident of mass missile throwing from Blackpool fans took place during the vital last home game of the 1995–96 season. The sell-out crowd was issued with tangerine plastic noses to wear to celebrate what could have been the team's promotion as part of the club's 'carnival atmosphere' initiative. However, when the team started losing, the opposition goalkeeper came under a barrage of the lightweight noses. United fans also set off red distress flares or smoke bombs at several important away matches, a practice that, while illegal under the Sporting Events Act 1985, was supported by carnival fans as a way of creating an impression for opposing fans and television viewers of both colour and disrespect for authority.

Another element of carnival introduced to the stands was the occasional use of musical instruments. At England, this came in the form of the Sheffield Wednesday brass band, who would start chants by playing favourite England anthems such as the theme from *The Great Escape* at matches. The attitude towards the England band was mixed from carnival fans; while some appreciated the noise and entertainment brought by the band and the fact that it encouraged singing, others objected to the noise (especially for those sitting nearby), and the fact that they tended to dominate and control the atmosphere, taking away from the traditional spontaneity of supporting England. One fan on Blackpool's South Paddock brought a trumpet along for a number of matches, although he appeared to be at an early stage in learning the instrument and was largely limited to playing the melody from a dance anthem (Alice Deejay's 'Better off Alone'). Although this tune had no connection to Blackpool at all, it soon became popular with the fans and long after the trumpet had disappeared the fans would spontaneously start singing the tune. An attempt by the club to create a 'carnival atmosphere' at Bloomfield Road, with drums, however, did not gain much support and was soon abandoned. As a general rule for Blackpool, England and United, the more 'official' the attempt to improve the atmosphere at grounds was, the less support it would receive from carnival fans, who remained the driving force for noise inside football stadiums.

For the duration of the match, of course, the carnival fans were observing what was happening on the pitch, and this would define much of their expression of fandom. Certain moments in the match would result in certain responses. An impressive piece of skill from a player would result in a chant of his name (if such a chant existed), and the winning of a corner would usually result in a simple chant designed to inspire the team and intimidate the opposition ('U-ni-ted'; 'Come on You Pool'; 'Come on England'). Carnival fans would attempt to sing for as much of the match as possible, but inevitably there would be quiet moments, particularly at home. At quiet moments in the match (for example while a player was receiving treatment or the opposition was making a substitution), fans would chat to each other about the match, plans for future games, stories of previous matches and social issues generally. For carnival fans the match provided a social function, enabling them to meet friends and family that they may only see at the football, so it was an opportunity to catch up on news and gossip generally. Fans would also make comments about the ongoing match to each other continuously, shout encouragement to the team, and abuse to players of both teams. Generally, abuse shouted at players from the supporter's own team was only given on the occasion of a mistake, and, even then, if it was perceived to be too abusive or if a particular player was seen as being 'scapegoated', fans nearby may challenge the supporter about their actions. Typically the criticism of the supporter's own players would be limited to expressions like 'For fuck's sake, Smith!', 'Do something, Smith!' or sarcastic cries of 'Oh, fucking brilliant Smith!'. When former Liverpool player Michael Owen joined United, many of the carnival fans were disappointed at the signing and upon his first appearance for the club he was greeted with (non-ironic) chants of 'You scouse bastard'.

The rules about what behaviour was acceptable when supporting the team were therefore complex and also varied from team to team. Booing individual players from your team, however badly they were playing, was generally perceived to be unacceptable as it could destroy their confidence and damage the team, but players perceived as poor or – even worse – not trying, would be abused and might be booed when they were substituted. Booing the team after a poor performance was more acceptable, particularly at home, but fans' views on this were mixed; at United in particular, the booing of the team was frowned upon. Away from home, however poor the performance, most of the carnival fans would applaud the team at the end of the match. In return, the team were expected to walk over to the away end and applaud them, and real anger and vitriol would be directed at players who did not do this, particularly after a poor performance.

The highlight of the action inside the stadium was when the team scored a goal. Reactions to goals varied wildly depending on the importance of the goal and the opposition. Goals scored in games that were being won or lost heavily would usually rouse little more than a cheer and a round of applause. However, for vital goals, the celebrations would be wild and occasionally dangerous. As we have seen, important goals scored in front of the South Paddock would lead to surges and often pitch invasions, and the celebrations would go on as fans tried to get back to their feet or reclaim their position on the terrace. At United, a number of vital last-minute goals were celebrated wildly in ST2, with fans jumping up and down screaming, falling over seats and hugging each other. A winning goal in the sixth minute of injury time in a 4–3 victory over Manchester City was described by a number of fans as 'making it all worthwhile' ('it' referred to the price of the season ticket and the perceived routine drudgery and poor atmospheres of normal home matches). Goal celebrations of this nature were no safer in all-seated areas than on terraces, with fans climbing onto the backs of seats in moments of high excitement and sometimes falling; at Nantes in 2002, a last-minute equaliser for United saw a crowd surge down a packed stairway and a crush when a fan near the front stumbled and those behind him fell over the bodies in front. For celebrations of vital goals, fans would often be out of breath and exhausted afterwards, describing themselves as 'buzzing' off the elation of the moment for days afterwards.

Identity and division at Manchester United

Attending football performed an important social function for carnival fans, enabling them to meet with friends who they may see infrequently, and in a context which allowed them to behave informally and expressively. The experience also provided an opportunity for them to exhibit their connection with the club and their geographical and social identity. Carnival fans needed to feel and express a connection with the club that went deeper than the mere wearing of a replica shirt or sitting in the stadium. Instead, they revelled in their ability to create the atmosphere within the stadium that would become an important aspect of the match for the other fans, the players and those watching on television. They spent time creating, learning and then teaching chants to others. For some that involved 'buying into' aspects of the carnival, dressing in a particular way or singing particular songs that did not actually reflect their own 'non-football existence'. At United, London-based fans would chant 'Manchester la la la', and female supporters would declare, 'We are the Manchester boys'. For many 'armchair' fans who only attended a few games a season, the excitement of going to a game came from not just seeing the players live, but being part of the crowd and experiencing the atmosphere initiated – in the main – by the carnival supporters.

The reasons that the carnival fans invested so heavily in becoming part of this carnival were complex and so were the internal social rules dictating the standards of behaviour expected in the areas of the stadium frequented by them. An unwritten code of conduct laid down minimum standards of support and maximum levels of abuse and criticism than could be made of the team. However, these standards shifted and changed depending on team's performance (both in that game and over the season), the players on the pitch, and – most importantly of all – the opposition. Those perceived to overstep this mark risked censure from other supporters, usually consisting of a put down or criticism designed to humiliate the supporter in front of other fans. If the supporter and his friends objected to this censure vociferously, then conflict could escalate between the groups. While this usually remained on a vocal level, at all three clubs I witnessed fights break out due to fans disagreeing on whether they were permitted to abuse an underperforming team.

A significant factor in United's match-going support was the number of non-Mancunians who followed the team. Although two local media surveys in the early 2000s indicated that United's support outnumbered City's in the Greater Manchester area, their support both home and away contained large numbers of fans from all over the country and, increasingly, the world. At home matches in particular, an Irish or London accent was as likely to be heard as Mancunian (although the language, tone and delivery of many of the chants forced non-Mancunian fans to depart from their normal accent and dialect). This led to both abuse from rival fans claiming, 'We support our local team', and occasional tension between Mancunian United fans and those from elsewhere. However, non-Mancunian fans who had 'bought in' to the Manchester subculture of supporting United (in terms of attitude, dress-sense, music, etc.) were welcomed into the heart of the carnival. As we have seen, another feature of the United's carnival fans groups that set them apart from most other teams' fans was their overall indifference, and in some cases genuine antipathy, towards the England national team. The attitude of United fans for being contrary, aggressive and arrogant is summed up in one of their most popular chants:

> We are just one of those teams that you see now and then,
> We often score six, but we seldom score ten,
> We'll beat them at home and we'll beat them away,
> We'll kill any bastards that get in our way.
> We are the pride of all Europe, the cock of the north,
> We hate the scousers, the cockneys of course – and Leeds!
> We are United, without any doubt,
> We are the Manchester boys, la la la ...

London-based supporters (viewed as 'cockneys' by Mancunian fans) were expected to join in with this declaration of support for the club.

Opinions of United carnival fans on their wider worldwide fan base was not usually complimentary; they were often derided as 'glory-hunters', 'hangers on', 'JCLs' ('Johnny-come-latelies') or, for those who only attended occasionally, 'day trippers'. At away matches in particular, fans taking photographs, asking others to sit down, or not joining in with vocal support of the team risked being at best ignored, and at worst, bullied. The question, 'how did you get your fucking tickets?' was put to those perceived as United 'tourists' at numerous away matches by carnival fans who believed their own access to away tickets was insufficient. At matches at Old Trafford 'day trippers' were tolerated to a much greater extent, but fans with Megastore bags, flags of their home country, or wearing 'jesters hats' would often be derided and made fun of behind their backs.

The division between the fans who perceived themselves to be 'genuine' and those they perceived to be tourists or glory-hunters was a major feature of the make-up of United's support. These 'non-genuine' fans were often ridiculed more than the genuine fans of other teams, and their presence at away matches often resented as denying access to 'proper' fans and 'killing the atmosphere'. The antipathy in the relationship between these two groups of fans did not appear to be as hostile in the other direction, but on occasion the 'tourists' complained about issues like standing, standing in the wrong seats, abusive chanting and pushing. On occasion, 'tourists' were observed making complaints to stewards about the behaviour of the carnival fans and when this led to censure or ejection, relations between the groups would sour even further. On some internet message boards, the carnival fans would be referred to disparagingly as 'top reds'. This label alluded to the fact that they perceived themselves to be genuine fans who set the rules about acceptable behaviour.

The divisions between these two groups were not as clear-cut as the carnival fans believed; many loyal and local fans did not fall into the subculture of the carnival fan, and also complained about standing and rowdy behaviour, some wore replica shirts and some shopped at the Megastore. Conversely, many tourists 'bought in' to the hard-core carnival fan culture at United in terms of dress code, alcohol consumption and singing. However, carnival fans had a very clear opinion about the 'right' behaviour for 'real' supporters, and also clear (and exaggerated) stereotypes about the demographic and behaviour of the different groups (see Table 3.1).

Table 3.1 Carnival fan and tourist fan stereotypes

	The carnival fan	The tourist
Demographic	Usually male, 15–60, local (either born or resident) or 'time-served' (non-Mancunians usually had to prove they had supported the team pre-1993). Possessing working-class roots/adopted what they perceived to be working-class norms.	Any age, both male and female, non-local/foreign, probably a 'new fan' who was not interested in United before 1993. Perceived to be typically middle class to upper-middle class.
Dress	Would typically not wear replica shirts, although pin-badges were popular and scarves were sometimes worn.	Official merchandise, replica shirts and, at the extreme, a United 'jester's hat'. Often carrying a United Megastore bag.
Expression	Carnival fans were expected to know United songs and chant them at matches and in pubs.	Did not sing/know the lyrics to chants. Would occasionally clap along to officially sanctioned club songs played over the tannoy.

Pre-match behaviour	Going to the pub/off-licence and meeting 'mates' to 'have a laugh', drink and chant before arriving at the stadium just before kick-off.	Visiting the Megastore, taking photographs outside Old Trafford, visiting the official United 'Fan Zone' and entering the ground well before kick-off.
Match behaviour	Chanting and, where possible, standing. 'Getting behind the team' when things were going badly was considered essential.	Sitting in silence, taking photo graphs, not 'getting behind' the team, leaving before the final whistle.

Research with all three clubs found support from previous work on wider football fandom and the rules for being considered a 'real' fan (Back *et al.*, 2001), although the perceived high quota of irregular and 'tourist' fans at United appears to exaggerate these divisions. Back *et al.* argued that being a 'real football fan' involved not only attending matches but also an, 'assimilation of masculinist/class inflected argot of consumption (involvement in the spheres of football fandom: pre-match drinking, familiarity with networks of rumour, gossip and football folklore)' (*ibid.*: 95). The divisions in United's support in particular have already been noted by Anthony King's research in the 1990s of the (largely) Manchester-based hard-core: 'the lads also see themselves as a distinct body within the following of the club as a whole', being fans but not 'customers' (2003: 153). For this hardcore, a replica shirt, 'which for so many is a symbol of allegiance, ironically denotes inauthentic support; it is worn by part-timers and by individuals who do not come from Manchester' (King, 2003: 156). His summary of the relationship of the hard-core with their team is also still appropriate (and this applied equally to the women in this subculture as to the 'lads'):

> The lads conceive their relationship with their team as a love affair. This conception links back to the creation of ecstatic solidarity in 'the craic' when the boys are 'buzzing'. On the one hand, the ecstasy of football fandom engages their emotions so deeply that they build up an affection for the club which is seen as love. However, the lads are only able to raise themselves to the level of excitement in their spectating because they invest the game with so much importance as a result of their love for the club. The ecstasy of the lads' support and the love they feel for the club are symbiotic, therefore. Yet the lads' relationship of love is more significant than merely reinforcing the fans' ecstasy. The love which the lads feel for their team is simultaneously also a love for the feeling of solidarity which they experience every time they see their team and participate in the communal practice of drinking and singing. (*ibid.*: 152)

Since then, there have been significant developments and changes within the United support, both politically and at the level of match-going fan culture. The most dramatic development occurred in the summer of 2005, when the club was purchased by the Glazer family in a heavily leveraged takeover which placed the club in around £700m. of debt. Fan groups and fanzines vehemently opposed the takeover, believing that it would place the club in financial jeopardy and that it would be the fans who would end up paying for the debt the Glazer family had taken on, through increased ticket prices. As a result, there have been a number of significant changes to the make-up and attitude of United's support since the writings of King (2000, 2003) and Brown (1998). Politically the fans appear weaker in terms of their influence on club policy, and the connections between the carnival fans and the club (as a commercial organisation) have weakened even further. While King noted a reluctance to purchase replica shirts (2003: 154), for many carnival fans this has been extended to all club merchandise and food and drink at official kiosks (a number of fans referred to their preference not to buy 'Glazer pies'). Furthermore, the connection between how many matches were attended and how much of a 'real' fan you were has been weakened, with thousands of United fans now boycotting home matches in protest at the Glazer 'occupation', and many of these supporting a breakaway non-League club, FC United of Manchester. This is turn led to a schism and considerable antipathy between the 'scabs' who remained at Old Trafford, and the 'judases' who left to support the new club.

However, despite the difference between the outlook of the disparate sub-groups, the carnival fans (of both United and FC) retained much of the culture that set them apart from other fan subcultures. The social networks, supported through a number of interlinked internet forums meant that fans from the opposite ends of the political spectrum on the 'Glazer issue' still drank in the same Manchester pubs, contributed to the same internet message boards and attended away matches and Euro aways. This meant that most of the views on what it meant to be a 'real' fan (with the exception of attending home matches) remained the same as pre-2005. To be a 'proper red', you had to adhere to an unwritten code that had the potential to influence everything from the clothes you wore, the songs you sang, the music you listened to and the way you supported the team. You needed to know the history of the club and the locality, and also know others from within the United-supporting network with whom you could converse, both at matches and through the internet. Carnival fans had their own style of verbal expression (again both spoken and virtual) and even its own words and phrases, some of which will be recognisable to other football fans, others which had evolved from other northern or Mancunian expressions. A 'brief' was a ticket for the match, and if you failed to get one you had been 'chubbed' (derived from the former ticket office manager Mr Chubb, who signed the letters informing applicants that they had been unsuccessful). If you had been chubbed and wanted to attend the match, your choice was either to 'jib' into the stadium without a ticket, usually by 'doubling up' with a fan with a ticket as you went through the turnstiles or by using a 'snide' ticket (a counterfeit). If you were successful, then you would be able to see 'the shirts' (the team), if not there might be 'mither' (trouble/aggro). Additionally a number of phrases were shortened to acronyms, normally for the ease of posting on internet forums. An ABU was 'anyone but United' (a fan of another team who supported whoever United were playing), a JCL was a 'Johnny come lately' (a new fan), an OOT was an 'out-of-towner' (not from Manchester) and a WUM was a 'wind-up merchant'. The shortened versions of all of these terms (ABU, JCL, OOT and WUM) were also used verbally in conversations. Although less pronounced, similar codes, modes of expression and language bound together carnival fans at Blackpool and England, allowing those who might not share this 'lifestyle' outside of football to assimilate into the carnival fan groups.

Conclusion

There has been considerable misunderstanding about the composition and behaviour of football crowds. One of the most fundamental mistakes has been to see football fans as a homogeneous group who attend matches with the same desires, motivations and expectations. Observations indicated that there were many different subcultures within even a single team's match-going support and within these subcultures there existed many different sub-groups. Often there was considerable antipathy between different subcultures and groups, who had more in common with similar subcultures supporting rival teams than other fans of their own club. Carnival fan groups made up only a small proportion of match-going fans overall, but tended to dominate a club's support when it travelled away. These groups had a very clear idea about their identity and their place and duties within the wider support of the team. In addition to the prospects for hedonism, matches were seen as an opportunity for the carnival fan groups to express their identity to outsiders through numbers, noise and colour. A key feature of this expression came from football chants, which carnival fans were expected to know and sing loudly. Observations suggested that it was normally these carnival fan groups who created, reworked and introduced chants to the wider match-going support and in doing so provided a vital role in creating association football's unique atmosphere.

4

Fans or hooligans?

'You're not fans, you're football hooligans'[1]

There is no accepted or universal definition of what constitutes a 'hooligan' or an act of 'hooliganism'; the derivation of the words is unclear as is its current definition. A search of several dictionaries reveals numerous definitions, emphasising different characteristics of the hooligan. A person who is lawless, rowdy and violent may be considered to be a 'hooligan', although according to some definitions they also need to be either young or a member of a gang. It appears that the term started being applied to football fans in the mid-1960s and the earliest reference I uncovered was to 'handfuls of hooligans' being responsible for pitch invasions at Goodison Park in 1964 (Inglis, 2006: 144). By the late 1960s, the term 'football hooligan' had been established by the media (particularly the popular press) as a wide-reaching label for rowdy football supporters and it was soon appropriated by politicians, police, judges, football club owners and governing bodies. In the mid-1970s it was typically used to describe the activities of young football supporters travelling on football specials to matches, usually if they became involved in vandalism, rowdy behaviour or fighting with opposition fans (or the police). In the 1980s the term started to evolve with the fan culture and become used primarily to describe violent activity, rather than more general rowdiness and criminal damage. However, whichever definition was used by the media, it was inevitably accompanied by sensationalist reporting (Hall, 1978; Dunning *et al.*, 1988; Pearson, 1998) which contributed to creating a moral panic (Cohen, 2002) about hooliganism. This moral panic led the media to demand of politicians that 'something be done', which in turn resulted in a plethora of legislative provisions designed to defeat the problem. The whole process led to Steve Redhead observing that the term 'has no precise legal definition and remains more or less historical (and hysterical) mass media construction' (1993: 3).

By the 1990s, the term was – in the UK at least – being largely reserved for the activities of usually small and relatively tight-knit gangs who travelled to matches with the hope or intention of confronting like-minded 'firms'. However when English fans travelled abroad, the term continued to be used for less serious violence and disorder; in short, the label 'football hooligan' has a range of applications and means different things to different people. Even among football fans, and academics researching them, its meaning has changed and developed. In 1978, Marsh reported that, 'football fans have incorporated the term "hooligan" into their own social talk and use it as a term for referring to boys who commit acts generally thought to be worthy of some praise. Some acts involve minor damage to property or disruption of certain routine social events' (1978: 71). For Marsh's fans, the hooligan was more of a 'jester' and could be contrasted with the 'aggro leaders', 'nutters' and 'fighters' (*ibid.*: 71–2).

Attempts to find an accepted definition of football hooligan in the 1980s and 1990s came up with equally contestable conclusions (e.g. Roversi, 1986: 312) and my own attempts at wrestling with this problem concluded that when deconstructed, there was very little behind the 'common sense' understanding of the term at all (Pearson, 1998). Since the 1990s, academic use of the term has been largely narrowed to focus specifically on the activity of fighting opposition 'firms' (or police). Dunning *et al.*'s refined explanation of the causes of football hooliganism focuses on, 'the "core" football hooligans, those who regularly go to matches with the provoking and initiation of fights as a principle objective' (1991: 474); and King defines hooliganism as gang fighting between opposition fans, which can be contrasted with other instances of violence and disorder at football matches that existed long before the term was applied to football (2003: 54–5). This narrower definition was also one used by Clifford Stott and I in our work on the policing of English fans abroad when we wished to differentiate the activities of 'normal' fans (who under certain circumstances could become disorderly or violent) from the small minority who travelled with the intention of becoming involved in violence (Stott and Pearson, 2007).

For my research, the most relevant definitions of 'football hooligan' and 'hooliganism' were those of the carnival fans themselves, and it is these that will be used for the remainder of the book. However, even here there were considerable disagreements between research participants about what the label meant, and whether particular individuals or actions fell under it. Indeed, carnival fans suggested that differentiating a fan from a hooligan was not always possible: the hooligans were all fans of the team and not all hooligans engaged in hooliganism all the time. At many matches it was believed that a hooligan would not be interested in fighting; this was particularly true if there were not sufficient numbers to assemble a viable 'firm' or if there was no opposition firm to confront. Conversely, a small number of fans would join hooligan firms for a particular match in a season (usually one with a high risk of violence), but then would return to 'non-hooligan mode' for the following match. Some carnival fans claimed they had previously been hooligans, but had since 'retired'. Others, they suspected, might have a hooligan 'career' just around the corner. Finally, there was disagreement among carnival fans of what constituted hooliganism, and that while some fans considered particular acts hooliganism, when they were carried out in isolation of other similar behaviour, the individual would not be labelled a hooligan. Other factors also came into play when using the label, such as provocation, and even the gender of the fan. However, despite the fluid nature of the term hooligan, it was possible to draw out a definition which was recognised by most of those within the research field. It should be reiterated that this definition is not a universal one and may not be considered accurate by, for example, the media, police or members of the public. It may also not be a definition that is recognised by many of those identified by the carnival fans as hooligans.

The carnival fans of Blackpool, England and United considered themselves fans rather than hooligans and when asked whether others in the group were hooligans, the answer was almost always negative. They recognised the existence of hooligans, but differentiated them from themselves. There was some dispute about what constituted a hooligan. For most of the fans, hooligans were those supporters who travelled to matches (usually in 'firms' – a gang of other hooligans that could be anywhere between ten and 400 members strong) with the intention of violently confronting rival firms of hooligans. This understanding of what it is to be a hooligan appeared influenced by changing media definitions of the label and the vast amount of hoolie-lit. This literature had a significant influence on the research participants who were often interested in the accounts, but largely avoided the type of violence depicted in them. However, the fans were also of the opinion that hooliganism of this type was on the decline, mirroring Redhead's charting of the 'disappearance of soccer hooliganism into popular media and fan culture' (1997: 102–3). As Jay, a self-confessed former hooligan and member of the Red Brigade pointed out in a post on the forum, indicating frustration at those arguing about a particular incident: 'The old days of fighting on the terraces are not here anymore. Most people now attend football to watch the game, some even watch without singing'. For other fans, acts of vandalism and disorder were enough to lead to an individual being labelled a hooligan, especially if they had travelled with the intention of doing this.

This interview, carried out with Red Brigade carnival fans four days after disorder involving United fans robbing a refreshment kiosk at Barnsley and throwing missiles at riot police demonstrates the complexity of the issue:

Author: So would you say nicking pies was hooliganism?
Dave: Er ... no
Ruby: I'd say nicking tills and breaking down kiosks was.
Dave: No ...
Dog: I don't think of myself as a hooligan and that, but I enjoy being in the company of ... those types.
Author: 'Those types'?
Dog: Yeah it makes it better. A good atmosphere.
Author: What makes a 'hooligan' then?
Dog: Misbehaviour ... I don't think it's all about fighting.
Beaky: I think a hooligan is someone who goes purposefully to get involved with violence, and not to watch the football game.
Moston: [inaudible disagreement] ... they're football fans.
Dog: I think what happened [at Barnsley] could be described as hooligan behaviour ...
Author: I'm not asking whether it could be described as hooligan behaviour,

I'm asking whether you yourself would describe it as hooligan behaviour.

Ruby: Yes, I would.

Beaky: I'd describe the actions of the kids as hooligan behaviour, yeah.

Dave: [shakes head]

Moston: I wouldn't.

Beaky: Bloody hell!

Author: [to Dave and Moston] So what would you describe as hooliganism?

Dave: Depends really, to go with an intention is one thing. To get in a row at football is just like anything else. You go out to the pub on a Friday night and you end up in a row with someone else, is that hooliganism? No it's not.

Moston: Yeah, I tell you, I'd say hooliganism is more regular, like organised ...

Dave: Yeah, regular and organised ...

Ruby: But what about ... [inaudible arguments]

Dave: The stuff that happened at Barnsley ...

Moston: Just happened.

Dave: Is different because. For one, kicking off with the old bill is no problem for me, the old bill brought it on themselves at Barnsley anyway. In fact if they waded in ... Half the problem half the time, I don't know what anyone else reckons, yeah, but, you know when you get teams drawn with United, at home, right, and their supporters go fucking mad, like at Barnsley, yeah? At United? The old bill are just as itching to get hold of it as much as anyone else is. United, United. They want to make a name for themselves, 'oh yeah, I fucking twatted this bloke, I fucking twatted that bloke...' you know what I mean? But what went on in terms of the robbing and everything, nah, not for me ... If you go to an away game, right? And you're giving it [inaudible] near their ground, ten, fifteen of us, thirty of us, whatever, and something happens, it's nothing to do with football hooliganism ...

Moston: It just happens doesn't it?

Dave: Yeah, It's just boys being boys at the end of the day but ...

Moston: I'd say hooliganism is someone that went looking actually for it.

Dog: I'd say hooliganism isn't just about fighting, it's about bother making and going to places like a small Division One club intent on, not necessarily fighting, but on causing trouble, you know like what happened at Barnsley, with, you know, the reaction of the police and that lot and with what happened at half time, for me although it wasn't fighting, it was hooliganism.

Author: So where do you draw the line? When we walk down the road in a bit, and we have a bit of a sing-song, and we have cans [of beer] in our hands, and then maybe we have a swig of alcohol in the stadium again, is that hooliganism?

Dog: No. The thing is, there's no intent to cause bother. You're not doing anyone any harm, you're not barracking opposing supporters. You're just having a laugh with your mates. It's not hooliganism ...

Andy: I see hooliganism more as organised fighting ...

Beaky: If you're organised and fighting, you're a hooligan.

It was clear, therefore that carnival fans considered hooligans to be those who *attended matches with the intention of fighting (whether or not this violence took place)*. As a result, use of the term 'hooligan' in the remainder of this book reflects this agreed internal understanding of the carnival fans, and excludes spontaneous disorder, individual unplanned violence or non-violent criminal acts. This is because there was clear dispute about whether those involved in other forms of disorder were hooligans or not. The situation became even more complex when I asked the fans whether any of the Red Brigade were hooligans, and raised the example of a recent incident involving Denis (detailed below). It was clear that they believed it was possible for former hooligans to stop being hooligans, for normal fans to 'become' hooligans and for incidents of violence not to be considered hooliganism depending on the circumstances and, again, the intent of the individual.

Author: Is there anyone in the Brigade that you we would consider a hooligan?
Ruby: Well Denis was certainly back in the day ...
Dave: Well Denis and Jay have admitted ...
Ruby: They were back in the day.
Dave: But not now.
Author: Even though he [Denis] head-butted someone in the face at [team name]?
Ruby: That's just, that's just ...
Dave: [inaudible] ... if that cunt [the victim] had acted like that ... It's nothing to do with football. Had acted up like that, he would have got that anywhere.
Dog: I think he did that not for hooliganism ...
Dave: No.
Dog: But because of what the lad had said. I believe he made a racist comment. Or something along those lines. It was a consequence of that. It wasn't a football rivalry, it was sticking up for someone who'd been ...
Ruby: It wasn't the consequence of football, it was the consequence of him [the victim] being a bell-end.
Moston: Exactly, yeah.
Ruby: Moston is probably the one, out of all of us, who is more likely to [become a hooligan] ... He's the youngest, he's more likely to be impressed by that kind of thing.
Moston: I'd say hooliganism was more fighting though.
Ruby: That thing that went on at Barnsley, I'd imagine Moston was probably not right in the middle of it, but on the outside pissing himself about it.

While the carnival fans differentiated themselves from these hooligans, physically telling the difference could be difficult for an outsider. Although some of the carnival fans wore colours (this was more the case at Blackpool and England than at United), which the hooligan firms generally avoided, many of the carnival fans adopted similar dress to the hooligans. This was particularly true of matches away from home where there was a perceived risk to visiting fans of attacks by locals. At Blackpool, it was common for fans to cover up their colours upon visits to such high-risk venues or where it was necessary to gain access to 'home fans only' pubs. This meant that the riskier the environment for the fans, the more likely they were to adopt the dress style of the hooligan. For the carnival followers of United, wearing colours was even less popular, and the typical United away crowd would largely wear black coats and jeans. Of course adopting this dress had the potential to increase the fans' chances of being confronted by local hooligans; although non-hooligan fans were rarely attacked, it was more likely that a group dressed in attire popular with hooligans would be attacked by a rival firm. Sugden describes the casual hooligan wear from the 1980s onwards as consisting of 'Fred Perry, Adidas, Puma, Nike, Lacoste, Stone Island, Hilfiger and Hackett with hats by Burberry' (2002: 53). In 2011, brands such as Stone Island, Hilfiger and Burberry remained popular, although the new label of choice – for both those perceived to be hooligans and many of the carnival fans – appeared to be North Face.

There were other similarities between the carnival fans and the hooligans; with both tending to sing the same chants and express similar views on the team and their rivals. At away matches in particular, where away-fan friendly pubs were infrequent, carnival fans and those they defined as hooligans would also often end up drinking in the same places and would mingle together. Although the hooligan firms did appear to remain tight-knit and somewhat paranoid of outsiders, their members mixed socially with non-hooligan fans both around matches and on other occasions, for example through sharing the same local pub or workplace. Additionally, as we have seen, some of the carnival fans at United were previously involved in hooligan activity and as a result they, and those they vouched for, were trusted by many of the hooligans. At away matches perceived as being particularly high risk, some of the carnival fans even sought out the hooligans for protection (although ironically they may actually be putting themselves at a greater risk of attack from locals). On occasion, the hooligans and the carnival fans were also forced together by the local police. For example, if fans and hooligans arrived on the same train, wearing the same clothes and chanting the same songs, then some local forces simply corralled them all together in order to escort them to the stadium or funnelled them into the same designated away pub. O'Neill's ethnography of police at football matches noted that for many officers dress sense was a key method of differentiating between hooligans and supporters (this was also a finding from my attendance at a number of different banning order hearings).[2] Football intelligence officers (or 'spotters') on the other hand appeared more aware of the number of non-hooligans who adopted the casual style, and preferred to take into account 'attitude' and the way they walked in determining if they were hooligans (O'Neill, M., 2005: 104–6). Of course, spotters travelling with the fans were not always listened to by local police forces, group of fans looking like hooligans could pose a risk to public order should local hooligans attack them, and spotters themselves could make mistakes when identifying hooligans.

The divisions between hooligan groups and carnival fan groups were therefore blurred in a number of ways and the view often espoused in the media that firms were completely closed and tightly regulated with structured levels of leadership did not appear to be true (see also Armstrong, 1998). The blurring of the borders between the firm and the carnival fans, and the relative ease with which some members would slip from one to the other contrasted sharply with the more regimented 'career path' described by Marsh (1978) and his colleagues at Oxford United in the 1970s. In practice at Manchester United, fans were more likely to differentiate themselves along lines of seniority, rather than between hooligans and non-hooligan fans. Groups of younger carnival fans in their teens and early twenties would often 'hang around with' or follow more senior fans, such as Jay or Denis, who were respected for being able to 'look after themselves'. These younger fans would sometimes be involved in disorder and also theft,[3] and could often not afford to drink in the same bars or eat in the same restaurants as the older fans. The older fans were sometimes dismissive of the younger groups, especially when they were being disorderly, but others 'took them under their wing' and would sometimes help out, for example allowing them to sleep on their hotel floor or by purchasing them drinks. Jay and Denis in particular saw it almost as a duty to assist and guide the younger fans, pointing out that otherwise they would become unmanageable, with public order results that could adversely affect their own opportunity for engaging in the carnivalesque. In turn, the younger fans enjoyed the stories of the older 'heads' and did not want to disappoint them with their behaviour (although conversely some did feel the need to 'prove' themselves physically should confrontations occur). On one occasion an older fan struck a younger fan once about the face after his behaviour delayed the group and nearly led to them missing the match – this was accepted by the younger fan and the rest of the group in a manner that a father smacking a child might be in some households.

In four years of carrying out research at Blackpool FC, I did not identify an organised hooligan firm who regularly attended matches with the intention of confronting rival firms, although I did witness numerous violent incidents, and regularly saw low-level disorder and criminality. Only once, when Blackpool played at Preston in 1996, did I see serious and sustained violence (both inside and outside the ground) that might suggest some groups of fans from Blackpool had travelled with the intention of 'causing trouble'. It is not certain that at other matches, groups of Blackpool hooligans did not attempt to confront rival gangs, but this disorder must have been isolated and irregular. Fans and self-confessed 'former hooligans' also suggested to me that Blackpool's hooligan 'problem' had disappeared some years ago (this is, of course, not to say that post-1998 it might not have returned). Inside stadiums, disorder was also extremely limited and I saw no serious attempt by either Blackpool fans or their rivals to 'take' a rival end (despite terraces existing at most grounds at the time). Marsh (1978) identified the practice of 'taking ends' as typical of the ritualised aggression of fans in the 1970s,[4] but during my time with Blackpool fans I only witnessed five incidents where fans deliberately went in the wrong section of the ground. On two of these occasions, fans appeared to have infiltrated to cause disorder, but were too few in number for this to amount to more than a brief skirmish followed by ejection from the ground. The other occasions were the result of ticketing problems which meant that the fans in the wrong section were not there to 'take' the end, but purely in order to watch the match (their own allocation having already been sold out). At Blackpool, although there remained the potential for serious violence and disorder (thanks largely to ineffective legislation and poor crowd management decisions from the football authorities), the fact that serious disorder did not occur regularly was largely due to the fans generally adhering to quite rigid rules of disorder, in the manner described by Marsh's work of the late 1970s. At times, particularly at derby matches against Preston, these rules were broken and serious violence did occur, but much of Marsh's findings were still applicable to the football terrace of the Second Division twenty years after his work. Some Blackpool fans were clearly willing to fight, but generally what violence occurred was spontaneous, limited in terms of numbers involved and quickly over.

At Blackpool, despite the observed lack of hooligans intending to engage in violence, some of the research participants became involved in spontaneous violence, and on a number of occasions the groups I travelled with were confronted by rival fans looking to fight us. On one trip to Wrexham in 1997, a confrontation occurred in a pub next to the stadium as we waited for the train. In retelling, the account seems surreal and almost comical, but at the time it was genuinely frightening. Prior to the match, large numbers of travelling Blackpool fans had taken over the pub, singing and wearing colours with no confrontation with the home support. After the match, most of these had returned immediately but the fan group I was with decided to return to the pub while we waited for the train. As we sat playing cards in the pub, two Wrexham fans approached our table. Politely at first, the first fan ascertained that we were Blackpool supporters (we were not wearing colours) and then asked if we wanted to go outside to fight their group. After the initial surprise we explained that we were not interested, but the Wrexham fan then picked on Alan, the biggest of our group, compliment-ing him on his physique, suggesting that he looked like he would be a good rugby player and then saying, 'I bet you can look after yourself. You could do me easy I reckon'. By now we were aware that there was a group of men at the other end of the bar observing the conversation and two had moved to stand by the door. We looked at each other nervously and the cards were wordlessly put away. When, again, the invitation to fight was declined, the other Wrexham fan started speaking aggressively in Welsh, picked up a bottle from the table and raised it threateningly. The first fan, who claimed to be his brother, translated: 'My brother says, "death to the English"'. At this point we jumped up and made our escape from the pub, abandoning unfinished drinks (although a couple of us took our bottles with us in case we would need them to fight our way out) and pushing the two men apparently trying to block the door out of the way. We ran down the road followed by the group of Wrexham fans from the pub, and on to the train platform. Fortunately there was a train on the platform we were able to board (although we did not know where it was going). The Blackpool fans were clearly shaken and expressed relief that they had escaped unscathed.

However, on a number of occasions apparently spontaneous violent acts were carried out by fans such as Micky, with whom I had travelled to a number of matches but who had shown no signs of being a 'hooligan'. Near the end of the 1995–96 season, Blackpool played a crucial promotion match against Swindon Town at Bloomfield Road and trouble broke out in the ground between the rival fans (many Swindon fans had purchased tickets for the home sections once the away end had sold out). As I left the stadium at the end of the match, I saw Micky in the crowd in front of me but before I could shout to him to say hello, he suddenly gave a shout and ran to a lamp-post, where he proceeded to rip a litter bin from its fastenings. He then charged at a group of five Swindon fans, waving and then throwing the bin at them, before disappearing after them around the corner. As I never saw Micky again, it was impossible to find out the context for this act which appeared out of character for him and also a rare act of *apparently* unprovoked violence. This and the Wrexham incident suggested to me that the threat of low level and spontaneous violence was often present, particularly at away matches or derbies. However, although groups would form with the apparent intention of confronting rival fans (particularly for matches against Preston) this was exceptionally rare at Blackpool during this period (in contrast to my research with Manchester United supporters later on).

While planned hooliganism involving Blackpool fans did not appear to be a problem during my observations between 1995 and 1998, violence and disorder occurred regularly around their derby matches with Preston and Burnley. Two matches in particular demonstrate the varying extent of this problem. In the spring of 1996 Blackpool were top of Division Two and facing a visit to Burnley's Turf Moor stadium. The importance of this match meant that a travelling support of 4–5,000 could be expected but due to redevelopment work that had reduced the capacity at Turf Moor, Burnley made the match 'all ticket' and allocated Blackpool fewer than 1,000. This left thousands of fans who wanted to attend the match without a ticket. In the games building up to the derby, ticket-less Blackpool fans discussed buying tickets for the home sections (the idea was that if enough Blackpool fans gathered together in one section, this would provide security in numbers from the home fans). The weekend before the match, a Blackpool fan ringing up the weekly Radio Lancashire 'football phone in', announced that Blackpool fans without tickets would be buying them for the uncovered terrace behind the goal called the 'Beehole'. As a result, I telephoned the Burnley ticket office and asked for a ticket in that section, although I was only successful after I had negotiated a trivia question on Burnley FC (telephone operators at Turf Moor had obviously been warned only to sell tickets to home supporters).

On the day of the match, I boarded the train from Blackpool and quickly made friends with a group of ten supporters I had not met before; all had tickets in the home sections. However, these were scattered around the ground, and only four of us were in the Beehole Terrace. It was clear that unless there were significant numbers travelling by other means, 'taking' a section of the terrace was not going to be a safe option. All were nervous about being identified as a Blackpool fan in the ground, and one had even borrowed a Burnley FC hat to wear. We walked to the stadium nervously, splitting up into twos and threes so as to not draw attention to ourselves, but this meant that we lost each other in the crowd. As we approached the ground, the fan with whom I was walking became scared that we had been recognised as Blackpool fans, and ran off, meaning that by the time I entered the Beehole terrace, I was on my own and feeling very vulnerable. As the terrace filled, it became clear that there was going to be no significant group of Blackpool fans in the home sections. When Blackpool scored the winner in the second half, a couple of visiting fans in the main stand jumped up to celebrate, leading to pushing and shoving followed by ejection by club stewards, but there was no serious disorder. I met the group with whom I had travelled to the match on the platform of the station waiting from the train back. We all congratulated each other on surviving the trip to Burnley and on a vital three points in the promotion race. A small group of Burnley fans confronted us but after a brief stand-off in which insults but no blows were exchanged, an older Blackpool fan intervened and the situation calmed, with a couple of the antagonists even shaking hands.

Despite the hype on the terraces and the radio phone-in beforehand, a mass invasion of the Burnley stands had simply not taken place. This may have been because the all-ticket nature of the match had made it difficult for fans (particularly with Blackpool telephone codes) to obtain tickets for the home sections, but this problem should not have been insurmountable. Had Blackpool been given their usual allocation, it is likely that over 4,000 would have travelled for this key derby fixture. Instead, in addition to the official Blackpool section of around 800, probably fewer than one hundred Blackpool fans attended, meaning that over 3,000 chose to stay at home and listen to the game on the radio rather than risk the home sections of the ground. There simply did not appear to be the appetite for the 'taking' of a home end, in stark contrast to the tales of hooliganism from previous decades (e.g. Marsh, 1978). The incident also demonstrated that even those who did go to the trouble of 'infiltrating' the home sections did not do so because they wanted confrontation – indeed when the opportunity for confrontation with Burnley fans arose after the match, they did not take it, even with superior numbers.

The match at Preston the next season, however, demonstrated that violence and disorder was still a risk at derby matches. Preston's promotion that summer had seen the return of Blackpool's traditional local rivals and Sky Sports televised the derby live on Friday 13 December. In the build-up to the match, Blackpool fans expressed surprise that such a high-risk match would be played at 7.45 p.m. on a Friday, and many on the South Paddock expressed excitement at the potential of disorder at the match. A comparatively large crowd of 14,626 attended, with over 2,500 Blackpool fans on the all-terraced Kop behind one goal. Some fans on both sides had taken the afternoon off work to drink in Preston prior to the game and tensions were running high as the match kicked off. The match was one of the rare occasions during my observations that widespread disorder occurred inside a stadium. Preston's goals were celebrated by pitch invasions by their supporters, some of whom ran to the Blackpool end and goaded the visiting support (who in turn surged down the terrace towards them but did not go onto the pitch). In another incident, a Preston fan from the opposite end of the ground, ran the full length of the pitch towards the visiting fans. They in turn beckoned him on and surged down the terrace as he (and three police officers) flung themselves into the away end. The police were able to pull the Preston fan to safety, and when I attended the court hearing afterwards, it was revealed that he had been armed with a knife. Following the match, further disorder took place on the streets outside. In what the magistrate in one of the subsequent court hearings described as, 'one of the biggest scenes of public disorder this town has ever seen', groups of Preston and Blackpool fans fought each other outside the ground, on their way back to the city centre and in the pubs afterwards. After the Blackpool fans had returned, local gangs of Preston fans (many of whom had not attended the match) fought each other and with the police. There were seventy-eight arrests that were deemed by the prosecution to be connected with the match that evening, the last one taking place at 4.30 a.m., and the disorder made the front page of the *Blackpool Evening Gazette* and the *Lancashire Evening Post* as the 'Night of shame'.

At England matches abroad, as with Blackpool, there was again an absence of a regular firm of hooligans looking for confrontation. Once again, almost all disorder was spontaneous and involved fans who had not travelled with the intention of causing disorder. Around England home matches during the period 2001 to 2006, when the national team toured different cities while Wembley was being redeveloped, there were frequent clashes between rival club firms but only on one occasion did I witness members purporting to be from club firms congregating to cause disorder as an 'England firm'. The lack of rigid organisation of the firms domestically could also be seen with regard to their supposed labels. At Blackpool, for example, I never heard any reference to 'the Bisons', who were, according to the media and hoolie-literature, the firm at the time. At United, the label 'Red Army', which has been linked to the hooligan gang of United was actually used by all travelling supporters. The more recent label for United's hooligan firm, the 'Men in Black' was occasionally used by carnival fans to describe the firm, but more likely to be used by the media and opposition fans and hooligans (even foreign fans had come across the term). O'Neill, however, claims that the term itself was not used in a serious sense by the firm itself (O'Neill, T., 2006: 152). At United, some groups of rowdy fans were labelled by the carnival fans (e.g. the 'Moston Rats' and the 'Moston Mice') but very few gave themselves these 'hooligan-esque' labels except in jest (e.g. the 'Stretford Squirrels').

This did not stop the media from adopting, applying and often misusing the group names. One example of this occurred followed disorder involving United fans at Barnsley in 2009, when a newspaper seized upon a misleading account of events from an internet poster on the forum Red Issue:

Manchester United fans are blaming a dangerous new 'firm' of supporters associated with the club for the looting of a food kiosk during the Carling Cup fourth round game against Barnsley at Oakwell that will result in a Football Association investigation. The 30-strong group of teenagers thought to be aged between 16 and 18 years old style themselves as the 'Moston Rats' and come from the tough north Manchester district. They are thought to have been behind the raid on the kiosk which resulted in staff locking themselves in a stock cupboard as the till and food and drinks were stolen.

The Moston Rats have become a source of concern for more experienced United fans who follow the club home and away. Even by the occasionally wayward standards of the club's fans in the 1970s and 1980s, this latest phenomenon are thought to be the worst yet. 'The rats are an embarrassment to the Red Army', said one poster on an online United fans forum. Anecdotal evidence from United supporters among the 4,000 travelling fans at Oakwell who watched the 2–0 victory suggested that the lack of security around the North Stand kiosk had prompted the aggression from certain sectors of the United support. Many of the fans had made a day of the trip to Yorkshire and had been drinking all day before the game. (*The Independent*, 29/10/09)

The report drew both anger and mirth from the carnival fans, and was ridiculed as lazy and inaccurate journalism on various internet message boards. A number of posters pointed out that the label 'Moston Rats' had been applied to a group of around twenty teenagers from Moston (North Manchester) who had been involved in incidents of disorder between 1997 and 2001, but who were now in their late twenties and largely no longer attended matches. Those present at Barnsley agreed that the teenagers who had been involved in the disorder in question were neither the 'rats', nor from Moston.

A further complication in determining whether the carnival fans were in fact hooligans comes from the fact that although they did not attend matches with the intention of fighting, some of them did, on occasion, become involved in disorder and violence. Violence from research participants was rare and as likely to be against fans of the same club as opposition supporters. However, a number of incidents were witnessed each season and even more were recounted in conversation. Usually this violence was spontaneous, did not result in serious injury and the instigator felt provoked in some way. Several times, the carnival fans with me came under attack from fans of other teams (particularly abroad), and responded by fighting back rather than running. During my research I witnessed punches, kicks and head-butts by carnival fans of all three teams researched, as well as missile-throwing. During my research with England, there were several occasions where large numbers of carnival fans (and also the wider body of the England support) became involved in disorder in response to what was perceived as aggressive, indiscriminate and unjustified policing. Additionally, on occasion the carnival fans were also involved in acts of vandalism, criminal damage and theft. This ranged from sticking 'Blackpool FY4' or 'Love United Hate Glazer' stickers on lamp-posts, to smashing glasses or bottles and kicking stadium seats from their moorings.

Explaining hooliganism involving England fans abroad

The blurring of the boundaries between hooligans and carnival fans was espe-cially prominent during observations with fans of the England national team, where those with no apparent intention of becoming involved in violence were involved in widespread disorder on a number of observed occasions. The most serious sustained disorder witnessed during the entire research took place during the 1998 World Cup when England played Tunisia in Marseilles, a city well known for its large North African population. Rumours of small-scale distur-bances two nights before the match, including an English fan being run over and groups of local youths attacking and robbing English fans were circulating in the pubs and bars of Marseilles and the consensus among the England fans was that the locals were supporting Tunisia and would be looking for opportunities to attack or steal from the English. A siege mentality started to develop; if you wanted to be safe from attack, you needed to stay among large groups of England fans. Anyone of North African descent was viewed with suspicion and avoided (unless they were selling tickets) and some were verbally abused by the English. As the day progressed, groups of Tunisians and local North Africans were gathering at the opposite end of the Old Port from where most of the English were gathered, some marching past the English with flags and drums. This behaviour was seen by many of the English supporters as being highly provoca-tive. Riot police were deployed and had attempted to disperse English supporters who had gathered near the North Africans in order to create a sterile zone between the two groups. Tensions increased as the two groups taunted each other and when a few bottles were thrown over the police line, the police fired tear gas into the English fans and launched a baton charge to disperse them. Tear-gas canisters landed not just among the group of English taunting the North Africans, but also among those watching a match in the bars nearby. Within moments the Old Port had been transformed into a tear-gas-clouded riot zone, with fans and locals running from the police and a small number of English trying to urge others to stand their ground and fight back against the police.

This incident marked the beginning of twenty-four hours of crowd disorder in Marseilles and one of the most serious instances of disorder involving English fans abroad. The remainder of that evening saw a number of further baton charges and uses of tear gas as the police attempted to clear the area of the Old Port of English fans. Instances of English fans being attacked by local youths, some wielding sticks and knives, also increased, and the feeling among the fans was that simply looking English in Marseilles meant that you were a target for both the riot police and local youths. With England fans perceiving that the police were making no attempt to protect them from the locals, they started gathering in groups and ensuring that weaponry (mainly sticks, bats and bottles) were to hand should they be attacked. I spent the night huddled around a campfire on the beach with a large group of English fans, some of who were 'tooled up' and all of whom were expecting an attack from local youths at any moment. The match day saw further instances of disorder around the stadium, bottle-throwing, skirmishes between English and Tunisian fans, and use of tear gas by the police. When England scored their opening goal, around 2,000 English fans watching on the big screen at the beach were attacked with bottles by Tunisian supporters seated in the temporary stand behind them. When they fought back, police once again fired teargas into the crowd, before clearing the area with batons (for a full account of the disorder and the media and political response see Stott and Pearson, 2007: chs. 5 and 6). The media explanation for the Marseilles disorder was that it was caused by English 'hooligans' who travelled to matches with the intention of causing disorder and who were orchestrating the riot and encouraging the drunken majority of England fans to join in with the violence. However, as my research with England progressed, it became clear that this theory simply did not explain why serious disorder occurred, and why – equally importantly – on most occasions it did not.

Although in terms of seriousness and duration, the rioting in Marseilles remained unsurpassed from my observations, during the following eight years of research a number of serious incidents of crowd violence and disorder involving England fans were observed, most notably in Charleroi at the 2000 European Championships, Munich before a World Cup qualifier in 2001 and Cologne at the 2006 World Cup. Journeys abroad to support the national team meant travelling with the reputation of an England fan abroad – for travelling in large numbers, for heavy drinking, xenophobia, rowdiness, disorder and violence. England supporters were concerned about this reputation and its effect on their match-going experience abroad in two ways. First, England carnival fans were often targets for gangs of local fans who wanted to prove their masculinity against the famous English hooligans. Second, the local authorities, instead of treating the English as tourists to the area, often treated them as hooligans looking for a fight. As a result local authorities frequently issued warnings to travelling fans about their 'zero-tolerance' approach to antisocial behaviour and ordered bars to be closed or city-wide alcohol bans to be imposed. Fans also felt that local police were quick to don riot gear, and would overreact to minor incidents with batons and CS-gas rather than communicate with supporters. As my research with England fans progressed, it became clear that the reputation the fans had, and how the local fans and authorities responded to this reputation, played a fundamental role in determining whether disorder would occur.

Evidence of English fans travelling with the intention of fighting was scarce and while some fans would talk in excited terms about the possibility of confrontation with local hooligan gangs, these fans rarely made any attempt to turn this apparent desire into reality. As with my research at Blackpool, the prospect of confrontation added to the excitement of the event, although most preferred to avoid any violence. Minor incidents occurred with regularity and individuals or small groups would occasionally confront locals, but this rarely led to violence or more widespread disorder. During my research with England fans abroad, there was only one occasion where group violence appeared prearranged and unprovoked, prior to England's 5–1 victory over Germany in Munich.

Events in Charleroi during the 2000 European Championships in

Belgium/Holland were more typical of the nature of disorder involving English fans abroad. The focal point for the England supporters ahead of a match against Germany was the town square in Charleroi. As usual, the carnival England fans gathered together in order to display flags, drink and sing. By mid-afternoon thousands of England supporters had gathered in the square and the atmosphere was generally convivial with locals mingling with them and no large concentration of German fans. Some of the England fans were singing overtly racist songs, but there was no suggestion that the crowd was suddenly going to turn violent. In the middle of this throng an arrest took place, apparently of a German supporter, and a crowd started to move towards the incident. Weed argues that a large proportion of this crowd were journalists who had been tipped off about the impending arrests by the Belgian police and that this added to the appearance of a dangerous surge by England fans towards the Germans and the police (2001: 413). At this point a skirmish took place involving a handful of fans and riot police moved in, along with a police tank that drove into the square firing water cannon into the crowd indiscriminately. The force of the cannon knocked dozens of people, both fans and locals off their feet, and caused a stampede as the crowd tried to get out of the way. The English fans regrouped by a bar at one corner of the square and several of them threw plastic chairs back at the police, leading to another burst of water cannon. The entire incident lasted no more than a few minutes, but television footage was relayed around the world as evidence of another riot involving English football supporters (a more in-depth account of the Charleroi incident can be found in Stott and Pearson, 2007: ch. 7). Both Weed (2001) and Crabbe (2003) have criticised this media construction of the events as a riot and claimed that a riot was what the journalists there wanted.

The reaction by both the media and politicians to this incident, and the earlier arrest of hundreds of England fans in Brussels, was out of proportion to the actual severity of any violence. Although the disorder was used by the UK government to push through controversial plans for Football banning orders 'on complaint' under the Football (Disorder) Act 2000 (James and Pearson, 2006), only 3 per cent of the 965 England fans arrested in Belgium were known to the UK authorities as 'known hooligans'. Furthermore, the UK Police Football Intelligence Unit noted that very few of the 'known hooligans' they were monitoring were involved in the disorder which did occur (Stott and Pearson, 2007). Returning briefly to the events in Marseilles, an analysis of arrests and UK Football Intelligence Unit (FIU) comment there reveals a similar pattern – that the vast majority of those arrested or otherwise involved in the disorder were not known to the police; these were not hooligans travelling with the intention of fighting, but carnival fans who were primarily interested in enjoying themselves in a collective gathering in support of their team.

Most importantly, the events of Marseilles and Charleroi were the exception; England fans generally did not become involved in rioting, regardless of how drunk they became or how many gathered together. After the riot in Marseilles, the UK FIU warned that disorder at the tournament was likely to increase because 'most of the hooligans haven't travelled yet' (*The Guardian*, 06/06/98) but England's second match in Toulouse passed off without serious incident. England fans in Toulouse got very drunk and were loud and boisterous, but I did not witness group violence involving police, locals or rival fans and even the last-minute defeat in that match was taken in good spirit. For the final group-stage game in Lens, more trouble was predicted as the town was a short drive from the Channel Tunnel but although some minor incidents occurred, it was nothing that would have been out of place in an English city at pub closing time on a Friday or Saturday night. My observations suggested that the popular media view of English fans as being drunken louts who would be sparked into rioting by the actions of 'ringleaders' who travelled with the intention of 'causing trouble' could not explain what was occurring at England matches abroad. Why was it that when England fans were involved in disorder, those involved were typically *not* the 'hooligans' identified previously by the police? Equally importantly, why was it that large groups of drunken fans, with hooligan supporters among them, usually did not riot?

The most convincing academic explanation for this is drawn from social psychology and the research of Drury *et al.*, in particular, including observations of crowd disturbances at the 1990 Poll Tax riots, the 1990 World Cup and the 1998 World Cup. As was noted in the Introduction, the social psychology (or elaborated social identity model (ESIM)) explanation of crowd disorder departed significantly from the traditional views of the causes of hooliganism espoused by the media and also many of the findings of the Leicester School. The social-psychology approach acknowledged that there were usually individuals in a crowd who wanted it to 'kick off' but that they did not have the power to instigate large-scale disorder on their own. Furthermore, even without their presence, circumstances could arise where a football crowd could become disorderly. ESIM suggests that the most important factors are not individual ones such as alcohol consumption or the presence of hooligans, but intergroup interaction, predominantly the actions of locals, rival fans and, most significantly, the police. The research suggested that when fans perceived that the police were either not protecting them against attacks by locals or rival fans, or were being unreasonably aggressive, this led to a change in the social identity of the crowd and disturbances were more likely to occur (Stott and Reicher, 1998; Stott *et al.*, 2001, 2007). However, where the police facilitated the expectations of the fans and were seen to protect them from unwarranted attacks, the fans did not riot 'for the sake of it'. The ESIM explanation was compelling when applied to my own findings from observations and conversations with research participants, suggesting why carnival fans might occasionally become involved in group violence but in most cases did not. It also suggested that drawing a line between who was a 'hooligan' and who was a 'normal fan' might not be possible.

The next mass invasion by England supporters was at the 2004 European Championships in Portugal. It was impossible to draw a line between fans who had travelled purely for the football, those who were combining the football with a holiday and those who were in Portugal for a holiday anyway, but would be wearing the replica shirt, cheering on England in the local bars and maybe making an excursion to Lisbon or Coimbra to see if they could pick up a ticket. However it was estimated that around 250,000 'football tourists' would be supporting England at Euro 2004. The tournament threatened more serious disorder, especially as the Portuguese record of policing English fans was not a good one – in 1997 twelve Manchester United supporters had been shot with rubber bullets when disorder occurred at a Champions League match. By 2004 however, the ESIM had established its credentials to such an extent that their model of best practice for policing English football supporters was incorporated into the security strategy of the Portuguese Public Security Police (PSP). The central tenets of this policy involved peaceful interaction with English supporters, early identification of – and targeted responses to – incidents, and the use of riot clothing and equipment only as a last resort. In contrast, Portugal's second police force, the GNR, retained their traditional 'high-profile' approach. My research at the tournament identified not only a clear differentiation between the approaches of the two difference forces, but also a clear difference in the way that England fans responded to these approaches. In the host cities, PSP officers typically wore standard uniform and mingled in the crowd in pairs and small groups, interacting positively with smiles, handshakes and the occasional English phrase. Under the low-profile policy of the PSP, no serious disorder occurred around any of the four England matches. In contrast, in the GNR-controlled area of Albufeira, there were two nights of rioting. In Albufeira, the police were conspicuous by their absence for the duration of the day and only late in the evening did they appear, in large groups dressed in riot gear. Without any interaction or communication with the English supporters, snatch squads performed seemingly random arrests and then lines of riot police moved up 'the Strip' (a street full of bars populated by English supporters) with batons drawn, clearing the England fans away. Some English supporters responded by throwing bottles at the police, in contrast to the host cities, where English supporters had, on the whole, responded to police requests with good humour.

My final tournament carrying out research with England fans was the 2006 World Cup, in Germany. Due to the historical football antagonism between the two countries, this was also perceived to be high-risk in terms of the potential for disorder. Again, large numbers of English fans travelled (around 70,000 were estimated to be in Frankfurt on the day of England's first match), most without tickets. As expected, large groups again gathered to display flags and chant pro-English and anti-German songs and the England fans drank heavily throughout the day. On the day before the match, huge numbers of English fans gathered in the Romer Square, as thousands of German fans passed through them on their way to watch their team on the public screen at the other end of the city. As at previous tournaments, some of the England supporters showed an interest in violence against German fans; many talked about the inevitability of it 'kicking off', large numbers chanted abusive chants and some threw beer over the passing German supporters. When the German supporters passed back through the English crowd some hours later, a skirmish occurred on the scale of that which had sparked the riot in Charleroi. As in Charleroi, police were deployed into the crowd but this time instead of using water cannon and batons, they formed a cordon around a group of aggressive English supporters. After a tense stand-off in which some English supporters attempted to provoke the police by jumping up and down in front of them and shouting abuse, the police line suddenly stepped back from the English fans. Within minutes the situation had been defused, and previously aggressive English supporters were posing for photographs with the police.

Late in the evening of the following day, a group of German supporters approached the Irish Pub in which many England fans were gathered. As they did so, the rumour of an attack circulated around the pub and a group of around 200–300 English fans left the bar apparently to confront them. At this point, a German police officer with a loud-hailer and a 'Communications Officer' fluorescent bib intervened, asking the English why they were stopping their partying, informing them that the story of the German fans was 'just a rumour' and asking them to return to the bar (Stott and Pearson, 2007: 307). Once again, the 'friendly but firm' approach of the police, in contrast to the more aggressive high-profile approach shown in Marseilles and Charleroi, was successful. The fans who had moments before shown the intention of violently confronting German hooligans posed for photographs with German officers and returned to the bar to continue drinking. Confrontations between large groups of England fans gathering the day before an England fixture and German supporters watching their team play on the public screens remained a feature of England's stay at the 2006 World Cup, but resulted in disorder only in Stuttgart, when a number of England supporters threw beer and plastic chairs. The most significant violence during the tournament involving England fans (more serious disorder came from clashes between Germany and Poland fans) occurred in Cologne and was once again the result of a response by riot police perceived as illegitimate and disproportionate by English carnival fans. This occurred when an England fan climbing on a statue to hang a flag fell, injuring himself. A group of police and some England supporters moved to attend to the fan but a group of riot police watching apparently mistook the actions of the English supporters as being aggressive and used CS-gas against them. Disorder then escalated rapidly, with some England supporters in bars nearby throwing bottles at the riot police and the police then driving the supporters from the square with a baton charge.

Research with England fans demonstrated that the traditional media construction of England's followers as containing a large number of hooligans who travelled with the intention of 'looking for trouble' was not accurate. Certainly a large proportion of the English support between 1998 and 2006 was rowdy, drunken and xenophobic, but this did not mean that they were also inherently prone to incidents of serious disorder. Similarly, my observations suggested that the idea that hooligan generals travelled among the fans and were able to orchestrate riots involving the drunken hordes also appeared groundless. Excluding the issue of the lack of a hooligan firm, the composition of the England travelling support appeared no different than that of either Blackpool or United with two exceptions. First, the numbers that travelled with the England team (particularly to international tournaments) meant that small instances of violence were inevitable. Second, the reputation of the English support meant that when those instances occurred, local police forces were more likely to react with disproportionate force, and take action against the English support as a whole, rather than just the instigators. Where this sequence of events occurred, disorder could quickly escalate into a riot involving carnival fans with no previous history of football-related violence. However, where these instances of violence were dealt with in what was perceived to be a legitimate and proportionate manner, and where police interacted at times of both low and high tension with supporters, observations indicated that large numbers of drunken, rowdy and xenophobic Englishmen and women could be successfully policed. I would contend that the English football crowd abroad is not always one 'flashpoint' away from a riot; sensible and progressive policing such as that seen at Euro 2004 and in Frankfurt at the 2006 World Cup can ensure that it remains in a state of non-confrontational carnival.

The huge numbers of England football fans who travelled to international tournaments and important away matches went not to riot, but to engage in carnival. Drunkenness and rowdiness were essential, but there remained social rules which the crowd adhered to. Serious problems tended to occur when this carnival came under attack from outside, whether by locals, riot police or – rarely – rival fans. This is not to suggest that local authorities should allow England fans to act as they see fit in the hope that the crowd will self-police, although this will take place to a certain extent. It is true that fans will find their own levels of engagement with the carnival depending on how comfortable they feel – in this respect Fonarow's 'zones of participation' remain relevant; if fans did not want to risk being jostled and hit on the head during a mass game of football, there were always areas of space where they could sit and drink a beer in relative comfort and safety while still feeling part of the party. However, the levels of carnivalesque disorder considered appropriate by *some* of England's followers simply would not be acceptable to the authorities or local people and this crowd, left to its own devices without any regulation could become a danger, both to those within it and those outside.

My own findings, mirroring those of the ESIM school, indicated that in order to reduce the risk of mass disorder, it was important that local police engaged with the carnival from the outset, interacting with fans and permitting the carnival to continue within certain boundaries of social control. If the police were seen as facilitating rather than hampering the carnival, then their presence became accepted and sometimes even welcomed. Furthermore, from this position, it then becomes possible for the police to establish 'tolerance limits'; e.g. by allowing a game of street football to be played, but confiscating the ball if it is kicked at residential windows, or allowing fans to stand in the middle of the square chanting, but not to climb on to tables or statues. However, it was simply unfeasible to expect large crowds of football supporters to abide by the normal rules of everyday life, because that was to deny them the very reason why they are there. On no occasion did I witness a purported 'zero tolerance' approach by the authorities working (particularly, as we will see, with respect to alcohol consumption). Understanding the desire and motivation of fans to create and recreate football carnival is essential for those responsible for managing and controlling football crowds. The social-control arguments that have developed from my research emphasise the need to acknowledge the fact that many fans believe that it is their right to perform the rituals of carnival when they attend matches, particularly away from home or abroad. I do not argue that this means police or local authorities should not intervene, interact with or manage these fans, indeed aside from the obvious health and safety needs it is clear that *not* managing football crowds can lead to the escalation of minor incidents into full-scale riots. However, an understanding of the English football carnival for those hosting matches involving the national team, and English club sides, is vital to understanding the intentions of the crowd and reducing the likelihood of serious disorder.

Carnival fans following England, Blackpool and United were loud, often rowdy and usually under the influence of alcohol (or sometimes drugs). They frequently committed criminal offences connected to football or breached local by-laws (usually in relation to alcohol consumption). Some of the group were involved, on occasion, in incidents of violence or vandalism, and some were self-confessed 'former hooligans'. On rare occasions they also fought defensively as a cohesive group in response to attacks by opposing hooligan groups. Finally, under certain circumstances, they would be corralled in the same pubs or police escorts as the hooligan firm. However, as far as both the carnival fans (and as far as I could tell, the hooligans) were concerned, the research participants were not football hooligans, but merely fans. Their intention was not to fight or become involved in disorder, but to watch their team and engage in good-natured carnivalesque activity around the match. Accounts of incidents in this chapter taken out of context paint a picture of violent and disorderly groups, but it needs to be remembered that the vast majority of matches and trips passed off without violent incident, even when emotions were running high and when the fans were being provoked by rival groups or the authorities.

Carnival fans attitudes to hooligans

In the same way that they differentiated themselves from 'part-time' or 'armchair' supporters, carnival fans also differentiated themselves from those who gather in firms with the intention of confronting rival hooligans. However, there was one big difference in their attitude to these two extremes of the football supporting spectrum; while 'part-timers' and 'armchair fans' were referred to in disparaging terms, there was a great deal of respect shown to the hooligans attached to their team. This respect was not merely a show or performance when confronted with a perceived hooligan, but was also apparent in conversations among the fans and when posting on internet forums under pseudonyms. The research participants lacked the inclination – or believed they lacked the ability – to engage in hooligan activity, and a few felt that they had 'grown out' of it, but they largely admired those who fought 'on behalf' of their club. This is not to say that all of those researched shared this view – there were many fans who saw little or no value in the activities of the hooligans. However across the culture as a whole, the respect for them was evident.

This mirrored Joel Rookwood's (2008) findings in his ethnography of Liverpool and Cardiff supporters, and we identified a number of reasons why non-hooligan supporters admired the activities of hooligans (Rookwood and Pearson, 2011). Some fans felt that there were practical reasons why 'their' hooligans were valuable. For many of the carnival fans, hooligans were *perceived* to perform two important match-day functions – distracting the opposition's hooligans (who they believed otherwise might attack normal fans), and protecting normal fans from attack (particularly abroad). This second function was witnessed following an FA Cup semi-final in 2004, when United hooligans chased away a gang of Arsenal fans attacking what were perceived to be non-hooligan fans as they exited the stadium. This protective function was considered to be most important at European away matches in high-risk locations such as Italy, Turkey or Eastern Europe, where the carnival fans (and other travelling fans) would sometimes gather with them for protection. Of course, this is not to suggest that the fans' belief in the protective function of the hooligans was correct; in some cases gathering with the hooligans may have made them a more likely target for local hooligans or police.

However, most of the recorded support for the hooligans came not from any perceived practical value, but from the fact that many carnival fans were proud to have a 'respected' firm. The reputation of the team's hooligan element was largely viewed with pride by the research participants, who enjoyed being part of a feared away contingent (Rookwood and Pearson, 2011). Furthermore, when the team's hooligans were perceived not to have 'done their job', some of the carnival fans would complain. In response to a post on RedBrigade.net about United's 'lads' not confronting a group of Rochdale fans who were ridiculing the Munich air disaster at a pre-season friendly, a debate broke out about the value of hooliganism to the match experience:

Posted by Spence – If the lads were just letting 'em get away with murder, then he's got a sort of point though. 15–20 years ago they wouldn't have dared would they? Seems any old two bob cunts can take the piss out of us nowadays.

Posted by Dog – I think it's pathetic how some of the scrotes go around nowadays looking for trouble trying to act like there is still a scene going on. I think if I had gone to the footy back in the '70s and '80s I probably wouldn't have enjoyed it. I don't like fighting me.

Posted by Spence – You're a lover mate, not a fighter. I'm the same, but watching someone else commit violence is fun. I personally believe that football should and will always have an element of violence about it. Once that has been completely eradicated from the game, I'm not gonna bother anymore, once they take that 'standing by the divide goading the home fans' element, that swearing, shouting, singing, drinking side of things, once that's gone, I'm gone.

So for many of the carnival fans it was not just their own hooligans who were appreciated; many believed that hooligans – or at least the risk of 'hooliganism' – improved the atmosphere. The element of risk and danger from attacks by local hooligans was perceived by many to provide an element of 'edge' that enhanced the 'buzz' or atmosphere. Despite the fact that Dog claimed he did not like fighting, his comments a few months later (detailed above) show that even he saw a positive role for hooligans in the generation of an enjoyable match experience. One of the defining aspects of Manchester United's match-going culture was an honouring of, and a wish to re-enact the 'red army years'. This referred to the period in the club's history following relegation into the second division in 1974, when large numbers of United fans travelled to smaller lower-division grounds. The interpretation of this period in the club's history by contemporary fans was that the red army 'took over' stadiums and even whole towns, terrorising local fans and police and causing mayhem and disorder wherever they went. Carnival fans (including those not even born at the time) frequently expressed a desire to return to those unregulated days and the shadow and influence of the red army 'hooligans' still hangs over United's travelling support.

To certain extent, support for the hooligans went beyond the carnival fans and permeated the ranks of many other groups of the match-going support. It was evident in the popularity of hoolie-lit among supporters (fans would often read these books on planes travelling to matches abroad), in discussion of recent incidents involving the hooligans of the team, and also speculation about how they would defeat the hooligans of rival teams. For example, ahead of matches against hated rivals, normal fans would often express the desire that 'their' hooligans gave those of the rival club 'a good kicking'. Additionally, support for the hooligan culture among the wider support was most evidently shown in terrace chants sung by a wide cross-section of the support, including women, children and senior supporters. Blackpool's version of the Blaydon Races claimed, 'hardest fans in the land, you'll never seen us running' and following a derby match in 1992, after which Blackpool hooligans apparently chased Preston fans to the train station, Blackpool fans sang 'Did you run down Central Drive?' at their rivals at every derby for the next five years. Blackpool fans also sang 'Seaside Aggro, hello hello', when disorder involving their supporters broke out (United fans sang 'United Aggro' in similar situations). Dozens of other popular United chants referred to the glory of hooliganism, including:

With hatchets and hammers, stanley-knives and spanners, we'll show the City bastards how to fight
If I die on the Kippax Street, there'll be ten blue bastards at my feet
How we'll kill them I don't know, cut them up from head to toe, all I know is City's gonna die

He's only a poor little scouser, his face is all tattered and torn, he made me feel
sick, so I hit him with a brick, and now he won't sing anymore

The threat of violence and the buzz around it was particularly noticeable at
derbies. The biggest dates on the calendar for Blackpool fans were the local derbies
against Burnley and, to an even greater extent, Preston. For the home leg of these
derbies, Bloomfield Road would be sold out, with large numbers of irregular and
travelling fans bolstering the normal numbers and Blackpool would take between
2,500 and 4,000 fans for away derbies. Both home and away matches were tense
affairs with the potential for disorder. Usually this appeared to be a spontaneous
result of the expressed hatred between the two sets of fans, although some fans
believed that older hooligans would make a rare appearance. However, rather
than worrying the fans, the threat of hooliganism added to the excitement. In the
build up to a derby, the talk on the terrace was all about the plans for the following
week, and in the match directly before the derby, the fans would often sing not
about the game they were watching, but about next week's match; 'One week till
Preston', 'Bring on the Preston', 'If you're all going to Preston clap your hands'. The
derbies showed that for many Blackpool fans, the 'needle' of these matches (and
the potential danger of them) was something to be relished, a high point in a
season that would usually otherwise consist of playing routine mid-table league
matches in front of half-empty stadiums. The derbies were also a departure from
the norms of terrace behaviour; it became accepted that missiles would be thrown
at opposition players, and that rival fans would confront each other. This is
certainly not to say that a large number of Blackpool fans were involved in any of
these activities, merely that these activities happened with regularity around the
derbies, and that there would be little disapproval or censure from non-violent
fans (in contrast to non-derby matches).

Carnival fans' wider attitudes to violence

For carnival fans, the subject of violence – whether in a football context or not –
was never far from conversation. From time to time, they were involved, usually
unwittingly, in instances of threatened or actual violence. This often occurred
because they were mistaken for hooligans, such as occurred to the Blackpool
group at Wrexham, or in Kiev, when a bar containing United carnival fans was
attacked by Dynamo Kiev 'Ultras'. Where escape was possible, the fans would
usually take this route, as occurred in Wrexham. However, in Kiev, they had no
option but to fight, barricading the doors and fighting with chairs, bottles and
fists to prevent the ultras gaining access to the building. These stories were then
lavishly retold in pubs and on forums. On other occasions, the carnival fans
would simply ignore invitations to fight, even in situations where they felt that
their numbers and personnel would mean they would win any confrontation
(one such incident occurred at Southampton when Denis was confronted by a
rival fan). When United travelled to Derby for an FA Cup match in 2009, I was the
victim of an unprovoked attack by a group of Derby fans after Ben and I had been

split up from the rest of the group. One Derby supporter identified us as United fans and started questioning why we had been singing anti-England songs in the ground. When Ben answered, 'because I fucking hate England', he was punched from the side, breaking his nose. When I moved to intervene to stop the attack, another Derby fan ran and attempted to karate-kick me, catching me on the leg. Following this attack, a further group of Derby supporters charged down the road and chased me for around 100 yards, trying to trip me up, before I finally managed to outrun them.

Another incident where research participants were attacked occurred in a pub before a match at Wolverhampton Wanderers. Various sub-groups of United carnival fans numbering around twenty in total had gathered here to drink, surrounded by greater number of Wolves fans. The United fans had commandeered the jukebox, playing Manchester band the Stone Roses, and chanting, which may have been seen as provocative by some Wolves fans. However, there was no sign of imminent violence, until a United fan sat on his own wearing a replica shirt stood up and threw his plastic glass of beer at the Wolves supporters. A beer glass was thrown back in return, hitting Pete a glancing blow on the head, cutting him. Another individual (believed to be a Wolves fan, although one account said this was another United fan) then attacked from the opposite direction, breaking his glass over Martin's head from behind, splitting his scalp open and sending blood everywhere. The incident was over in seconds and the bar was shut. Martin's head was bandaged up so that he could still go to the match and a number of Wolves fans enquired after his health. It was agreed on all sides that the United fan who had thrown the first glass was to blame for the entire incident and it was claimed that another United fan had punched him as a result (although I did not witness this). Missile-throwing as part of crowd disorder was worryingly indiscriminate for the carnival fans, and observations suggested that you were as likely to be hit by a missile thrown from your own fans as from those of the opposition. At a number of European away matches, missiles thrown from rival fans were inches from causing me serious injury, the closest when a bottle thrown by an England fan in Munich in 2001 deflected off the peak of my cap and smashed against the wall behind me.

On a few occasions, however, carnival fans were themselves the instigators of aggression or violent confrontation (e.g. the incident with Micky noted above). On one occasion Little Jim from the Red Brigade head-butted a Manchester City fan the evening following the match ('He was a City fan taking the piss so I nutted him', he explained). Another incident observed occurred at an away match in 2010, this time involving a female supporter. Riot police were deployed into the concourse area under the stand in order to control a crowd of United fans. As these officers entered the concourse, Caz was standing nearby finishing a cigarette.

> Caz: About twelve of these riot cops came through out of a corner at the far end
> ... these were the same lot that had been shoving us about for smoking
> that had gone and regrouped ... I have to confess, I had had a drink ...

> This lot suddenly appear to get the shout that something horrific has gone on and start running with their fucking riot shields up and fucking batons ... and start running towards where all the United fans are all jammed in. And it's like, 'well that can't be right' ... and I thought 'd'ya know what? You shouldn't be doing that'... and I used to play football a bit, and I was a dirty bastard ... so I legged one of them up ... I just put my foot there and took him out at the knees. And the lad goes skidding across the floor [laughs] and I was just stood there just laughing because it was one of the funniest things I'd seen ... But what were they going to be doing? They were going to be running in and assaulting my fellow fans ... if you're going to do that, then why shouldn't I do that? It was a bit of a giggle. It wasn't meant to be being an awful hooligan ...

Caz stood laughing for a moment before she was grabbed by a two police officers, dragged across the concourse and pushed up against a wall. She was informed that she would be arrested for assaulting a police officer, but the arrest never took place, possibly because the police could not afford to lose personnel needed to control the crowd and rescue officers who had become trapped further up the concourse. 'You, you can just fuck off right now', shouted the officer releasing her.

Another physical assault involving a research participant occurred during a United match in Turkey. In a bar before the match, Denis had become involved in an argument with another United fan who had racially abused a Turkish United fan. Although this incident had appeared to calm down, Denis identified the fan in the stadium and went to confront him. The confrontation ended with the other fan attempting to head-butt him and Denis responding in kind, splitting the fan's nose open and sending him tumbling down three rows of seats: 'I turned round and stuck one on him. I didn't expect him to bounce like a fucking bowling ball down the fucking steps'. Denis was questioned by police who then released him at the end of the match. Discussing the incident in the bar later, Denis was more concerned that he had made an error of judgement in the way he had handled the situation than the injury he had caused the other fan:

Denis: What I feel now is ... a slight amount of embarrassment because what happens is that lots of people will be talking about it and that's not what I went to the match for – I went to support United. For all the excuses I make, I could have done it much better, I could have ... waited till later ... But I just feel a little bit embarrassed because, it turned out well, but it could have been horrible. [inaudible, but says he could have been arrested and put in jail]. And my wife would have said to me 'you're a fucking idiot' and that would have been absolutely spot on. And I embarrassed my mates, Jay was worried, you know, lost my phone ... However I make no excuses for it. The only reason it happened was because I got the hump. No matter what he did wrong ... I went up the stairs deliberately to have a little dig at him. No one – you had a little word with me – but no-one was going to stop me cos I had the hump. He was going to get twatted. So I don't say, 'oh no he asked for it', I don't make excuses it was me ... The only reason violence happened was because I decided I wanted to twat him ... I'm putting my hands up ...

But to my own credit, I didn't hit him ever again. I never punched him and kicked him. I did have a few words, I said 'come on you fat cunt, get up'. 'I'm not a fifteen year-old boy. You know, I'm here now you mug'. I did have a bit of a rant. But I didn't kick him or hit him. That's really not my style.

Becs: If the guy did racist comments I believe you did the right thing and he deserved everything he fucking got because I hate racist ...

Denis: So do I, but to be honest that wasn't the driving force ... I'm not going to say 'hey I'm the enlightened one' ... A few people I've spoken to tonight have said, 'no it weren't clever, but ...'

Becs: I do not want someone like that being a fan of United ...

Denis: And to be fair, if I hadn't had a drink, I wouldn't have got that extreme ... However, I really do not regret it.

For the carnival fans this type of incident was generally not welcomed or condoned (although the fact that the victim had racially abused another fan meant that fans such as Ruby, Dog and Becs who had expressed anti-violence opinions defended Denis's actions). However they were accepted as part and parcel of travelling to matches, especially away. The views of United fans of the incident involving Denis also revealed a lack of surprise that such an incident had occurred on the away terrace and a certain amount of good humour about the assault. One fan at the airport on the journey home recognised me as a friend of the assailant and thanked me for 'the half-time entertainment'. Accounts of all the above incidents were sometimes repeated as 'amusing' tales at subsequent matches, demonstrating – as with Caz's response to her assault on a police officer – that occasional violence of this nature could be viewed as a humorous part of the football carnival.

Violence was seen as an inevitable part of following your team away from home, and not only from confrontations with rival supporters. At Blackpool, England and United, dozens of violent incidents between fans of the same team were observed, on terraces, on concourses at half-time and in pubs. Counter-intuitively, the fewest instances of this type of intra-group violence witnessed were among the England support, made up from fans of many rival clubs. In 2009, a number of United fans commented on what was perceived to be a worrying increase in 'red on red' violence, and at one match at Wigan, I witnessed three separate violent incidents between United fans, two in the concourse and one in the stands. My own personal experience of confrontation between fans of the same team came from an incident of being pushed and threatened by a Blackpool fan who perceived I was not getting 'behind the team' sufficiently, and being head-butted by a replica-shirt-wearing United fan after his friend had become involved in a disagreement with me about an anti-Glazer protest. Taken in conjunction with the incident at Wolves (above) and Rome (below), it was clear that despite the common belief that hooligans do not wear colours, actual physical violence affecting the carnival fans was as likely to be instigated by those wearing replica-shirts as those wearing designer 'hooligan clobber'. Observations of disorder abroad involving England (particularly in Marseilles and Charleroi) also demonstrated that the wearing of a replica shirt was by no means an indicator that a fan would not become involved in violence.

To a lesser extent, violence was also seen as part of everyday social life and occasionally a perfectly acceptable way of solving problems and avoiding humiliation. A number of researchers into the night-time economy (e.g. Tomsen, 1997; Winlow and Hall, 2006, 2009) note a similar prevalence of violence on 'nights out', and similar attitudes towards this as I observed among carnival fans. Indeed, their accounts indicate that there was far more frequent interpersonal violence in the night-time economy than around football matches, where much of the apparent threat appeared to be highly ritualised displays rather than genuine attempts at violence. This difference possibly results from the relative lack of state regulation (Winlow and Hall, 2006: 188) in contrast to the high level of regulation at football. It should therefore not be a surprise that carnival fans also experienced violence in this environment. Similar to Armstrong's (1998) findings with the Blades, carnival fans under observation often saw violence as an acceptable response to assaults upon them, and were sometimes willing to assist friends in getting revenge. When Gary from the Red Brigade was assaulted while drinking with his girlfriend in London, a number of London-based members of the Brigade offered assistance for violent revenge (which was declined). 'I'll pop in with a few pals', offered Jay, 'If you want this sorted proper ... I'll get the chaps to do it ... Trust me ... it will finish sharpish'. Rich, among others, suggested Gary take up the offer, 'I'm not one for violence but if it happened to me, I'd be taking Jay up on his offer, no questions about that'.

Observations indicated that violence was also seen as justified within a group when they were confronted with overly aggressive police and stewards at football matches (see also Stott and Reicher, 1998; Stott *et al.*, 2001, 2007). When United fans in Rome were attacked by baton-wielding riot police in 2007, the crowd cheered when a fan threw his seat at the police, striking one officer on the visor of his riot helmet. Similarly, when riot police attacked a group of England supporters trying to assist a fan who had fallen from a statue in Cologne during the 2006 World Cup with CS-gas, the watching crowd felt justified in throwing bottles at the riot police. What was viewed as disproportionately aggressive policing against United fans at Barnsley in 2009 and Birmingham in 2010 also led to some carnival fans feeling justified in shouting abuse and throwing missiles at officers.

However, certain forms of violence were viewed as unacceptable. On the train back from Derby following the attack on us, Ben's complaints were not that we had been the victims of an unprovoked violent assault, but that he had been hit from behind. My own interpretation of this attack was also affected by the amount of time spent in the field, and the appropriation of the belief that violence was part and parcel of following your team away. My initial feelings were of relief I had not been seriously injured; my only anger was that we had been assaulted by superior numbers. Around fifteen Derby fans attacking me and Ben did not seem 'fair'. Likewise, the Brigade's views on the assault on Gary in London were not that the attack itself was unfair, but that it was unreasonable to 'gang up' on him while he was out drinking 'with his missus'.

The throwing of dangerous missiles into crowds was one practice that caused more consternation among those on the receiving end than other forms of confrontation (although as we have seen, the throwing of missiles at the police or in defence against a hooligan attack was often seen as acceptable). The indiscriminate nature of missile-throwing into crowds meant that fans seen as more vulnerable (senior supporters, children and women) were often put at risk. For example, following a derby between Preston and Blackpool in 1998, Blackpool supporters came under a barrage of stones from the other side of a police cordon outside the turnstiles, leading to angry shouts of 'there's women and kids here'. The throwing of bottles and glasses into a crowd of United supporters gathered outside a pub near Wembley in 2009 drew similar anger and condemnation from the Red Brigade:

Dave: Bottles and glasses is a fucking cunts trick. You want to go at it with fists they could have brought it on . . . and would have got served up a treat by the look of 'em and they knew that. Everyone there was game if they wanted it . . . but some cunt wants to get a pint pot involved.

Ruby: I was proper scared that day. I hate mither.

Another incident that demonstrated unacceptable violence came from 'red on red' violence at the 2009 Champions League Final, when a United fan had his ear bitten off following a dispute about a ticket. The nature of this attack drew universal condemnation from United supporters for a number of reasons. The victim was not perceived to have been 'up for it' and had tried to walk away and the injury caused was deemed to have gone 'too far', again echoing the findings of Marsh (1978) about the 'rules of disorder'. The condemnation of this attack was also assisted by the common knowledge about the alleged perpetrator of the attack that circulated in the social networks (both physical and virtual) of United's carnival supporters. The victim was described as a normal match-going fan who had tried to intervene when a female United fan's ticket had been stolen. The attacker, on the other hand, was suspected to be responsible for a number of previous incidents of 'red-on-red mither'. He was also denigrated for wearing a replica shirt (apparently with his wife's name on it), and for being a 'Johnny-come-lately' fan. A forum-led witch-hunt then took place to locate the attacker and arrange violent retribution. Again, this retribution was perceived as legitimate:

Posted by Spence – [the] cunt fucked someone over in Porto, and again at a domestic away, then he bit that poor cunts ear off in rome. Shithouse. I personally hope (he's a big lad see) that 5 or 6 big nasty fuckers get hold of him (he wont be hard to find, blue shirt, [the name of his wife] on it), and fucking muller the cunt, i mean bounce him up and down Chester road for an hour. I WOULDNT BITE A LEEDS FANS FUCKING EAR OFF, NEVER MIND ONE OF ME OWN. Utter fucking shithawk of the highest order, needs a really severe fucking up. Bring your stanley blades if you like, this cunt deserves it.

Posted by Jay –   I'd gladly smash the cunt. I'll keep my eyes peeled for him.

Posted by Spence – Every nasty cunt in United's following knows who [he] is now.

Posted by Jay – Do we need all the nasty cunts to deal with him? I'm not a nasty cunt, and I will put him in my pocket. Many other non nasty cunts may well do the same. Let's leave the nasty cunts to deal with serious business.

Posted by Jenny – Biting someone's ear off isn't being 'up for it', it's being a complete cunt. A fight is a fight but biting someone's ear is pure scumbag behaviour.

A few weeks later, the victim approached the police and following an appeal for help circulated across the United internet forums, the police issued a photograph of the suspect. The hunt for the assailant also led to disputes about whether it was fair to 'grass' the attacker to the police, and while the majority of United's carnival fans considered that in this case it was acceptable, generally 'grassing' to police or stewards was frowned upon. The 'us and them' mentality of football supporters and the authorities, particularly at away matches, meant that supporters would often even hide fans being pursued by police or stewards. Numerous times with England and United, supporters who had been engaged in unlawful activity (often jibbing into the stadium) sought sanctuary in crowds of fans who would not reveal their location. Some supporters in these crowds would even assist in their escape from the authorities (e.g. by suggesting they change their coat, or by lending them a hat). In one such incident a Blackpool a fan who had thrown a missile on to the pitch was protected in this way; when two police officers entered the terrace, they were met with shouts of 'I'm Spartacus' from the crowd as they hid the escaping fan.

My observations indicated that very few of the home-and-away match-goers considered themselves 'hooligans', or were thus labelled by other fans. However, the attitudes towards violence and disorder of those under observation revealed that this behaviour was accepted as part and parcel of the match-going experience, particularly at away games and matches abroad. Although it was rare to see any of the research participants become actively and physically involved in violence, they were largely unmoved by what violence did take place in the context of football matches. Fans would often observe violence taking place between others dispassionately, or with mirth, and under certain circumstances – where the violence was deemed justifiable – would even encourage those involved. The idea of primarily non-violent individuals gaining voyeuristic pleasure from witnessing violence is by no means confined to football (see Winlow and Hall, 2006: 96, 101–3), but the relish with which these encounters (both real and mythical) were anticipated and relived remained a dominant feature of match-going culture for many of the carnival fans.

Violence at matches was certainly not confined to the traditional view of hooliganism – i.e. groups of rival supporters clashing. This was in fact very rare and the instances of rival fans confronting each other normally comprised of one side being the aggressors and the others unwilling participants, and were usually solved with the latter backing down or escaping. Much more common were confrontations between fans and stewards, police or security at bars and clubs, and the most common form of *observed interpersonal physical violence* was between fans of the same team. Similarly, from my observations of carnival fans, those wearing colours were as likely to launch a punch, head-butt or pint-glass as those wearing supposed hooligan attire. As with Winlow and Hall's work on the night-time economy, violence was viewed in a 'fatalistic' manner (*ibid.*: 96) – it could happen to you at any time, and the more matches you attended, the more it became inevitable that you would be a victim. This was evidenced by a short discussion between two United carnival fans shortly before a match at Manchester City:

Baz: Surprised to see you've got your glasses, Jonno. I thought this would
        have been a contacts [contact lenses] match.
Jonno: Eh ... well if some cunt smashes my glasses, it's just a day off work isn't
        it?

Conclusion

The spectre of 'hooliganism', 'trouble' or 'mither' was never far from the thoughts of carnival fans. The risk of being the victim of a violent attack, particularly at an away match, was considered part and parcel of the carnival fan subculture. Fans would talk about fights with relish, contemplate how they would react under threatening situations and show respect and admiration to those considered to belong to the 'firms'. But despite considerable confusion and disagreement over what constituted hooliganism at football, the carnival fans distanced themselves, both psychologically and (if possible) physically from those they considered to be hooligans. They did not consider themselves or those in their groups to be hooligans and did not attend matches with the intention of becoming involved in disorder. Actual acts of violence involving the carnival fans were rare and consensual fights between carnival groups supporting different teams were not observed. However on occasion individuals in the groups – both male and female – would become involved in violence (often against fans of their own team), and on several occasions carnival groups were attacked and forced to fight back. Large-scale football riots were exceptionally rare, but when they did occur, their causes bore little observable relation to the explanations of the media for such disorder. Observations of the rare instances that large-scale disorder took place, and the frequent occasions it did not, also supported the ESIM of crowd behaviour, indicating the importance of numerous factors bringing an otherwise disparate crowd together in the belief that its legitimate aims had been unfairly infringed and that a violent response was both justified and necessary.

The existence of hooligan groups who went to matches with the intention of fighting rival firms was acknowledged by the carnival fans, and in some cases the research participants socialised with these hooligans or admitted to having been hooligans in the past. Moreover, most of the carnival fans showed a considerable respect for their 'own' hooligan firm, and would read books about them, discuss their activities, and generally wish them well in confrontations with rival firms. Furthermore, many of the fans – particularly following United – would dress in a similar manner, avoiding colours and wearing labels that were considered popular with the hooligans. As a result, it could be very difficult differentiating between those hooligans who attend matches with the intention of confronting rival supporters and the carnival fans who mimicked their style. This became virtually impossible when the hooligans and carnival fans drank in the same pubs, travelled on the same trains or were corralled in the same police escort. Some of the research participants even enjoyed being treated by the authorities as a 'hooligan' by being put in an escort or prevented from leaving a pub, which provided them with the opportunity to mimic the hooligans without fear of being involved in violent confrontation with rival gangs.

The observed blurring of the boundaries between the carnival fans and the hooligans has a significant potential impact upon policies for controlling football crowds if it reflects match-going fan behaviour more widely. Many policing and public order strategies for managing potentially high-risk matches focus on segregating rival supporters, but one potential outcome of this is to force the hooligans and the carnival fans together. This can be a problem because the ESIM theory of crowd management suggests that one strategy for reducing the likelihood of disorder from 'non-hooligan' fans is to encourage them to exclude elements of the crowd looking to cause disorder (see Stott and Pearson, 2007: 281–3). The ESIM school has demonstrated that positive interaction between police and fans such as those under observation for the purposes of this book can prevent disorder involving these fans, but treating these fans as potential hooligans has been shown to make disorder involving non-hooligan fans more likely. (Stott *et al.*, 1998, 2001; Stott and Pearson, 2007).

This chapter shows that those responsible for policing football crowds are faced with serious problems when it comes to identifying those fans who attend matches with the intention of becoming involved in disorder and those who merely want to be involved in a carnival of fandom, usually entailing drinking, humour and song. Where this latter group are treated as potential hooligans, they too have the ability to become involved in disorder. This situation occurred in both Marseilles and Charleroi with England, and during United's visits to Rome in 2007, Barnsley in 2009 and Birmingham in 2010. Understanding the motivations of the carnival fans, and understanding their attitudes to both hooliganism and violence and disorder more generally is vital. The traditional view that 'non-hooligan' fans abhor hooligans did not hold true for carnival fans. Finding a way of satisfying their complex objectives when they attend matches, without forcing them into the same spaces as the hooligans, would seem to be a serious challenge for those charged with managing large football crowds but it is one that, if achieved, will make management of both carnival fans, and the hooligans, simpler.

Notes

1 This chant, apparently more popular in the 1970s and early 1980s, was heard only once during my observations (with fans of Blackpool) in response to disorder by visiting supporters.
2 Trafford Magistrates' Court: 14–16/02/06; Leeds Magistrates' Court 21/06/10; Leeds Crown Court: 6–8/02/11; Bristol Magistrates Court 27/01/11.
3 One sub-group of younger United fans were constantly 'on the rob', particularly on Euro aways. They would steal alcohol to drink and also luxury items such as perfume and designer wallets which they would try to sell on in order to fund part of their trip.
4 Although primary observations of this practice are lacking.

5

Authority and social control

Maintaining order at football matches

We have seen that while the carnival fans did not attend matches with the intention of causing disorder, they were affected by violent incidents. On occasion, the dress code and the 'attitude' of the fans led to them being mistakenly targeted as hooligans by rival groups, particularly abroad. One might therefore assume that carnival fans viewed the role of the police in maintaining order positively; on numerous occasions I witnessed the intervention of police officers preventing violence against research participants occurring or escalating. Also, because the motives of the carnival fans were to have good 'craic' without confronting rival supporters, it might be assumed that the police would play a positive role in helping them achieve their aims. In reality, the situation was far more complex; often the intervention of the police into the carnival was resented and under some circumstances it could lead to bad feeling and even disorder and violence. This chapter investigates the relationship between the carnival fans and those responsible for maintaining order at and around football matches attended by them – police, private security staff and match-day stewards.

The relationship between the police and the 'hooligans' is one that has been considered in ethnographies from both sides with similar conclusions. Marsh (1978) notes that part of the 'illusion of violence' from football fans in the 1970s resulted from the fact that fans involved in a confrontation relied on the police to intervene so that aggression remained ritualised and did not escalate in severity. Armstrong (1998) also implies that the role of the police as 'umpires' in confrontations between firms was all too readily accepted. O'Neill's ethnography of the policing of football found that the police believed that, 'the hooligans need the police to be close by so they do not get too seriously injured or need to risk losing face if a fight happens, and they need the police for an extra element of chase and escape during the football day' (2005: 127). She also suggests that, 'The police and hooligans are not adversaries, but partners in one large production, though this may not be something of which they are aware. Although they may present themselves as involved in a 'war' with each other, none of them actually want to win' (*ibid.*: 130). My findings suggested that in domestic football in particular, carnival fans wanted, and expected, a police presence. Abroad this desire was less apparent, and the appearance of foreign police was often feared. Both home and abroad the appearance of riot police or police dog handlers was always viewed with resentment and suspicion.

The relationship between the carnival fans and British police

The fans' relationship with the British police oscillated from complete loathing, anger and hostility on the one hand, to friendly chatter and deliberate interaction on the other. Most of the time good-natured tolerance was the order of the day; carnival fans accepted that police at and around matches were necessary and the police largely left the carnival fans to their own devices, often turning a blind eye to minor infractions of the law. Under the normal circumstances of a low- to medium-risk football match, the two groups treated each other with outward courtesy and respect, although the carnival fans would make fun of certain officers behind their backs after interactions. O'Neill (2005) found that officers behaved in a similar manner, and on one occasion I overheard a police officer who had just confiscated cans of beer from a group of carnival fans commenting disparagingly that, 'they've not even got the wit to hide their cans'. This also suggested that the police were often aware of illegal activity by fans, but were not interested in taking action unless they felt compelled to do so by public shows of illegality. Observations of police in England and Wales throughout this research suggested that peacekeeping was the primary objective of those officers policing large groups of football fans rather than strict 'law enforcement', in line with Bittner's findings that the police's 'overall objective is to reduce the total amount of risk in the area. In this, practicality plays a considerably more important role than legal norms' (1967: 713–14). This is not to say that strategic decisions by either match commanders or individual officers always achieved this aim.

The relationship of outward courtesy usually shown between fans and police could break down in particular circumstances depending on both the attitude and character of individual officers and fans. Additionally, both police units and coherent sub-groups of carnival fans were protective of their members. If one police officer was insulted by a fan, the attitude of other officers would typically turn hostile. Similarly, where it was perceived that a member of a carnival fan group was bullied by a police officer, the attitude of that group could become more hostile towards that force as a whole. One way in which police officers could avoid the 'us and them' mentality between police and carnival fans developing was through positive and friendly interaction. As we have seen, positive interaction is viewed by crowd psychologists employing the elaborated social identity model (ESIM) as a key factor in laying the foundations for successful management of a football crowd (Stott and Reicher 1998; Stott et al. 2001, 2007), and could often be based upon such minor social signals as a smile. Caz: 'People have got a natural distrust of coppers, certainly at the football … but if they're [walking past] and they're smiling, it's amazing how much [tension] that takes out of the situation. *If* [her emphasis] you see a smiling copper, because one is such a bloody rarity. And it's like, there's no need to have a go at these, because they're not having a go at us'.

In particular, carnival fans expected the police to have a sense of humour. If a police officer recommended a pub to a group of fans, it was not uncommon for a joke to be made by one of the fans – 'are you on commission?' or 'can you radio ahead and order us a round?'. However weak the joke, the officer was expected to make a humorous retort, or at least to laugh, and a failure to do this would inevitably result in a comment a while later that he or she was a 'miserable bastard'. A couple of police officers from a particular force on away trips who failed to engage in light-hearted banter could lead to the entire constabulary being labelled 'humourless cunts'. Fans also seemed to expect more in terms of behaviour and attitude from women police officers (WPCs) or officers who were deemed short in stature or 'skinny'. Orders from these officers risked being treated with more contempt and some of the female fans in particular complained about the attitude of WPCs. Smaller male officers acting officiously were often deemed to have a Napoleon complex, or were seen as 'little Hitlers'. Behind their backs some carnival fans were heard to comment that but for their uniform, they would have 'laid him out' with ease.

It was also believed by some carnival fans that many of the police officers on the ground saw dealing with them to be a challenge of masculinity. United's carnival fans in particular thought that many police officers wanted to 'test' themselves against them due to their reputation for disorder. As Dave argued, when discussing what was considered to be an 'over-reaction' by police at a match in Barnsley in 2009:

> You know when you get teams drawn with United, at home, right, and their supporters go fucking mad, like at Barnsley, yeah? At United? The old bill are just as itching to get hold of it as much as anyone else is ... They want to make a name for themselves: 'Oh yeah, I fucking twatted this bloke, I fucking twatted that bloke ...' You know what I mean?

This view was also shared by Caz following quite serious disorder which occurred in a concourse at half-time during a United away match at Birmingham; 'Those riot police ... From the very beginning they were itching for a fight'. While, as we will see, this attitude was not prevalent among all carnival fans, and varied from police force to police force, the belief that for high-risk matches in particular the police were simply a 'third firm' in a hooligan battle (the other two 'firms' being the home-and-away hooligan groups), was noted on a number of occasions.

On journeys to away matches, the appearance of police officers was normally tolerated but not welcomed. British Transport Police (BTP) officers on platforms and on trains were generally perceived as being unnecessary and an imposition on a very low-risk part of the match-day without providing any value in terms of protection. However if alcohol was permitted and fans were not prevented from catching the train of their choice they were not resented and particularly after matches carnival fans on trains home often engaged BTP officers in conversation, sometimes discussing the behaviour of other groups of fans or even the behaviour of the local police force (grievances about incompetent or heavy-handed policing by local forces were often met with sympathy). However, where alcohol restrictions were in force on trains, BTP officers were viewed as being overly officious and kill-joys. For fans travelling to matches on buses and minibuses, police in patrol vehicles were resented, as it was common for vehicles to be pulled over, searched for alcohol, and then led to a car park or service station where fans would be forced to wait for a police escort. Many fans set off early with the intention of drinking in a local pub, only to find their time instead wasted sat on a stationary vehicle before being escorted to the ground just in time for kick-off (or sometimes afterwards). As a result, fans altered their strategy to try and avoid this – minibuses would stop off at pubs before entering the area of the local police force, or chose back roads to avoid police patrols. This meant that the location of the carnival fans would often be unknown by the police until they arrived at the stadium or (rarely) were involved in an incident.

With the exception of these patrols, the attitude towards police at away venues was generally positive. Carnival fans usually welcomed the sight of police at away matches because they performed a role that in the main facilitated their own intentions; the police would provide a perceived deterrent against attacks by local hooligans and give the carnival fans a feeling of security in an often strange city. The police could also be a useful source of information when it came to which pubs were best to drink in (either because they were good venues or safe for away supporters) and where they were, or how long a walk it was to the stadium. Usually local police were both helpful and friendly towards the fans, appearing genuinely interested and honest when it came, for example, to pub recommendations. This was appreciated by the research participants and appeared to have an effect in making many of them more good-natured and receptive towards other members of the local police force later that day. Many carnival fans believed that their first interaction with a police officer from the local force at an away match would indicate how they would be treated through-out the day. A friendly police officer in normal uniform interacting in a positive way to them was seen as boding well but a humourless officer suggested that the local police force had been briefed that the travelling fans were troublesome. Police in riot gear indicated that there would be trouble. At one match in 2009, for example, the first experience of the group of United carnival fans with whom I travelled was of humourless officers whose interaction consisted of little more than pointing them in the direction of the designated drinking establishment (which turned out to be a sports hall with a bar). Outside the hall were officers in riot gear with police dogs. Several fans commented that the local police looked ready for trouble, and by the final whistle riot police and dog handlers had been deployed in the stadium, with some United fans throwing missiles at them. Large scale police deployments could also have the effect of leading to previously peaceful and disparate sub-groups of fans adopting a unified aggressive attitude towards the police; previously quiet and good-natured United fans were observed suddenly directing collective and aggressive chants of 'United' and 'Attack, attack, attack!' at the police.

Carnival fans were also suspicious of local police forces who 'read the riot act' in advance of any trouble. Before a United match at Blackburn in 2008, fans disembarking from the train were immediately corralled by police. They were then addressed by a senior officer whose opening words were 'Welcome to sunny Darwen!'. The officer was attempting to be friendly and was using humour (it was overcast and raining), but the context of his speech did nothing to allay the concerns of the fans about what to expect. The content of the pep-talk also caused disquiet. While the officer said that he hoped the fans enjoyed their stay, and recommended a pub, he ended the address by noting that police cells in Blackburn and Burnley had been cleared for any troublemakers. The 'welcome to Darwen' speech became infamous among United's travelling support, especially in the light of perceived heavy-handed policing in the marquee of the recommended pub and a high number of arrests (fifty-nine) that day. The fans believed the talk served no purpose whatsoever, other than leading them to suspect over-the-top policing, and did not appear to deter the fans from being rowdy in the pub later on.

One of the victims of the perceived illegitimate and indiscriminate policing at this match was Freddy, who was arrested at the pub and charged with disorderly behaviour after he had finished his can of lager and thrown it onto the ground. He missed the game and spent the next six hours in the cells before being released after his final train home had departed (this appears to be a common occurrence and many fans believed it was done deliberately). Freddy had to spend over £100 on a taxi home and then make two appearances at the magistrates' court. The police alleged that Freddy had been warned on a number of occasions about his conduct by officers and they also testified that he was a 'ringleader' in the disorderly crowd. Although Freddy admitted that he threw the can to the ground, and that he should not have done that, he was angry at what he considered to be deliberate lies by the police to justify the arrest. He was found not guilty and the magistrate noted that this was 'a clear case of mistaken identity'. It was typical, however, for carnival fans to simply plead guilty to such charges, fearing a heavier sentence if they fought their case, and believing that the police would simply corroborate each other's version of events leaving little chance of a not guilty verdict.

In the main, however, the appearance of local police officers in pubs was accepted as legitimate, so long as they were not interfering with the fans' drinking. It was common at many pubs where the fans gathered for a pair of local police officers in luminous jackets to walk in and converse with the bar staff. If, as fans suspected, the police were simply asking the bar staff if everything was all right, the fans were usually sure the answer would be affirmative as they prided themselves on treating bar staff with respect. So long as the police carrying out this function were courteous (e.g. by saying 'excuse me' as they moved through a crowd, and smiling at fans or responding to questions), their imposition was accepted. The appearance of police Football Intelligence Officers (or 'spotters') from the fans' home police force was treated with more suspicion; it was rare for spotters – whose role is primarily to identify the location of 'risk supporters' – to converse with the carnival fans, so these appearances were usually uncomfortable (with conversations often dying) but also transitory.

Carnival fans travelling to away matches usually expected, and many wanted, to see police on the walk from the city centre, train station or pub to the away turnstiles. This was again primarily for security, with fans at away matches usually heavily outnumbered by home fans if they were allowed to walk to the stadium on their own. Indeed, despite the posturing and clothing of many of the research participants, if elements of the home support confronted them, inevitably in greater numbers, it was common for them to later ask, 'where were the police?'. Of course, the chances of being confronted by local fans was increased by the fans' tendency to chant their team's songs as they approached the stadium, so the presence of sufficient numbers of police to deter confrontation allowed them to enjoy one of the elements that made up the away day carnival – the practice of announcing to the locals that you had arrived. As we have seen, creating an impression on the locals, in terms of numbers, colour, noise and behaviour is a key driver for many of the carnival fans. Giulianotti's appropriation of Goffman's 'dramaturgical model of impression management' to describe the activities of Scottish fans at international tournaments (1991: 506) also reveals a key driving force behind the behaviour of English fans at away matches. Leaving the 'audience' with a lasting impression of the supporters' visit was highly important for all English fans, although the exact nature of this impression varied from team to team. For Blackpool fans, colour ('painting the town tangerine') played an important role, whereas for United's carnival fans, noise and variation in song was more important. For England fans, the Cross of St George played a huge role. For all fans, the number of travellers and the amount of noise made was vital.

Police escorts and policing in the stadium

As a result, any police activity that assisted fans to create this impression would usually be appreciated, even if this was merely by being present as a visible deterrent against the perceived risk that home fans might confront them. The one potential exception to this rule came from the corralling of fans in police escorts. This provided an excellent opportunity for travelling supporters to congregate in large numbers, walk to the stadium together and create a visibly and audibly vivid impression upon the home supporters. However, attitudes to police escorts were mixed among the carnival fans. Most of the fans claimed they hated being put in police escorts, but in reality only a few of these actively tried to avoid being corralled in them. Indeed, some fans sometimes deliberately attended pubs that they knew would be escorted to the ground before kick-off, and complied with police requests to join the escort. This was even when it was made clear these were just requests rather than orders, which was not always the case: 'At times the peacekeeping officer and the law enforcer are difficult to separate. Police will occasionally give supporters instructions in an authoritative manner that are for the supporters' own good and produce overall social tranquillity, even though the supporters are not legally obligated to follow them' (O'Neill, M., 2005: 140).

The 'order' for fans to join a police escort is one such example. On numerous occasions at away matches with fans of Blackpool and United, police would enter the pub where the fans were drinking and clear it. Usually this involved a number of officers entering the pub and announcing to the fans that they needed to 'drink up' because they were being escorted to the ground. Normally fans were given a few minutes to finish their drinks, before police moved through the pub ushering fans outside. Depending on the police force, this would be done with varying degrees of physical contact; on occasion officers were observed physically taking half-finished drinks from the hands of fans and pushing them towards the door. Usually it was more consensual but, as O'Neill suggests, the request to enter the escort (which should legally be a voluntary decision on the part of the fan) was often given as an order.

On several occasions the fans with whom I was drinking refused, and were simply left in the empty pub as the escort moved off towards the ground. Many older fans objected to being 'herded' to the ground and 'treated like shit' by the police, and would avoid pubs where large numbers of away fans were gathering. At an away match in 2009, a group of around ten of the Red Brigade refused to join the escort and were left drinking alone in a pub near the station. Their presence meant that a police van and a number of officers remained outside the pub, presumably because the group were perceived either as a threat, or as potential victims of an attack. After a few minutes, the police re-entered the pub, explained the problem and suggested that, since they would have to escort the group to the stadium anyway, they could give them a lift in the police van. The police allowed the group to sit in the van and drove up to the away turnstiles, even allowing them to finish their beer in the van. This show of consensual policing by friendly negotiation left the Red Brigade with nothing but admiration for the local police and also reduced the level of risk posed by the group on the journey to the stadium.

The police escort consists of corralling a fan group and then moving them at walking pace towards the stadium. Officers surround the group to prevent them leaving the escort or local fans from confronting it. Usually police go ahead of the escort to clear the route and, if necessary, stop traffic for it. Depending on the number of fans in the escort, it may be surrounded by officers on horseback and by riot vans. It was also common for those in the escort to be filmed by Football Intelligence Officers. Most police escorts operated on a consensual basis and fans were normally happy to chat to officers escorting them, appreciating the role they are playing in protecting them. Also, many of the carnival fans, particularly the younger ones, or those fearful of attack by the local hooligans, enjoyed being in police escorts. Fans were observed eagerly joining escorts, and could often be seen filming the escort on their mobile phones. The escort provided a good way for fans to put on a performance to the locals, and fans in escorts would often chant and raise their arms to make themselves heard as they passed home pubs or crowds of onlookers. The escort also provided many younger fans who appeared to aspire to the hooligan lifestyle an opportunity to mimic an aspect of it.

On occasion, however, I found police escorts very unpleasant experiences. This was particularly the case at high-risk matches or where it seemed that the police believed there were hooligans among the away group. The following account comes from a match involving Manchester United at one of their main rivals: a high-risk encounter in terms of the potential for public disorder due to the historical antagonism between the two sets of fans. Many of the carnival fans arrived by train into the city centre and gathered in a nearby pub. Once they had entered the pub, the police formed a line across the doors, letting visiting supporters in but not out. Across the road from the pub was a line of riot and CCTV police vans, police on horseback and dog handlers, keeping the United fans in the pub and keeping any rival supporters (and curious bystanders) at a distance. Approximately an hour before kick-off, police entered the pub and officers shouted to the fans that they had two minutes to 'drink up' before the pub would be cleared. Then a line of police swept through the pub, guiding (often physically) the fans out onto the street and forcing them to leave any unfinished drinks (in one case pouring the beer on the floor). The police then corralled the United supporters, surrounding them with police vans and officers on horseback. This group was then joined by another group of United supporters who had just arrived by train, making a total of around 800–1,000 fans in the escort, mainly made up of males between the ages of sixteen and fifty, but also containing a number of women. The police then started to escort the group towards the stadium.

The police appeared to have in mind a pace that they wanted the fans to move at, and the officers at the rear of the escort started to shout instructions to those fans who found themselves at the back to walk faster. However, these fans had nowhere to go as they were penned in by the crowd directly in front of them. As a response to this apparent lack of cooperation, some officers pushed fans in the back. Police horses bumped into supporters on the edges of the escort and some officers at the rear stepped on the heels of fans directly in front of them. As far as the fans were concerned, these little knocks were quite deliberate. Officers shouted aggressively at the fans to walk faster and, penned in towards the back of the escort and seemingly with nowhere to go, I felt intimidated by the officers around me. After being pushed and kicked on the ankles a number of times, the little group I was with managed to jostle our way through the throng to the middle of the escort, presumably leaving a new group of fans at the back to be subjected to the same treatment. The escort lasted almost an hour and although we reached the stadium in time for kick-off (in contrast to some escorts which resulted in fans being taken on long detours and missing the start of the match), and without any confrontation with rival supporters, it was an experience full of low-level harassment, intimidation and general bullying. Fans were not permitted to leave the escort and any who tried were threatened with immediate arrest (although for what offence was never made clear).

As a result the fans were given no choice but to be marched along in the police escort and to suffer the intimidation from many of the officers, who gave verbal abuse to some, along with the kind of pushing and shoving noted earlier.

Requests by the fans (who had been drinking for the last few hours) for 'piss stops' were ignored. This meant that a number – on not being allowed to leave the escort – were forced to urinate in the street as they walked, all the time being jostled by the marching crowd. Intelligence Officers filmed the fans in the escort for the duration, and the impression of the fans both at the time and in conversations afterwards, was that much of the police action was deliberate provocation designed to illicit a response that would lead to an arrest or would be captured on camera and used as evidence to obtain a banning order. Although on this occasion I did not witness any arrests, at other matches involving both United and Blackpool I witnessed fans arrested for swearing at officers whom they felt were abusing them, and subsequently charged under the Public Order Act 1986, s. 5. This section makes it an offence to use words or behaviour that causes harassment, alarm or distress to those nearby (usually the arresting officer), and a conviction can lead to a banning order. The abuses witnessed in the escort to this particular match, although not routine, were not exceptional for police escorts to high-risk matches. The continual intimidation, both verbal and physical, was a feature of many escorts and a reason why many of the older fans in particular avoided being placed in them. However, for many of the younger fans, it seemed to provide an exciting way of getting to the stadium that enabled them to put on an impressive performance to the locals.

Conversations with officers about the role of the police escort, revealed that the overwhelming view was that fans who travelled to matches such as this in these groups had to accept that they would face this treatment. In other words it was seen as part of the 'price' of travelling independently and exhibiting their team or city's cultural values through alcohol, song and congregating in large groups in a rival city. In line with O'Neill's findings, the view among officers was very much that 'if they are going to act like children they can be treated like children' (O'Neill, M., 2005: 108). However, as we have seen, the fans did not always have the choice as to whether to participate in a police escort, often because they are unaware of their rights to refuse. Additionally, in the police escort detailed above, the supporters were not 'acting like children'. On the contrary, they responded to police requests as best they could and did not respond despite provocation.

To reiterate, not all police escorts operated in this way, even at high-risk matches, and an observation of the escort taking United fans back to the station after the same fixture two seasons later showed that some of the practices departed significantly from those highlighted above. First, the police gave visiting fans a choice as to whether to be escorted back or not, allowing those who did not wish to be corralled in this way the opportunity to walk back on their own. Second, police communication to the fans on their journey back to the station was improved, in terms of both amount of information provided and tone. Fans were constantly told to 'keep moving', 'fill the gaps' and 'go faster', but they were asked (often using 'please') rather than ordered, and some officers explained that this was in order for the fans to catch the next train back to Manchester. Some officers smiled and joked with the fans and firm action was taken against local fans and passers-by who attempted to antagonise those in the escort. However, even in this escort some low-level harassment occurred. A number of fans were pushed to speed them up, others threatened with arrest for very minor offences and at one stage a fan was bitten by a police dog. The following exchange from this escort demonstrates that some officers continued to bully and intimidate fans in the escort even though they had been compliant and non-violent throughout:

> United fans [chanting]: Champions of England! Champions of Europe!
> Officer 1: Is that the only song you know? It's getting boring.
> Group of 4–5 fans [chanting]: Oh [City Name] is full of shit . . .
> [Officer 1 moves quickly into the crowd and grabs one of the chanting fans (Fan 1), pulls him out of the escort, pushes him violently up against a fence and pins his arms behind his back as if to handcuff him].
> Fan 2: What's he done?
> Officer 2: That's disorderly behaviour.
> Fan 2: What did he do?
> Fan 3: He was singing '[City Name] is full of shit'.
> Officer 2 [shouting]: Stop swearing now!

As far as the fans were concerned, this exchange not only demonstrated that the police were being unfair and abusive, but that some of them were supporters of the home team and were unable to keep their professional objectivism in the light of chants designed to 'wind up' the home fans.[1]

Inside stadiums, there was typically little interaction between police and fans. At Blackpool and United home matches, it was common not to see police on general view from the stands, although in the Stretford End, pairs of police officers in luminous jackets were present. Most crowd management in stadiums was carried out by stewards, with police often only intervening in the stands when stewards requested it. At high-risk away matches involving both United and Blackpool, police were more visible, often gathering in groups in the corner of the stand between the rival fans, or being deployed across the front of the stand near the end of the match to prevent a possible pitch invasion. Such a deployment would often lead to a chorus of the theme from *Laurel and Hardy* from the fans, although by the late 2000s, this practice appeared to be on the wane at United at least and replaced with the chant of 'What a waste of council tax, we paid for your hats'. It was also common for fans to taunt police who were deployed in this manner with chants of 'we're going on the pitch' to illicit a police response, even though they had no intention of carrying out this threat.

This occurred towards the end of United's match at Barnsley in 2009, when, following the incident in the concourse described in Chapter 4, and general rowdiness by fans at the front of the stand, riot squads with police dogs were deployed to prevent a pitch invasion. Some of the police were then seen to try to confiscate a United banner, and at one stage a police dog started biting it. The appearance of the riot police increased tensions, and a number of them were struck with bottles (and pies previously stolen from the kiosk) thrown from the crowd. The match ended with three Barnsley fans invading the pitch, kicking the ball into the net and running around the pitch celebrating. With the police so concerned with United's support, it took a number of minutes for these fans to be caught. They were escorted off the pitch to a standing ovation by many United fans, demonstrating how the 'us and them' mentality of police and football supporters can resurface under certain circumstances and overcome rivalries between different teams' supporters.

The use of riot police made carnival fans feel uncomfortable. Police behind visors appeared less friendly and were certainly less likely to interact positively with fans. While police use of riot gear was occasionally necessary, usually when missiles were being thrown, it appeared to increase tensions between the fans and the police, not just at the time, but for the rest of the match day. Similarly, the use of police dogs was seen by the fans as unnecessary, and many were of the view that the police were unable to control them. I saw two incidents where fans were bitten because they strayed too close to police dogs, and on neither occasion were they acting aggressively. However, despite this risk, the use of police dogs in front of a crowd often resulted in that crowd deliberately trying to provoke the animals. The deployment of dogs at Barnsley resulted in a portion of the crowd chanting 'Woof woof!' aggressively at the dogs, before a more good-humoured chant warning that United's Korean player Ji Sung Park ate dogs. In contrast, mounted police were treated as part of the match-day experience, even though fans often ended up stepping in manure on their way to grounds and in unruly crowds they could knock fans off their feet by simply turning around (in 2000, a Swansea fan was killed by a police horse at Rotherham). However, carnival fans seemed to accept the role of mounted police and frequently stroked the horses or patted their noses as they walked by. In one incident at Old Trafford, a mounted officer was heard shouting, 'Do not feed my horse beefburgers!' at a fan offering the animal a bite of his burger.

Match-day stewards and security staff

The majority of interaction that fans had with the authorities in the ground and at the turnstiles came through match-day stewards and security staff (often hired through agencies). The role of the stewards in England and Wales is primarily to ensure adherence to ground regulations and compliance with the safety certificate. When fans enter a football ground, they also enter into a contractual relationship with the host club whereby they agree to adhere to the ground regulations or face ejection. Standard regulations throughout the league include restrictions on standing in seated areas, smoking, and the use of abusive language or behaviour. They also cover behaviour prohibited by criminal law, such as the throwing of missiles, 'racialist' and indecent chanting, invading the playing area, and drinking alcohol within sight of the pitch. Stewards are also permitted by the ticket contract to search fans entering the stadium. There is therefore considerable overlap between the role of stewards and police inside stadiums, and the division between the roles of stewards (in enforcing ground regulations) and police (in enforcing the criminal law) frequently broke down. On a number of occasions I witnessed stewards responding to breaches in criminal law, and police (unconstitutionally) becoming involved in disputes about ground regulations (although they are empowered to intervene if a fan resists ejection or becomes abusive towards a steward).

Carnival fans demonstrated considerably less respect for stewards than police (particularly away), viewing them as being 'jobsworths' and were often deliberately obstructive towards them. Fans also knew that in disputes with stewards over standing or the blocking of aisles, force of numbers would usually lead to success on the part of the fans; stewards here appeared quite powerless and often abandoned attempts to enforce ground regulations altogether. Disputes with some stewards could be either friendly (fans were occasionally seen sympathetically hugging stewards whose attempts to control them were futile) or aggressive – on a number of occasions individual stewards were targeted for abuse. On several occasions at Blackpool and United, stewards were punched by fans, whereas during the course of my research in domestic football, I never witnessed a police officer inside a stadium being punched by a supporter (the Caz incident noted in Chapter 4 was the closest to this). Some stewards punched fans back and at Old Trafford there were a number of on-running feuds between groups of United fans and stewards hired from private security firms, which normally arose from what were perceived to be unnecessary or overly aggressive ejections. On one occasion, a steward wearing a white coat at Derby who had been involved in a dispute with a number of unruly United fans at the front of the stand was seen to strike one in the face. This led to a surge down the steps as fans made a show of trying to attack the steward and chanting from the rest of the crowd of 'Who's the wanker in the white?'. Eventually the steward was led away by another member of security staff and the situation calmed.

How effectively stewards performed their job varied from ground to ground, with some being perceived as overly officious while others simply let the visiting fans behave however they liked regardless of the potential implications for safety. While individual stewards were generally helpful, in groups they were occasionally both aggressive and at times violent. On one occasion when passing through a ticket check cordon of stewards at a United match in the Midlands, Becs, a small, slight woman, was thrown violently against a set of railings by a male steward twice her size. This assault came without warning and appeared to be because she unwittingly walked the wrong side of a cordon. Although a police officer who witnessed the incident enquired if she was 'all right', no action was taken against the assailant. In carrying out their crowd management duties stewards at many grounds failed to communicate with fans or establish tolerance limits, failing to warn fans that they were transgressing regulations, explain why they needed to follow a particular instruction or what would happen if they refused (most police seemed better at communicating with fans). During my observations, both police and stewards occasionally lost their temper and swore at fans, usually at moments of high stress or tension.

In 2009, I was the victim of an assault by a number of stewards at the start of a high-risk away match. I was in a group of four of the Red Brigade that entered the away section shortly after kick-off and walked to the back of the stand, where my own ticket was located. While the rest of the away section appeared over-capacity, the back rows of the stand were empty. Upon arriving at the back of the stand, it was clear why this was the case – with the crowd in front standing, it was impossible to see even half of the pitch due to the angle of the roof above. We quickly agreed that this was not a good place to watch the match and started to move down the stairs to look for somewhere else to stand. As we did so, a group of three stewards moving up the stairs, seemingly attempting to clear the gangway, confronted us. The supervisor of this group instructed me to return to my seat, ignoring my complaints that I could not see from there. There was a brief dispute in which both the steward and the fans (myself included) raised our voices but at no stage was I aware of aggression or foul language towards the steward, and at the end of it, I started moving back towards my seat.

Then, without warning, the supervisor called to the other stewards and they grabbed my arms and propelled me forcefully down the stairs. Having been pushed and pulled violently down the steps (at one stage I had to grab onto another fan to prevent myself losing my balance), I was manhandled into the concourse below the stand and handed to a police officer, who pinned by my hand behind my back. The supervisor and another steward told the officer I was being ejected and without questioning the reasons why, another police officer demanded my name and address. The officer then radioed to check if my name appeared on their database of risk supporters. While we waited, I told the police officer restraining me what had happened, pointing out that I had been the victim of an assault. In response to this, the supervisor made a false accusation against me, claiming that I had punched him in the face first. This allegation was without foundation and I challenged him about this, pointing out that the incident would be captured on CCTV. While the use of camcorders by football intelligence officers infuriates many football fans, as I was being restrained in a concourse empty but for police officers and stewards, I felt that CCTV may be protecting me from a further and more serious assault, accounts of which had been relayed to me by carnival fans with regularity. The police officer appeared uninterested in both my complaint and the false accusation and when it was confirmed that my details were not on record he ejected me from the stadium, saying that next time I would know, 'not to argue with the stewards'.

The whole experience demonstrated once again the opportunity for abuse of the power possessed by both stewards and police. As a result of a civil law dispute, I had been assaulted by three stewards and falsely accused of committing a criminal offence. Additionally, I had my details taken and had been unlawfully restrained by a police officer despite having committed no crime nor (at the time of the initial restraint) been accused of an offence. At no point had I been asked to leave the stadium, become aggressive or abusive or resisted the ejection. I had simply tried to find somewhere that would allow me to watch the football match that I had paid for. A number of United supporters were ejected from the away end that day, and in the following weeks, several fans approached me to say they had seen me ejected, that they thought it was unfair, the stewards were 'out of order' and that they were acting in that manner all match. My ejection from the stadium was to prove the biggest personal academic crisis in the course of my research. During the whole incident, I was of course still carrying out participant observation – and had been literally propelled from overt participant observation into covert participant observation in seconds. The stewards and police who were assaulting me were unwitting research subjects, but for my research this situation provided the opportunity to gather data on how a normal fan might be treated. As a result, I did not inform the stewards or police that I was a researcher (although my name may well have been recognised by Football Intelligence officers).

After fifteen years in the field, I was forced to consider what action I could ethically take in response to the assault. As detailed in Chapter 1, my general principle, following the approach taken by Van Maanen (1983) was that my purpose was to simply 'tell the tale' of the behaviour and treatment of football fans, and that the safety and security of those under research should be sacrosanct (see Ferdinand *et al.*, 2007). Faced with this perceived personal injustice, both ethically and legally, I came closest to demanding to speak with the stadium manager and match commander (both of whom I had previously met in a professional capacity), but I remained in my participant-observational capacity and allowed the normal procedures to take their course. However, I was soon put under pressure by some fans to use my position to complain about the treatment that I (and others) received at this stadium. A number of fans suggested that I had a *duty* to take action as this might stop these kind of abuses (and worse) happening to other fans in the future. Van Maanen argued that in carrying out research with the police he had a duty to help them when needed (1983: 279), although in his personal dilemma (whether to report an assault carried out by police he was researching) this meant *protecting* research participants from harm. It was also pointed out that if I did not 'clear my name' there was the potential that I could be blacklisted as a 'risk supporter', be banned from Old Trafford or that the fan whose ticket I was using at the time could also be banned. In the end, I wrote to both the club to complain about the conduct of their stewards and to the local constabulary to ask for clarification about why I had been restrained and whether my personal details had been stored anywhere. Of course, this had the potential to cause harm to the stewards who had assaulted me, in possible contradiction of the principle that unwitting research participants should not be harmed. However, my view was that another supporter in my position would have also had the option to complain.

My complaint about my treatment came to a disappointing, but not unexpected conclusion. The local police identified immediately that I was a professional working in the field of football crowd behaviour and policing from my previous research and networks. This meant that I could not be sure that I was treated the same as 'normal' fan. That said, I did not appear to receive any preferential treatment. The police and club stated that CCTV footage had not picked up the ejection. The club interviewed the stewards in question but they claimed that I had punched the supervisor in the face (although one suggested this had 'on reflection' been 'probably accidental') and that this was the reason for the violent nature of my ejection. Without CCTV footage to prove that the stewards were lying, I was left with little option other than to drop the complaint, despite the support I received from fans who recognised me at later games and offered to act as witnesses. I could have pursued proceedings against the officer for restraining me without arrest, but it was probably only my legal expertise and previous work in the field that meant I knew the officer was acting unlawfully, so any further action would have both distorted the field and caused harm to an unwitting research participant. Furthermore, pursuing this complaint may have led to the police instructing officers that in these cases they should simply make arrests in order to avoid legal action. Obviously this would harm the interests of visiting fans returning to that stadium in the future.

The whole experience demonstrated the severe imbalance of power between fans and those responsible for maintaining order in stadiums. The paper slip filled out by the officer who had restrained me stated I had been ejected for 'disorder', and was retained on file by the local police. The lack of CCTV evidence was greeted with general suspicion and cynicism by all the supporters I spoke with, highlighting the air of distrust that exists, even in the UK where policing and crowd management is considered by fans generally superior to other countries. The view was summed up by Dog upon hearing about the lack of CCTV footage: 'I bet you're gutted you never punched him in the face now. Although the CCTV would have appeared … as if by magic'. Of course not all stewards or clubs treat carnival fans in this way. In contrast, at an away match in the same city several months later, club stewards assisted United fans in 'restricted view' seats to find better locations to watch the match, and a supporter who was becoming rowdy in the concourse at half-time was taken to one side by an officer and instructed merely to calm down with the words, 'We're all here to enjoy the football'.

The assault and the subsequent failure of the club and police to apologise also supported the view by the carnival fans that the police and stewards were usually 'in cahoots'. To a certain extent this was not surprising, especially given that police officers were often involved in civil actions such as ejection of fans for breach of ground regulations, and stewards also took action against criminal offences such as drinking alcohol within sight of the pitch and indecent chanting. It should also be noted that many of the club safety officers (who carry overall responsibility for crowd safety and stewarding at a club) are former police officers, and it was clear that at most clubs the links between the safety officer and senior match commanders were strong. The appearance of complete cohesion (and sometimes collusion) between the stewards and police officers was occasionally challenged, and cracks appeared in the 'machinery' of crowd control inside stadiums. These usually came in the form of disputes between the private security firms and police officers. In January 2010, Ben was one of a number of fans who unfurled a 'Love United Hate Glazer' banner during a match. Staff from the private security firm hired by United confiscated the banner and attempted to detain Ben. However a police officer informed the security personnel they were not permitted to do this and he was released. At the end of the match, a United-supporting member of the security firm was dismissed after he attempted to return the banner to the fans (*The Times*, 10/02/10). The carnival fans at United also drew a distinction between the security staff (generally viewed as 'hired thugs' who were bitter they were not police officers) and stewards employed by the club (who were usually seen as 'all right', not least because they were probably United fans). During the 2010 anti-Glazer protests, a number of fans claimed that stewards had wished them luck in their campaigns and turned a blind eye to various low-level infractions of ground regulations in the course of the protest. Some stewards would also turn a blind eye to fans gaining admittance to the ground on senior or junior tickets, with the 20-year-old Davo being allowed access to one match on a senior ticket with a wink from the steward on the turnstile who allowed him entrance. However, abuse of power from the machinery of crowd control inside the stadium was still seen during the anti-Glazer protests. Ben's flag was unlawfully confiscated by the security staff and although they took his details when the flag was removed and he was ejected, the club then refused to return the flag unless he could provide 'proof of ownership'. A visit to the police station to complain also drew a blank, with police refusing to take action on claims the banner had been stolen. Rumours circulated that the banner had been incinerated and only when the Independent Manchester United Supporters Association (IMUSA) became involved was it finally returned.

Abroad, stewards were again largely perceived in a negative way by the carnival fans. The fact that many stewards were also fans of the home team appeared even more pronounced, with some wearing the colours of the team and others openly supporting them as the game progressed. Fans also expressed annoyance at the failure of stewards in the home sections of the ground to prevent missile throwing at the English fans. The most notable instance of this was during United's visit to Rome in 2007, when stewards in the Curva Nord allowed Roma fans to pass through their cordon in order to pick up missiles to throw into the United section. During United's visit to Turkey in 2009 fans were also infuriated by local stewards confiscating all loose coinage to prevent its being thrown. However, the visiting section inside the stadium was surrounded on two sides by high plastic walls, covered on all sides (and above) by netting to prevent missiles, and was separated from the pitch by a running track. Despite these precautions, hundreds, if not thousands, of pounds was confiscated and those who protested were threatened with ejection from the stadium. Fans were further infuriated when they discovered that the refreshment kiosk inside the visiting section was handing out coins in change.

The policing of English fans abroad

The problems of harassment and occasional assault that were a feature of some policing and stewarding practices for domestic games were far more prevalent when England and United fans travelled to matches abroad. Some foreign police forces were considered to be good at managing English fans and preventing disorder; the Dutch and German police received specific praise (see also Stott and Pearson, 2007: 225–6), as did the PSP Police at Euro 2004 in Portugal (*ibid.*: chs. 11 and 12). However, many other police forces were considered to be at best incompetent, and at worst inherently violent and psychotic; forces in Italy, France, Spain and Turkey and much of Eastern Europe received particular criticism from fans. In contrast, the British police were often praised for their own methods, despite the regular complaints domestically. As research with Clifford Stott found, poor policing of crowds is typically characterised by a lack of positive interaction with supporters and indiscriminate and violent responses by riot police when incidents did occur, which tended to escalate rather than control disorder.

I observed numerous examples of aggressive policing of English fans abroad which increased tensions, inflamed situations and in some cases causing rioting. Two of the most serious involved England fans, one in Marseilles at the 1998 World Cup and one in Charleroi, in Belgium, at the 2000 European Championships have already been detailed in Chapter 4. Two other stand-out examples came from European away matches involving United, the first in Lille, France in 2001. Here, around 4,500 United fans were drinking in Lille and Lens (where the match was hosted) and interacting positively and peacefully with OSC Lille supporters; fans swapped scarves and shook hands, United fans sang an Eric Cantona-inspired version of the 'Marseillaise' and in the ground Lille supporters held up a banner stating, 'Mancs, We Salute You'. However, this did not stop the deployment of large numbers of riot police to surround the fans, leading to an increase in tensions between the United fans and their hosts.[2] Disorder occurred later on as United fans tried to gain access to the stadium; a crowd crush developed and some police struck fans with batons. Fans questioned about the policing at this match described it as 'frightening', 'threatening' and 'absolutely fucking terrible'. As far as many of the carnival fans were concerned, the deployment and behaviour of the riot police created an 'unsavoury atmosphere' and was 'inviting trouble'. Matches in Lens proved to be a problem for English supporters in other matches too, with fans of Arsenal reporting difficulties there (Stott and Pearson, 2007) and a later visit by United fans in 2007 seeing a dangerous crowd crush in the stadium and the use of tear gas and batons on fans attempting to escape the crush over the perimeter fencing. Similar problems with police using batons on United fans were observed in 2011 in Marseilles when police attempts to manage the flow of fans in and out of the stadium led to long delays and crowd crushes.

The final example of this type of violent and indiscriminate policing response faced by English fans abroad was observed during United's visit to Rome in 2007 for a Champions League quarter-final. Here, United fans were subjected to a number of attacks by both Roma 'Ultras' and Italian riot police inside and outside the stadium. For the duration of the match, 4,000 United fans were pelted with missiles from the Roma fans in the Curva Nord adjacent to the away section. The rival groups were separated by a two-meter high clear Perspex barrier, but stewards and police made no attempt to prevent Roma fans running up to this barrier to hurl bottles and other missiles. When Roma scored the opening goal, around two hundred of their supporters ran to the barrier and started beating at it and in response around fifty United fans also ran over to the barrier. At this point, riot police started moving up the terrace, hitting United fans at or near the barrier with batons. Soon after, another group of riot police who had gathered near the main entrance to the United section also started lashing out at fans around them with batons, at one point repeatedly punching and striking with batons Carly, a female supporter who was trying to record evidence of the violence for the IMUSA.[3] Other United fans were struck by batons as they tried to escape the police, as they lay on the ground, or as they tried to help up friends. As a result, disorder escalated, with some United fans fighting back against the police, and others throwing missiles. The mini-riot, lasting around five minutes, was the worst disorder inside a stadium that I witnessed during my research and demonstrated the extremes of policing abroad for English fans.

However even outside of the type of disturbances seen in Marseilles, Charleroi, Lille and Rome, instances of fans being hit for no reason with batons by riot police were not uncommon. At a match in Turin in 2002, a solitary United fan being chased by a group of Juventus fans was struck on the back with a baton as he ran, and in Rome before a group-stage match in December 2007, a police officer struck a fan across the face with a baton when he asked directions to the stadium. Generally, fans travelling away with England and United were wary of police forces in Southern and Eastern Europe, and would, where possible, keep their distance. This, of course, meant that the opportunity for positive interaction and communication between fans and police that has been identified by the ESIM school as a vital feature in keeping order at football matches was significantly reduced. However, some foreign police forces were able to successfully manage large numbers of drunken English fans abroad, even in high-risk situations. One such example, which demonstrated how effective deployment and strategy have a direct impact upon the behaviour of carnival fans, came from the policing of England fans in the Romer Square in Frankfurt detailed in Chapter 4. In Frankfurt, the police seemed to be aware of the driving forces behind the England fans' behaviour, rather than interpreting it as hooliganism, and fans were allowed to gather in large numbers in the square, to put up flags and chant songs, and no restrictions were placed upon the opening hours of the bars. Potential flashpoints and confrontation with German fans were managed by clear communication and deployments that were seen as proportionate and events which led to significant disorder in Charleroi in 2000 (see Chapter 3), were diffused without the use of a single police baton. Carnival fans in Frankfurt had nothing but praise for the police and many actively sought them out for conversation and photo opportunities.

Conclusion

Whenever carnival fans attended matches, the police were never far away and in this sense were as much a part of the match-day experience as the rival supporters. As a result, being aware of the relationship between the fans and the police is vital to understand the interpretations, behaviour and attitude of carnival supporters. However, describing how the fans view the police is not a straightforward task. First, the views of the carnival supporters were not uniform; some are more sympathetic to the police than others, often based on personal experiences following football. Second, how the fans reacted to police officers could vary wildly. Fans and police could be either participants in the same carnival, helping each other in the creation of a peaceful environment, sharing jokes and posing for photographs together, or they could be violent adversaries. Most of the time at domestic matches the relationship between the two parties fell somewhere between the extremes, with both parties tolerating the presence of the other and accommodating their motivations in a form of (usually unspoken) negotiation. For the fans, the relationship was renegotiated for each individual match, depending on whether the police force were seen as friendly, accommodating and, overall, fair. Where the police were perceived to be unfriendly, humourless, violent or (at away matches) biased in their treatment of the home supporters, relations would sour.

In high-risk matches in particular, research participants believed they were frequently subjected to low-level bullying, intimidation and harassment by officers (and occasionally stewards). This could be a perceived 'lack of respect', for example officers ignoring fans, giving curt and unhelpful responses to questions or being 'rude'; at one away match, Baz and Robbo objected to an officer on horseback grabbing their half-finished beer cans from their hands and emptying them on the ground next to them (Baz: 'He was like an eagle swooping in and snatching it'). They had previously been asked to finish their cans before moving on by another officer and were happy to comply with this politely spoken request, whereas the action of the mounted officer made them angry. At the other extreme, officers could engage in verbal barracking and physical abuse; mainly pushing and shoving, occasionally kicks to the legs and even slaps to the head. On a few occasions fans were knocked over by horses or bitten by dogs. Police would also often order fans to comply with instructions by claiming it was a criminal offence not to comply, relying on a lack of knowledge and confidence on the part of the fans to challenge their version of the law (e.g. on one trip to Lancashire, members of the Red Brigade in a pub were told they had to show their tickets to a police officer or they would be sent back to Manchester). However, more serious assaults on carnival fans – punches, strikes with batons and the use of CS-gas – were very rare in England and Wales, although they were more common in Italy, France, Turkey and Eastern Europe.

For carnival fans from Blackpool and United, this type of low-level harassment by domestic police forces became assimilated into the normal 'away day' experience, leading them to normalise this treatment and adapt their own behaviour for the match-day reality. The typical reaction of fans subjected to both verbal and physical intimidation was not one of resistance but reluctant acceptance. Their demeanour when faced with verbal and physical abuse, confiscation of alcohol and constant threat of arrest was often one of good humour, resignation and only mild annoyance. Fans would grumble, be sarcastic and occasionally complain, but they knew that anything more forceful (on an individual basis) could result in an arrest. On journeys to and from matches and in the pubs, the fans would occasionally complain about policing, but real shows of anger were normally only witnessed on the occasion that police officers made what were seen as unjustified arrests, or where fans were more seriously assaulted. This may be surprising when one considers that crowds of football supporters have often been portrayed as having a propensity towards violence and disorder. When the research participants travelled abroad, their attitude towards the police was likely to be more suspicious and unforthcoming than with domestic forces as a result of previous encounters where fans had been subjected to violent and indiscriminate treatment. On occasion, however, a positive relationship could be established with foreign police forces when English teams played away from home. Where police officers approached English supporters and were friendly and both able and willing to speak some English, trust could be established. Similarly, on occasion carnival fans would approach police officers who had been observing the group for a while and ask to pose for photographs. Here, officers who were willing to pose with fans were treated as friends rather than adversaries and this often had a positive impact upon relations between the groups for the rest of the trip.

As the ESIM school of crowd psychology suggests, both domestic and foreign police forces appeared to play a significant role in influencing whether disorder involving the research participants would occur. A police force that was perceived as treating the fans fairly by facilitating their desire to create a non-violent football carnival of drinking, colour and song, was likely to be one that was respected and listened to. Friendly communication also played a significant factor in whether the police would be able to manage carnival fans successfully. Police forces who interacted in a positive way with fans were much more likely to be well received when they gave instructions. In contrast, forces that ignored the fans entirely and then suddenly attempted to move groups of supporters about, or close pubs, were often met with resistance. A police force that from the start of the day was dressed in riot gear and appeared 'ready for trouble' was less likely to be engaged positively by the fans and would therefore be placed at an immediate disadvantage when it came to managing the crowd. From my observations, 'high-profile' policing of this nature was often likely to become a self-fulfilling prophecy when it came to crowd disorder. Of course, these kind of high-profile police responses were typical when the police had intelligence that trouble involving 'risk supporters' was likely; but non-hooligan fans were not always aware of the potential dangers, and for carnival fans, whether the policing was seen as legitimate depended very much on the levels of risk that the fans *perceived* there to be. However, in the UK at least, the police were welcome participants in the match experience where this was deemed to be necessary, proportionate, discriminate and fair.

Notes

1 O'Neill notes that many police officers choose to work at football matches precisely because they are football fans themselves (2005: 67).
2 More detail on this is presented in Stott and Pearson (2007: 219–24). The decision to deploy riot police in this instance was made despite the fact that both UK and French Football intelligence officers were of the opinion that there was little risk of hooligan confrontation (*ibid.*: 223).
3 At the time of writing, footage of this assault can be found at www.youtube .com/watch?v=oH7ODTRmxjw.

6

Alcohol and the effectiveness of alcohol controls

On the lash

One of the fundamental aspects of the football carnival was the consumption of alcohol. Whether this was a slow steady intake over a twelve-hour period, or even over several days, or a quick (or 'cheeky') couple of beers in the half-hour between arriving at the venue and the kick-off, obtaining and consuming alcohol was one of the most significant driving forces guiding the behaviour of the research participants. At many matches the consumption of alcohol with friends appeared more important than the match itself; carnival fans would often miss kick-off, would occasionally leave early in order to get a beer, or would go down to the concourse with ten minutes of the first-half remaining to avoid the queue at the bar. However, it was not just the consumption of alcohol that was driving fan behaviour here – carnival fans were not all alcoholics (although many of them were highly and unhealthily dependent upon it). Instead it was the practice of *social consumption of alcohol* (usually beer) that was so important. 'Having a beer with your mates', was a phrase often used to describe what was so great about the match day and carnival fans would go to extraordinary lengths to achieve this, particularly if the authorities attempted to restrict this social drinking.

Understanding the role of alcohol consumption in the fan culture of English supporters is therefore essential to understanding carnival fan behaviour. Following in the footsteps of their ancestors in the traditional carnivals that took place throughout early-modern Europe (Burke, 2002: 183), and were idealised by Bakhtin (1984), 'excessive drinking' formed a major part of the festivities. The social historian Burke provides the following example described by Kolve of the St John's Eve festival in early-modern Britain; much of which bears striking similarities to the carnivalesque expressions of football fandom observed during my research. 'People danced, sang and lept with great pleasure, and did not spare the bagpipes ... many loads of beer were brought ... what disorder, whoring, fighting and killing and dreadful idolatry took place there!' (quoted in Burke, 2002: 195).

The importance of alcohol to the carnival of British fandom is already well established (e.g., Armstrong, 1998; Sugden, 2002; King, 2003; Millward, 2006, 2009) and Giulianotti notes that while alcohol consumption at, or in transit to, matches in Scotland has been prohibited since 1980, 'gett'n' skittled affor the fitba' is also integral to Scottish fan culture (1991: 505). This is incontrovertibly true for the subculture of English carnival fans and more widely with match-going supporters. During the course of this research, the time I spent inside football stadiums was dwarfed by that spent drinking with fans in pubs, town squares, street corners and on buses, trains, planes and cars travelling to and from matches. Indeed, getting a strong stomach and head for alcohol was an important research skill if I was to get anywhere near the intersubjective 'life world' of the carnival fan groups. It should of course be noted that alcohol plays an important part in the wider social life of the English and excessive or 'binge' alcohol consumption has become an essential driver of the night-time economy (Hobbs, 2003; Winlow and Hall, 2006). It should also be noted that heavy social drinking and drunkenness is by no means a new phenomenon; in Manchester in particular, heavy social drinking by the working classes was identified as a serious cause for concern (Engels, 2009; Davies, 2009) and was used to support the campaign for a national police force (Hobbs, 2003: 57).

The taking of drugs – cannabis, cocaine and, towards the end of my research, mephedrone (known by the fans as 'plant food') was also important to some of the carnival fans, but by no means the majority. Some fans took drugs some of the time at football matches. But even those fans who liked to use drugs regularly could sometimes not get hold of them, particularly abroad (although a few risked smuggling them through customs). It appeared that towards the end of my research with the Red Brigade, mephedrone in particular was becoming increasingly important for many of the fans (and for some possibly a chemical or social addiction), to the extent that they were discussing how to smuggle it across the border into Turkey for a match. However, many of the carnival fans did not take drugs even when offered them for free by their friends. In short, they were not seen as being so essential to the fans as alcohol. Neither did they appear to have the cultural significance to the carnival groups as beer.

For both Blackpool and United carnival fan groups, finding a pub to drink in prior to the match was essential. For home matches, many of the fans at Blackpool would gather in the club's 'Tangerine Nitespot' by the stadium, while others, depending on their locality, would frequent pubs either side of the ground. United fans had a number of favourite pre-match pubs near the stadium where they would gather to drink. Some of these, such as 'The Trafford', 'The Bishop Blaize' and the now demolished 'Dog and Partridge', were also venues where the fans could be rowdy and chant United songs. These pubs were *not* dominated by the carnival fans, and many of those who favoured these venues fitted the stereotype of the 'tourist' that many of the carnival fans derided. For the tourists, these pubs appeared to perform an important function for learning new songs, being able to feel part of United's culture and for those with tickets in quiet parts of the stadium – to actually sing their support of the team. Other pubs, including the one most usually frequented by the Red Brigade before and after matches, were quieter establishments where fans could sit down and talk in peace. For the Brigade, their pub of choice also provided the opportunity to smoke and consume their own cans. It was also popular for many of the carnival fans at United to stand on the corner of the Chester Road and the Sir Matt Busby Way around 200 yards from the stadium. Drinking by 'Lou Macari's chippy' was popular for being cheaper than the pubs and avoiding queues for beer. Although drinking in the streets around Old Trafford was technically illegal, until the end of the 2009–10 season, the police turned a blind eye to alcohol consumption here, and even placed an alcohol cordon consisting of 'wheelie-bins' at the top of Sir Matt Busby Way for fans to leave their 'empties' prior to arrival at the stadium. At away matches, both Blackpool and United fans would attempt to either find pubs that were safe for visiting fans or would simply attempt to take over a pub providing safety in numbers from potential attacks by local hooligans. At matches abroad where large numbers of fans travelled, particularly in the summer, crowds of both United and England fans would gather in town squares or on popular pedestrian streets to drink cans and bottles and engage in chants.

For carnival fans, football and alcohol were inseparable, and the beer-fuelled 'craic' around matches was at least as important as what occurred on the pitch. As we have seen, the success of the team in a particular game was not how many of these fans judged whether the trip had been a success. For many of United's carnival fans, for example, the Champions League final in Rome in 2009 was considered a memorable trip, in contrast to the previous year's match in Moscow; beer was cheaper, more carnival fans travelled, and the opportunities for social drinking were greater. This view was held despite the fact that United lost the Rome final, whereas they had won the previous year in Moscow. At the end of the 2009–10 season, fans from the Brigade argued that they were not 'that bothered' about losing the league because the season had been good fun anyway. For Dog, the highlights of the season were not important victories, but the games at Barnsley and Birmingham, both of which saw considerable incident: 'For me it's more about the good times and the people you associate with, than whether we [the team] are successful or not. It's been great'.

For the Red Brigade, the role of alcohol in their match-day experience was set out on the flag they took to matches which proclaimed the name of the group, United's (traditional) crest, and the words 'On the lash' (i.e. 'on the piss' or 'getting drunk'). This tenet was followed even for matches scheduled by the police for early kick-offs in order to reduce alcohol-fuelled disorder:

Author: What time did you start drinking for the derby [United vs. City]?
Ruby: It was nine o'clock [in the morning]. We got to the pub and it was closed. So we went round the corner to the Working Men's club and got a beer even though ...
Jay: Oh yeah, we're always bang on it ...
Ruby: Oh no, we had a drink first at our house didn't we, me and you? So half eight it was ...
Jay: Because I was driving I couldn't have a drink on the way. However this morning I got a lift up so I had my first beer at approximately nine o'clock ...
Author: So did you start drinking earlier for the derby because it was an early

	kick-off? Or would you have started drinking that early anyway?
Ruby:	It was because Jay got here and said 'why aren't you drinking?'. Like on the Charity Shield morning where if Gary and I could have stopped vomming [being sick as a result of drinking the night before] we would have been given ... He actually walked into our bedroom and threw a can at each of us and we just told him to fuck off ...
Jay:	My match-day policy is as soon as you wake up, if you've got cold beers in the fridge, get bang on it straight away. That's my match-day policy ... I'd expand that by saying if there's others staying with you, expand your match-day policy and, and force it onto others so they also join in. And the party just gets going earlier, doesn't it? ...
Author:	So would you all say that beer is an essential part of the match-day experience?
Jay:	Absolutely. I drove to Aston Villa away last season and it was the most ... it finished 0–0 as well ... but it was most fucking dire experience I've had ... I went there, didn't have a drink. And what I didn't take into consideration was that everybody else ... I thought, I can handle not having a drink ... But everybody else is bang on it and I wasn't. It killed it stone dead.
Ruby:	When I was dieting last year I used to drive down [to the games] quite a bit and not drink. But it does ... and you definitely find that after the match everyone is having a bit of a party as well ... And that would mean that I would generally go home 'cos there's nothing worse than being around a load of pissed people when you're sober ... As a general rule, yeah, drinking and football. It does tend to go hand in hand.

So not only was alcohol an important part of the match because it was necessary to get the 'party' started, but also that the absence of alcohol could spoil the experience. Being sober in the middle of a carnival of drunken fans was to be avoided, as evidenced by arguments and negotiation when someone needed to drive to an away match, and by the lessened enthusiasm for European away matches if carnival fans were unable to drink for health reasons.

Because fans reflected on trips where beer was cheap and plentiful as successful, this in turn meant that when fans organised future excursions, creating the opportunity for heavy social drinking became a vital part of the plans. In 2009, United's group-stage Champions League fixtures were in Moscow, Istanbul and Wolfsburg. The first two ties would guarantee tickets for the research participants due to the lack of numbers of fans travelling, but the Wolfsburg trip was always going to be popular due to the novelty of a new club for United to play against. Most importantly, the trip would prove to be cheap in travel costs and German Euro aways had good potential for hedonistic experiences. Another important aspect of the fans' plans was where they would travel to, as Wolfsburg was considered to be of little interest as a town. Instead, fans planned to travel to Bremen, Hannover, Berlin and – for the Brigade – Hamburg. All of these cities were considered to provide excellent 'craic', in terms of beer and – for Hamburg at least – prostitutes. For the Brigade, the general consensus was that it would be the evening in Hamburg that would be the highlight of the trip, not the match in Wolfsburg (which most acknowledged they would be lucky to get into).

Regulating alcohol at football matches

The value to English football fans of alcohol has long been a matter of concern for those policing football matches. In the UK, the correlation between alcohol consumption and violent behaviour has long been established (e.g., DHSS, 1981; Lipsey *et al.*, 1997: 245; Shepherd *et al.*, 1989: 1045); Hobbs notes that instances of crime and disorder increase with the numbers of licensed premises (2003: 41) and Marsh highlights that 50 per cent of all offences of violence or disorder in the UK occur around the traditional pub or club closing time on Friday and Saturday (1992: 38). Several studies demonstrate that alcohol consumption increases the likelihood of young men in particular perceiving the behaviour of others as insulting or challenging and makes it more likely that they will respond to this perceived hostile behaviour aggressively (Gibbs, 1986; Pernanen, 1976; Pihl, 1983). However, although it is established that alcohol acts as a chemical disin-hibitor, a direct pharmacological causal link between alcohol and violence has yet to be scientifically proved (Gibbs, 1986: 133; Lipsey *et al.*, 1997: 246; Marsh and Kibby, 1992: 37). 'The causal issue is still cloudy and uncertain', explains Lipsey *et al.* (1997: 277); 'there is no broad, reliable, "main effect" of alcohol on violence, analogous to the easily demonstrated and almost ubiquitous effects on motor and cognitive functioning that occur at significant doses. If alcohol has any causal effects on violence, they almost certainly occur only for some persons and/or some circumstances' (*ibid.*: 278).

Studies have suggested that it may be situational factors, particularly crowd 'congestion' and 'clustering' around alcohol outlets (Tuck, 1989), that actually increase the likelihood of confrontation occurring among drinkers. Additionally, learned social 'expectations' of what happens during social drinking (Deehan, 1999: 8; Hobbs, 2003; MacAndrew and Edgerton, 1969) may play a significant role in leading to the increase in violent incidents connected to alcohol consumption. Tomsen argues that 'a powerful link between many incidents of public violence and the social process of collective drinking' exists, which is the result of 'cultural understandings of the connections between rowdy and violent group drinking, the construction and projection of an empowered masculine identity, and the symbolic rejection of respectable social values' (1997: 100).

However, this causal complexity is often overlooked:

> The popular view, in this country and some others, is that alcohol consumption by males inevitably increases their likelihood of engaging in aggressive behaviour. It is also popularly assumed that the causal factor is either a direct, chemical one, or relies on a mediating process of disinhibition. In the latter case, aggression is said to erupt because people feel more able, after consuming alcohol, to express their 'true' feelings or release 'pent up' emotions. (Marsh and Kibby, 1992: 35)

This is often reflected in government, football governing body and media discussions of football crowd disorder involving English fans, and also – to a lesser extent – by the police themselves. For example, the McElhone Report into football crowd behaviour concluded that, 'Nearly all those who gave evidence were firmly of the view that a strong relationship exists between alcohol and violence and that a good deal of the disturbances associated with football is due to the amount of alcohol consumed before, during, and after matches' (1977: 5).

The Sporting Events (Control of Alcohol, etc.) Act 1985 was also based on this apparent link, and the second reading of the Bill was introduced by the home secretary declaring, 'There is widespread agreement that alcohol is a major contributory factor in violent and disorderly behaviour in football grounds' (Hansard, Commons, 03/07/85: col. 333). Even the pressure group Alcohol Concern has referred to the link as if it has been proved, commenting that 'Having match packs of twelve cans [of Manchester United's own-brand lager 'Red Tribe'] encourages binge drinking by fans on match-days and we all know what that leads to – football hooliganism' (*Daily Telegraph*, 03/11/96).

As was detailed in Chapter 4, official and media responses to 'hooliganism' involving English supporters, particularly abroad, also often focus on 'causational' mass drunkenness. Returning to the disorder in Marseilles at the 1998 World Cup, all parties were in agreement that alcohol was a major, if not the most significant, causal factor. The minister for sport claimed the disorder was caused by 'brainless drunken louts' and a 'crowd of mindless drunks' who were exploited by a minority of organised hooligans, while the Football Association stated that, 'there were a lot of English people and they had all had too much to drink and ... were behaving in a disgusting way' (BBC Radio 5, 15/06/98). Media responses similarly blamed the amount the English had been drinking: 'Drunken thugs filled England's World Cup with shame last night' (*Daily Mail*, 15/06/98); 'Only a small number of English supporters were involved – probably those who had drunk the most' (BBC1, Six O'Clock News, 14/06/98). In contrast, the UK police delegation at the World Cup considered the early closing time of bars to be, 'an important factor in how matters were dealt with' at England's relatively trouble-free second match in Toulouse (Stott and Pearson, 2007: 139), despite the fact that almost all of the mass disorder in Marseilles took place during the day, and not the late evening/early hours.

The view that English fans become involved in disorder when under the influence of alcohol is also one that is shared abroad. Around United's 2009 Champions League Final in Rome, Arianna Sale, then a Ph.D. student at the University of Milano Bicocca researching policing of fans in Italy interviewed senior Italian police officers about the behaviour of English fans. Their answers revealed that they considered drunkenness to be the major factor behind disorder:

> I'm not saying English fans are bad. Actually they're not. But the problem is they drink. And when they drink, they become violent, they don't respect people and things any more. You know, it becomes like a barbaric invasion.

[Matches] can never be quiet with English fans, because they always get drunk, and when they're so pissed, they become uncontrollable.

nine times out of ten, English fans cause trouble just because they are drunk, so if we prevent them from drinking, we solve the problem. (trans. A. Sale; Pearson and Sale, 2011: 12)

The view that plying a crowd of English football supporters with alcohol will necessarily lead to them becoming disorderly did not stand up to scrutiny. My own experiences in the field suggested that alcohol consumption made *some* fans (whether they were young, old, male or female) more likely to become involved in violent incidents or disorder. However, other fans did not appear prone to becoming violent under the influence of alcohol, and some became *less* likely to become involved in confrontations. Overall, research participants were far more likely to burst into song, hug another fan or make amorous advances to members of the opposite sex than to punch someone as a result of heavy alcohol consumption. Furthermore, while heavy alcohol consumption was part of every England match abroad, serious disorder did not regularly occur and where disorder did occur the spark for such incidents (and subsequent escalation) was usually connected to external factors such as the influence of groups of local fans and the police controlling the English supporters rather than 'internal' factors such as excessive alcohol consumption or the presence of hooligan fans (see Chapter 4). The argument that alcohol consumption leads to hooliganism fails to account for that fact that crowds of drunken English fans usually do not become involved in hooliganism or that other fan groups with a match-going culture based on heavy drinking (e.g. Scots, Norwegians and Danes) do not normally become involved in disorder. It also cannot explain the situations where fans who are not drunk become involved in violence and disorder, as was observed on a number of occasions both domestically and abroad.

However, while the social-identity model of crowd behaviour is of increasing influence on the policing of football crowds, a key element of social control policies at and around football matches both domestically and abroad remains focused on limiting access to alcohol. As a result, football fans have seen their use of alcohol around matches heavily regulated and curtailed by legislation, local authorities, police and event organisers. Given the importance that English carnival fans place upon alcohol as part of their football experience, these restrictions obviously result in a tension between the desires of the fans on the one hand, and the authorities on the other. The remainder of this chapter will detail the way in which the research participants responded to alcohol restrictions upon them around matches. As we will see, regulations and laws prohibiting alcohol consumption were often simply ineffective, due to lax enforcement, ingenuity on the part of the fans or in many cases a combination of the two. Furthermore, in some cases, attempts by the authorities to restrict alcohol consumption by fans had the effect of *increasing* both alcohol consumption and potential flashpoints for disorder.

Alcohol bans in stadiums

For English carnival fan groups, the experience of drinking alcohol while watching the game live is largely forgotten. Consuming alcohol within sight of the football pitch is a criminal offence in all designated football stadiums[1] under the Sporting Events (Control of Alcohol, etc.) Act 1985. This act also made it illegal to enter a designated football stadium while drunk, to consume alcohol on officially organised transport to matches and to take alcohol into a football ground. Where stadiums or stands did not have the structure for a bar and drinking area positioned out of sight of the pitch, this meant they were alcohol-free zones (as was the case with Blackpool's South Paddock). Bigger and more modern stadiums contained bar areas in the concourse under the stand where fans could drink before matches and at half time. Additionally UEFA also banned alcohol from being served in stadiums for its competitions (although executive sections are exempt from this ban). This led to a situation where Heineken beer sponsored the UEFA flagship club tournament with the slogan, 'Heineken and the Champions League: Great Together' but at which their product could not be consumed, presumably because the event organisers feared it would transform the consumers into rampaging hooligans. Alcohol was also usually not on sale at England matches abroad, although observations revealed the many fans mistakenly purchased alcohol-free beer in kiosks in and around stadiums.

Observations indicated that stadium alcohol bans were usually effective in preventing fans taking their own alcohol into the grounds or drinking within sight of the pitch. At one match a group of United fans were observed hiding cans of lager under a police traffic cone before kick-off, and collecting them after the match, knowing that it was too risky attempting to smuggle them into the ground. However, some fans did smuggle alcohol into stadiums. For home matches – where body searches were usually non-existent – fans hid cans and bottles in their pockets. At away games this was more difficult, although some fans smuggled miniature bottles or sachets of spirits into the stands, or mixed vodka into bottles of soft drinks. Other fans smuggled bottles of beer from the half-time bar up into the stands, and dozens were observed being ejected (and possibly arrested) as a result. However, for the most part the fans did not risk smuggling alcohol into the ground, knowing that to have it discovered would mean missing the match. This did not mean that the alcohol ban achieved its more overarching aim of reducing levels of drunkenness inside football stadiums. One of the main reasons why most fans did not feel the need to risk smuggling alcohol into grounds was because they were able to drink beforehand and also, if necessary, get a 'top up' at the half-time bar.

Despite the Sporting Events Act, intoxicated fans still attended matches in large numbers, with police and stewards at turnstiles rarely stopping fans for being drunk. Occasionally police were observed using drunkenness as an easy means to exclude a fan acting in a disorderly manner from the stadium. However, during the entire period of my research, I witnessed only a handful of supporters stopped from entering the stadium because they were drunk. Of these, most of these were physically unable to stand without assistance from friends. Stewards appeared unwilling to risk confrontation with groups of drunken fans by denying one or all of them entrance, and may have been aware of the potential risks to safety of turning fans away due to crushes at the entrances. Police appeared to have fewer concerns with confronting drunken fans, but were also faced with the same difficulties regarding crowd safety. Interviews with a number of match-day commanders also revealed that police often preferred not to make arrests of drunken fans at the turnstiles because it would deplete police resources at a key moment in the build-up to the match. As a result, police who did stop fans entering the ground while drunk usually did not make an arrest, but simply told them they were not permitted to enter. In some cases, the drunken fan would wait to sober up before trying again or would simply attempt another turnstile. I also observed several instances where police advised drunken fans to sober up and try again later.

It was common knowledge to carnival fans that drunkenness was not usually enough to see them excluded. Indeed, many of the research participants were not even aware the law existed. This meant that the ban did not act as a deterrent to drinking pre-match in pubs and outside off-licences near the ground (although friends of fans who were so drunk they could not walk would sometimes suggest that they stop drinking to avoid the possibility of not gaining entrance).

> Author:　Does the law influence how much you drink before a game? [The question led to research participants acting out a pretend scenario where one fan stops the other from drinking too much due to fear of being refused entry to the stadium, to illustrate how absurd they perceived the concept to be].
> Dave:　Not a chance.
> Moston:　I'd not even thought about that 'til you said it.
> Dave:　Could you imagine your mate putting his arm round you to say, like [puts on serious voice] 'Look, you've had a couple now, right? ...' [laughter]
> Dog:　'Sit down, you've had a couple ...'
> Dave:　'Now you do know it's illegal to be drunk inside a football stadium'. 'Really?'
> Dog:　'You've had a couple, now sit down!'
> Dave:　'Ok, I won't have a beer, get me a water, that would be lovely ... hey, I know the law' [laughter and applause].

Being intoxicated while the match was taking place was an important aspect of the culture of the carnival fan. In order to achieve this, and knowing that access to alcohol in the stadium was strictly curtailed (and would be expensive, of poor quality and would require considerable queuing), most of the research participants engaged in pre-match 'binge drinking' so that they would be drunk while watching the match. The intention was to achieve a state of drunkenness, although for different fans this meant different amounts and speeds of consumption. Observations outside Old Trafford revealed large numbers of fans arriving at the time of, or even after, kick-off due to this 'binge drinking'. Many were still drinking from cans and bottles as they approached the turnstiles. While the cordon of 'wheelie-bins' noted earlier was largely effective at preventing fans taking their alcohol to the stadium, it served no purpose in stopping drunken fans gaining access to the stadium (some of whom gathered by the bins in order to 'down' their cans before rushing to the stadium). The rush to consume large amounts of alcohol before entering the ground meant that many fans were drunk by kick-off (typically the later this was on a weekend, the higher the level of intoxication; levels were typically lower for midweek evening matches).

The legislation (and other restrictions) also had an observable negative impact upon stadium safety and public order. One observed consequence of stadium alcohol bans was that it was usually the fans who had been drinking the most that arrived at the stadium latest (because they were drinking until the last minute). Particularly at away matches, crushes developed at turnstiles as these fans tried to get in for kick-off, which in turn increased the risk of disorder. This was particularly problematic at matches abroad where the local fan culture is to arrive at the stadium at least one hour before kick-off. For away matches, this crush of intoxicated fans often caused further problems in the stadium; many of the carnival fans arriving late found the away end appeared already full and gathered by the entrances, or on stairways rather than find their seats. Stewards who attempted to move these fans were frequently ignored or abused and on a few occasions fans trying to push through the crowd to find their seats were assaulted. On one occasion at a play-off match involving Blackpool at Bradford in 1997, the stewards attempted to fill the unreserved seating from back to front, meaning that the drunken fans arriving late found themselves on the front rows. These fans then invaded the pitch when Blackpool scored.

Another impact of the Sporting Events Act was that the concourse under the stand at half-time was the only place alcohol could be consumed. This meant the concourse usually became crowded; pushing, shoving and jostling was commonplace, beer was spilled and arguments sometimes broke out. Three times in the 2009–10 season alone, I observed United fans fighting each other in the concourse at half time, usually as a result of initially minor altercations brought on by the number of fans in such a tight and enclosed area. This supports the views of Tuck (1989) on 'congestion' and 'clustering' causing much alcohol-related disorder. As has already been detailed, when United fans travelled to Barnsley in 2009, disorder broke out in the concourse after a kiosk was closed, leading to the shutters being broken, food being stolen and the deployment of riot police to disperse the fans. Similarly, when United played at Birmingham that same season, only one bar was left open, leading to a crush of fans gathered by it at half-time. When a disturbance occurred at the bar (probably about beer being taken without payment), six riot officers pushed through the crowd to assist. However they found themselves surrounded by an angry crowd of United fans, some of whom threw beer over the officers. Some of the United crowd then surged towards the officers, and a scuffle broke out, trapping the officers. More riot police were sent to their assistance, pushing through the crowd to assist their colleagues, but occasionally pushing fans who were not involved out of the way, and in some cases hitting them with their shields (one of these officers was tripped earlier by Caz, detailed in Chapter 4). This led to one of the worst violent disturbances I witnessed inside an English football stadium, with fans surging back and forth at riot police for over five minutes until further reinforcements finally meant the officers could clear the concourse. Conversely, at a subsequent high-risk away match at Manchester City despite significant disorder occurring outside the stadium, all concourse bars remained open for United fans, and officers in normal uniform patrolled the concourse. The interval passed off without incident, although it should also be noted that due to the modern stand design there was considerably more space in the concourse at Manchester City than there had been at either Barnsley or Birmingham.

An interview with a senior police match commander about this type of problem following the Barnsley match, demonstrated that it was difficult to deploy officers into crowded concourses to keep control: 'Concourses can be quite dangerous areas ... You can have officers getting trapped and ... some of our staff have suffered severe beatings on concourses, because if you go down, you're down, there's no getting back up. You know, you're down until they've finished kicking you basically' (interview, 09/11/09). This can be problematic in terms of public order because, as we have seen, the lack of presence and interaction between police and fans can lead to disturbances escalating. My observations suggested that this lack of interaction contributed to disorder occurring at Barnsley and Birmingham. Furthermore, had fans been able to return to the stands with their beer, the pressure of the crowd would be been alleviated and disorder may have been reduced.

A final consequence of the lack of provision for the consumption of alcohol inside stadiums was that fans were likely to spend more time in pubs immediately before the match, rather than drinking in the stands. This meant that instead of drinking in highly regulated and segregated stands, with high levels of CCTV and police observation, they often found themselves drinking alongside rival supporters outside the ground. This obviously increased the chance of confrontation between rival fans and also meant potential weaponry such as bottles, glasses and pool cues were to hand. Whether a relaxation of the law on alcohol consumption in sight of the pitch would lead to the research participants gaining admission to stadiums earlier is unclear, particularly for home matches where they were split up into separate stands. However, for small groups of fans sitting together, the potential to reduce possible confrontation was clear.

Alcohol bans in transit to and from matches

As we have seen, restricting alcohol consumption within stadiums did not have a significant impact in reducing the ability of carnival fans to watch the match while drunk. As well as restricting alcohol consumption in stadiums, the Sporting Events Act also criminalises drinking on coaches or trains organised to transport fans to and from away matches. Furthermore, some scheduled train services are designated 'dry' around high-risk matches. The intention here appeared to be to reduce overall levels of alcohol consumption, following the perceived link between drinking and football violence. However observations again revealed that this policy was largely ineffective in achieving its aims due to the determination of carnival fans to engage in pre-match drinking. For example, in 2009, United played in the League Cup Final at Wembley and all Manchester to London trains (a journey of just over two hours) were designated dry. In order to enforce this, police established a cordon on the platform, using body searches, sniffer dogs and an airport-style scanner to search for alcohol and drugs. In the days preceding the match, many fans expressed concern that there might be an alcohol ban on the train and, concluding from previous experience that there would, many set off early in the morning in order to give ourselves 'drinking time' in London. It is possible that without the ban, some of these would have departed later in the knowledge that they could start their drinking on the train.

In light of the predicted ban, many of the more experienced carnival fans decided to smuggle alcohol onto the train. Fans mixed bottles of soft drinks with spirits and some smuggled miniature spirit bottles or sachets in their underwear. The most confident simply replaced the contents of mineral water bottles with vodka. For the carnival fans, it was not just a matter of practicalities, but an opportunity to demonstrate disrespect for authority, experience, cunning and also 'bottle' to each other. All the fans observed succeeded in smuggling alcohol through the police check, which they then consumed on the journey. This meant that when the train arrived in London at 11 a.m., some fans had already consumed half a bottle of vodka. It is likely that there was more alcohol in their bloodstream than would have been if they had been permitted to take beer onto the train or purchase alcohol from the bar on the train. A number of groups of United fans with apparently less experience of matches at Wembley arrived at the station with 'slabs' of beer, only to be denied access through the police check. As we queued to get through the alcohol cordon, we could see these fans making a brave effort to consume their purchases before the train departed. Again, the end result was that fans were more drunk, earlier in the day, than they would have been had there been no alcohol restrictions. Furthermore, many fans arrived in London earlier than they otherwise would have, increasing the potential of confrontation with rival fans.

The attitude of carnival fans to the alcohol ban on the trains to Wembley in 2009 was typical of how they responded to such controls. They perceived alcohol restrictions as being unfair (because they were penalised just for being football fans), unnecessary and pointless. As a result the bans were not respected and those enforcing the restrictions were ridiculed as 'jobsworths' who should be dealing with 'real criminals' rather than simply trying to spoil a peaceful carnival. Every Cup Final trip embarked upon with the research participants saw similar patterns of behaviour. On one such occasion, United fans who had smuggled cans of beer onto the train home were initially frustrated by BTP officers patrolling the carriages to stop alcohol being consumed. However, almost immediately after the train departed, the lights on the old carriages failed[2] and the sound of beer cans being opened could be heard in the darkness, with some fans goading police by asking if they wanted a drink. United fans travelling on official coaches to Manchester (who were subjected to this section of the Sporting Events Act on a weekly basis) also explained how they would breach the ban regularly. For these out-of-town fans, consumption of alcohol was a symbolic show of resistance not only against the authorities but also the 'new consumerism' of modern football (see also King, 2003).

Alcohol bans abroad

Carnival fans travelling abroad often encountered even more restrictions upon their alcohol consumption. Here, the fear of the local authorities about English hooliganism occasionally resulted in the entire host city being designated dry for a period of twenty-four hours on the date of the match. Alcohol bans abroad were not the norm, and for matches in Germany for example, it was often easier to find bars serving beer around the match than in the UK (at one match in Germany, fans were even allowed to take their beer into the ground itself and drink in sight of the pitch). In Italy, however, city-wide alcohol bans were imposed regularly, and attempts to impose similar bans were also observed in France and parts of southern Europe. Typically the ban would prohibit the sale of alcohol in bars, restaurants and shops, and would criminalise public consumption. During my research I encountered city-wide alcohol bans in Rome (three times) Milan and Turin. In 1998 I also witnessed an attempt to create a seventy-mile 'alcohol free corridor' between the channel ferry ports and the town of Lens in northern France, where England played in a World Cup match. For carnival fans, this attempt to interfere with one of the most fundamental parts of their trip was severely resented and encouraged them to avoid interaction with local police. As we have seen, this can increase the risk of disorder, and Giulianotti notes that for Scottish fans at the 1990 World Cup, an alcohol ban 'led to the strongest collective feeling against the Italian authorities' (1991: 511–12).

Due to the fundamental value of heavy alcohol consumption at matches abroad for fans (Brown, 1993; Sugden, 2002; Millward, 2006), not only did they resent alcohol bans and share a collective feeling against the authorities, but they also had no respect for these laws. Research participants would go to enormous lengths to find and consume alcohol during these city-wide bans, and those who failed were often both pitied and ridiculed for being inexperienced or 'green'. Normally, however, it was easy to avoid the restrictions as owners of local bars, restaurants and fast-food outlets (as well as locals wanting to make a quick profit) were usually willing to assist them. The risk of losing their licence appeared to be outweighed by the opportunity to profit from the English fans on the day of the match. Additionally, bar owners who had good experiences of the fans prior to the ban (through both their behaviour and the profit made), were more likely to ignore the prohibition when they returned on the match day.

There were four ways in which carnival fans were observed to obtain alcohol during these large-scale prohibitions. Upmarket restaurants often sold alcohol, usually wine, with meals. Often this was due to pressure by locals who did not see why they should drink soft drinks with an expensive meal simply because of 'English hooligans'. On a number of occasions this led to fans purchasing small quantities of food which were then washed down with numerous bottles of wine or glasses of beer over a long period. A second way to obtain alcohol was from fast-food outlets and bakeries, which would often sell bottles and cans of beer from their fridges to take away; it appeared that these venues were not targeted by the police looking to enforce the ban in the same way that bars were. Third, fans obtained alcohol from unlicensed street traders, usually local youths; they would purchase cans and bottles of beer from supermarkets prior to the ban and then sell it onto English fans who had gathered on the street, in town centres or near the ground (sometimes from cool boxes). This meant that alcohol was very cheap (fans were able to bargain lower prices with the vendors) and fans did not even have to queue to obtain it, providing more opportunity to get drunk than if they had been sitting in a bar.

Typically, however, fans simply gathered in and around bars that were located away from the main streets or town squares and so were out of immediate sight of the police enforcing the ban. These bars would often ignore the ban, although their owners sometimes demanded that fans did not chant, so as not to alert the police. On the day of the 2009 final the Brigade concluded that around one-third of bars in Rome continued to serve alcohol. Even an alcohol ban that was rigorously enforced would not prevent drinking occurring; the network of carnival fans communicating by mobile phones enabled different sub-groups of fans to gather together when bars serving alcohol were located. These bars were mainly found away from the main squares (the bar chosen by the Brigade for the 2009 final was on a side street behind the main station), and some bar owners went to great lengths to avoid the ban. Even in one of the squares where police were present, one bar was serving alcohol; any fan buying beer here was also given an empty Tourtel alcohol-free beer bottle to place next to their glass to mislead the police. At the same match, fans were told that they could drink beer in a bar, but that if the owner shouted a warning, they were to hide the bottles under the table and replace them with Coca-Cola bottles. Other bar owners locked United fans into their premises so that they could drink undisturbed. All this occurred within the twenty-four-hour 'dry' period in central Rome. Noticeably, one Barcelona fan at the same final complained that the alcohol ban meant he was not able to buy a single beer on the match day, demonstrating the varying subcultural interpretations of what such alcohol bans meant and the knowledge of how to get round them.

In short, on no observed occasion that alcohol bans were enforced upon English fans did this prevent binge-drinking around a match. The fans' previous experience of this also meant that advertised alcohol bans did not prevent them looking for alcohol. Interviews carried out at the 2009 Final with the match commander by Arianna Sale indicated that it was clear the authorities knew the ban had been ineffective: 'We are fully aware that the alcohol ban hasn't been working. The area subjected to the ban is too wide to make controls effective. And both sellers and buyers are too willing to make their deals to be able to stop them' (trans. A. Sale; Pearson and Sale, 2011: 10–11). The Italian press also noted the ineffectiveness of the ban, with *La Repubblica* reporting: 'Beer flows. There is the ban, that's true, but who's respecting it? This is Rome' (28/05/09, trans. A. Sale, *ibid.*: 11).

City-wide prohibitions therefore did not appear to reduce alcohol consumption by carnival fans; the carnival simply went underground. Their observed effect was to push alcohol consumption away from popular drinking areas to bars and restaurants hidden down side streets and to kebab shops and stalls, meaning that fans gathered out of sight of the police, again reducing the possibility of positive interaction between fans and the authorities. In hostile cities, these groups of visiting fans gathered away from the view of the police had the potential to become targets for any groups of local 'hooligans'. These establishments often only served beer in bottles, meaning that groups of fans had potential weaponry to hand if disorder occurred, and if disorder did occur – either with locals or between different groups of English fans – the lack of police meant that it could easily become more serious in their absence. From my observations, rather than reducing the likelihood of 'hooliganism', alcohol bans did not limit alcohol consumption but created other factors that had the potential to increase the risk of disorder.

Research with carnival fans of England and United travelling abroad demonstrated that alcohol was an essential part of the trip, and a tool for creating a memorable carnival experience. Contrary to claims by the media that many English fans travel to matches abroad with the intention of becoming involved in disorder, creating a noisy, rowdy but peaceful party was actually the driving force behind their actions. Where alcohol restrictions attempted to prevent this, fans would simply recreate this carnival in less controlled areas where opportunities for interaction and control by police were fewer. The experience of a visit to Italy on a Euro away for carnival fans was completely different to that of England fans observed in Germany at the 2006 World Cup. Here, the authorities in all host cities where England played generally allowed bars to remain open as long as they liked. Alcohol was even served inside stadiums and could even be drunk within sight of the pitch. The only condition was that beer was served in flimsy plastic glasses that could not be used as weapons or thrown any distance. As a result of this policy, English carnival fans gathered in large groups in the town squares and created a carnival atmosphere of song, dance and colour, drinking heavily throughout the day and at times throwing beer over each other. All this took place in sight of the police who, in Frankfurt and Nuremburg especially, made a number of interventions into the crowd to warn individuals becoming abusive or aggressive (Stott and Pearson, 2007: ch. 13). Despite the vast number of travelling English fans, and a number of 'flashpoints' (mainly involving confrontations with fans of the German national team), the 2006 World Cup was viewed as a huge success in public order terms.

Early kick-off times

Bringing forward the time that matches take place is a common police tactic in northern Europe (especially the UK and Netherlands) to reduce the risk of disorder at high-risk matches, particularly local derbies. The purpose of early kick-offs (which are generally unpopular with both match-going fans and television companies) is to reduce the amount of alcohol consumed prior to kick-off and therefore the likelihood of drink-related disorder. Observations suggested that early kick-off times *did* reduce the amount of alcohol consumed before kick-off, although some pubs and clubs would deliberately open early ahead of local derbies, and some fans would begin drinking earlier than for later kick-offs. However, even when pubs were allowed to open early, carnival fans on the whole consumed less alcohol and were less drunk by kick-off time as a result of early kick-offs. Observations suggested that high-risk matches which kicked off earlier also typically resulted in less disorder in and around the stadium. In contrast, on the rare occasion that high-risk matches took place in the evening, there were several instances of serious disorder. Two of the most significant incidents of public disorder domestically during my observations both took place around evening matches (Preston vs. Blackpool, 1996 and Everton vs. United, 2005).

The extent to which this was caused by increased alcohol consumption, however, is unclear; and many of those involved in the serious violence at 'Everton Valley' in 2005 were, by the accounts provided, not drunk at all. In 2009, the Sheffield derby was scheduled for a 7.45 p.m. kick-off on a Friday night, but when I interviewed the match commander for this game about his experiences, his view was 'never again'. Although he felt that alcohol did play a part in the disorder that took place that night, he also felt that the darkness played an equally significant role. His view was that playing games at night meant that 'hooligans' looking for confrontation were deterred less because police were less visible Furthermore, his view was that what violence or disorder did take place was *perceived* to be more serious by fans because they felt less reassured by this reduced visibility, even with the police's use of luminous jackets. A final problem as far as the police were concerned was that when disorder occurred, organising a rapid, targeted and effective response was more difficult than in daylight when:

> it's just easier to see what's happening. You've got aircraft footage that shows you [what's happening] you're not on infrared, it's easier to get your cops in place to get it back under control ... But if it breaks down like this at night-time you've got huge problems getting it back under control ... I would say that if we've got a high tension game, a night-time makes it worse ... night-time and drink make it more difficult to police. (interview, 11/09/09)

My own research suggested that matches taking place at night-time (or early evening in the winter) certainly *felt* more dangerous than those taking place during daylight. My own perception at higher-risk matches that rival fans looking for confrontation might be nearby was much more pronounced in darkness than during daylight. However, when I asked the research participants about this, there was a surprising amount of disagreement as to whether night-time games were more dangerous than those taking place in daylight.

When viewed purely in terms of alcohol consumption, early kick-offs for high-risk matches were not always effective. While for high-risk matches between rivals in different cities (e.g., Blackpool vs. Preston or United vs. Liverpool), early kick-offs appeared effective at reducing the amount of alcohol consumed by rival fans during the period that they were in contact with each other (as visiting supporters usually travelled back soon after the match), for same-city derbies, early kick-off times did not appear to reduce the overall levels of risk of confrontation. They even had the potential to increase the amount of disorder; overall levels of risk for these matches were not reduced by an early kick-off because rival fans remained proximate throughout the entire day. Although early kick-offs may have reduced disorder immediately around the stadium, my own observations illustrated that they could increase the likelihood of problems later. United's carnival fans would typically start drinking early, and following the match would often return to city centre pubs for drinking throughout the afternoon and evening. Research at several Manchester United vs. Manchester City games which kicked off early revealed that violence and disorder was likely throughout the entire day. In terms of the overall amount of alcohol consumed, early kick-offs for many fans (particularly those of the winning team) may have increased it considerably. When United won the Manchester derby, the Manchester-based research participants would return to the city centre to drink, usually in 'red pubs' (i.e. pubs that had a reputation as being for United fans). On a few occasions these pubs came under attack from groups of City hooligans, and incidents between drunken rival fans were numerous and continued into the early hours.

From news reports and interviews with police, this story appears to be repeated for same-city derbies that kicked off early throughout the UK. Statistics released by Strathclyde Police in May 2009 for example showed that 'serious crime on average during the last three Old Firm games was *113 per cent higher* than during any other weekend'. Reported instances of domestic violence, for example, showed a 41 per cent increase.[3] It may actually be that 7.45 p.m. weekday kick-offs, rather than weekend early kick-offs, lead to the least amount of alcohol consumption and the least amount of contact between rival fans around a same-city derby; many fans would be at work until shortly before the match and most pubs will close soon after the match finishes. The Sheffield derby match commander agreed that early kick-offs had the potential to exacerbate disorder in the city throughout the remainder of the day. However, as far as he was concerned, keeping public order in the immediate vicinity of the stadium was the priority: 'you have to have a hierarchical strategy for the way you approach this. If we say, as we do, that the primary safety focus is around the stadium, then you take the stadium out of the context later on ... We try to protect the stadium and take it out of the alcohol-threat' (interview, 11/09/09). My own observations suggested that early kick-offs largely achieved this aim, in contrast to many of the other alcohol restrictions that simply irritated carnival fans and created additional risk of violence and escalation of disorder.

Conclusion

It is impossible to understand the motivations and behaviour of English carnival fans without recognising the fundamental role of alcohol. For different fans within these groups, alcohol consumption was either a tool for engaging in the carnivalesque, or an objective in itself. For carnival fan groups, communal drinking was an essential part of the practice of watching football and they would go to great lengths in order to achieve a stage of drunkenness prior to a match. The fans were not deterred from this by restrictions on alcohol consumption by clubs, governing bodies and local authorities, and observations suggested that such restrictions failed to reduce alcohol consumption by carnival fans and in some cases may have increased it. Furthermore, some restraints had a side effect of increasing the likelihood that carnival fan groups would be exposed to the risk of confrontation with rival fans or would become involved in disorder. In contrast, although observations demonstrated that some fans were more likely to be involved in disorder when drunk, there was no clearly observable link between the amount of alcohol consumed and the instances of group disorder engaged in by carnival fans or those perceived to be hooligans.

Notes

1 Currently grounds above 5,000 capacity or of teams playing at conference level or above are designated for the purposes of the legislation.
2 It was typical for additional trains, with old and dilapidated rolling stock, to be laid on for fans travelling to the Cup Final.
3 www.strathclyde.police.uk/index.asp?locID=1430&docID=6735: accessed 19/10/09.

7

Attitudes to gender, sexuality, race and disability

Shag your women and drink your beer

One key feature of the carnival fan groups under observation was that fans were overwhelmingly white and male. For Blackpool, the domination of white supporters appeared to reflect the population of the areas from where most of the team's support was drawn. For England and Manchester United, black and Asian fans were under-represented. At both United and England home matches, however, the proportion of ethnic minorities in the wider crowd was much higher; at Old Trafford, there were a significant minority of black and Asian fans in Stretford End Tier 2 (ST2): this seemed to increase when other parts of the ground were taken into account and was swelled by the number of foreign tourists (particularly from the Far East). A number of these tourist groups were also witnessed at United away matches, particularly in London, to the anger of many carnival fans who resented their ability to obtain tickets without going through the normal process of application, loyalty and networking, and their refusal (or inability) to participate in terrace culture (e.g., through not knowing the words of chants, and their constant taking of photographs).

The contrast between the constitution of home and away crowds was also noticeable in terms of the ratio of men to women. At home games, the proportion of women to men appeared to be as high as 40 per cent in 2011 (having increased gradually since the start of my research). Again, this depended on the area of the ground observed; Blackpool's South Paddock, for example, contained very few regular match-going females, although it is generally acknowledged that the number of women attending football in the UK has increased since my research finished there in 1998. However, in the rowdiest section at Old Trafford, the back of ST2, women made up a significant proportion of the fans, probably around 30 per cent. At away matches for all three teams, the number of females fell dramatically, and for carnival fan groups, travelling independently and engaging in the more 'traditional' fan culture, the proportion of women could be lower than 5 per cent. It should be noted that these figures are estimates based on crowd observations over a period of time, and compared with the views of the fans being interviewed, and should not be treated as quantitatively verifiable. However, it provides a flavour of how male dominated the carnival fan groups were, and also how these groups were only one element of the overall match-going support for a team over the course of a season. This chapter considers the attitudes of carnival fans to issues of gender, race and – briefly – sexuality and disability. Since the overwhelming majority were white and male, these views will be predominant in this chapter. However, this chapter will also detail the behaviour and experiences of the women in and around the Red Brigade group of United fans.

Prevailing attitudes to gender

The whole culture of football support is one built upon dominant masculine attitudes, making the activities of fandom 'essentially a male domain' (Armstrong and Young, 2000: 175). Sexist terminology, metaphors and chants prevail in comment upon the game and in fan culture. Calling players who are perceived to exaggerate injury 'girls', or a complaining manager 'a moaning old woman' was typical, as was chanting 'she fell over' when a player was perceived to have dived. Jones (2006) goes as far as to claim that the prevailing and accepted football fan culture in the UK is 'anti-women'. Footage of matches from the immediate post-war period onwards clearly shows women in football crowds, but many carnival fans bemoaned the number of women who now attended, accusing them of only attending because football is now 'fashionable', and blaming them for harming the atmosphere at matches (an accusation made by female as well as male research participants). Although the number of women going to games has increased (*The Independent*, 21/09/03), fan culture has remained embedded in its male-dominated traditions. Crolley bemoans that during the 1990s revolution of football, the 'discovery' of football by middle-class culture and the apparent civilising process the game underwent at this time was not reflected in more liberal attitudes to women either playing or watching football. In fact the 1990s football boom went hand in hand with 'new laddism' (1999: 59–70), reinforcing traditional sexist views which in turn were magnified by the attitude of many of those in the carnival fan groups.

Popular chants at both Blackpool and United reflected this dominant masculine culture, and we have already seen the importance of fans being able to 'fight' rival supporters in the singing culture of British football fans. Chants threatening rival supporters with violence or celebrating hooliganism were popular, and from observations were as likely to be sung by female carnival fans as male ones. In addition, non-violent chants with a clear sexist bias were also popular; one of the United fans' anthems ends with the declaration: 'We are the Manchester boys'. Furthermore, one of the most traditional, generic and popular chants in British football, to the tune of 'When the Saints Go Marching in', praises the location of the team for the quality of its women as well as its football:

> It's full of tits, fanny and Blackpool/United,
> Oh Lancashire/Manchester is wonderful.

And it is not only traditional chants that reflect this sexist outlook. United's 2008 chant in honour of Anderson (Chapter 3), praised him for his alleged skill with a prostitute following a story about his personal life in one of the tabloids with the line: 'He is class with a brass', rather than focusing merely on his footballing abilities. Of the popular terrace chants, only one was observed to refer to the fact that the support for the team was made up from both men and women:

> All the lads and lasses, smiles upon their faces,
> Going down to Bloomfield Road/ Walking down the Warwick Road
> To see the Blackpool/Matt Busby's aces.

This chant derives from the Blaydon Races folk song, which makes a number of references to the 'lads' and the 'lasses', so we should not jump to the conclusion that the inclusion of the line in the later versions tells us much about the attitude to female fans other than the fact that it was accepted they attended matches.

Internet message boards used by the carnival fans also espoused sexist language and dominant traditional masculine norms. As we will see in Chapter 8, message boards were used to discuss far more than just football issues, and frequent 'threads' were started on the subject of sex (from a male perspective) or women. On the first day drafting this chapter, I took a sample of the most popular threads open on two message boards frequented by United's carnival fans. The Red Issue forum's top-twenty threads at the time[1] included a thread entitled 'Sex with sluts', another on whether a character on a popular soap opera had recently 'got her tits out' and two more where posters had linked pictures to women on the social-networking site Facebook (one of which promised 'a nice bit of upskirt'). Another thread was entitled 'Brass help':

> If a lad I know who runs a coach to away games for United fans *cough cough* fancied, as a Christmas treat, arranging a brass to come on board his coach for the Fulham game so that whoever fancied it can chip in and have a go of her, do you reckon there will be a brass out there willing to be dicked by up to 50 horny Reds? And if so, would 50 horny lads be prepared to get knee deep in front of 49 other horny lads? The brass could jump on in town, stay on board for 2 hours and get dropped off somewhere like Birmingham. All lads who fancy a go throw in 20 dabs each she could earn herself a nice bit of wedge for Christmas for 2 hours work. Will there be anyone willing to do this do you lot reckon?

While this message may have been a 'wind up' rather than a serious proposition, the responses to it were all in favour of the idea and some carnival fans certainly used 'Euro aways' as an opportunity for using prostitutes. The top-twenty threads on Red Brigade at the same time included a vote for whether a female celebrity was 'worth a rinse', and a thread entitled 'The perfect vagina'. Both these message boards also contained forums which contained links to pornography (entitled 'Not safe for work' and 'Gashpad' respectively), with thread topics clearly aimed at the male posters. Additionally, male posters on many of these message boards often used images of female models for their distinctive 'avatar', meaning that even opening a thread on a football topic would mean being confronted by a series of soft-porn images. The Red Brigade's 'On the lash' banner was also called 'Gashout' (another flag was known as 'Minge').

Some of the language used in discussions on these message boards was not only sexist, but openly misogynist. On the boards frequented by United carnival fans, women were frequently dismissed as 'snakes with tits' and the recommendation given to any poster who asked for advice about a problem involving a woman was inevitably, 'kick her in the cunt'. While this was not a serious suggestion (and was occasionally used by female posters), the phrase was used with such regularity that it had its own acronym, KHITC. Another acronym that was commonly used on United message boards was NWAF, meaning 'no women at football'. This would be typically used following a post about women stood near to the poster at a match, or when the poster's wife or girlfriend (usually described as 'the missus') wished to attend a match. NWAF was referred to by many of the United carnival fans (both male and female) as a 'movement', but it was actually merely a belief held by many supporters that the perceived increase in the number of women at the match was having a detrimental effect on the atmosphere at matches, the support given to the team and the ability of 'the lads' to have a good time without the civilising presence of women. For many carnival fans, NWAF was merely a way of 'winding up' the females who followed United away, but the underlying belief about the impact that women had on the unwelcome civilising process was expressed seriously.

With very few exceptions, the women who travelled away with the carnival fan groups could expect to be subjected to sexist language and comments, and also be sexually 'objectified' by many of the male fans. Flirting and comments of a sexual nature were commonplace, and women were frequently asked for hugs, or to sit on the knees of male fans. Male carnival fans would also often talk about the females in a sexual way when they were absent, and on one occasion, Robbo from the Red Brigade ran a quiz on the message board inviting other posters to identify female members of the group from photographs of their cleavages. In another incident, a female England fan standing at a window was chanted at to 'get your tits out for the lads' by male fans below. She was eventually persuaded to do so by a couple of (male) England fans in the room with her, to the cheers of the crowd. For some of the female carnival fans, this type of treatment appeared to be largely tolerated as a price for being accepted into the masculine-dominated world of the carnival fan. For others, however, it was clear that the attention received was part of the enjoyment of being part of the group, and they would play along with the sexual banter. Two examples of this came from members of the Red Brigade who were the particular focus for many of these type of comments. Becs, for example, became famous for wearing a combination of fishnet tights and Doc Marten boots to matches, and would happily pose for photographs showing these off. Ruby, on the other hand, received a considerable amount of attention for the size of her breasts. She continued to wear low-cut tops at matches and would on occasion pose for photographs showing off her cleavage and bring attention to her breasts in conversation and posts on the forum. While both fans drew limits on the banter and physical proximity of other members of the carnival groups, they appeared to enjoy both the attention and the sexual banter.

Burke (2002: 186) suggests that the three major themes for the traditional carnivals of early modern Europe were 'food, sex and violence', and replacing alcohol for food probably provides the three major themes for a Euro away for many carnival fans. Sex was certainly a major theme, with numerous incidents of carnival fans having one-night stands with local women, or visiting lap-dancing bars or brothels. The frequent use of prostitutes on away trips abroad is recorded by both Sugden (2002: 74) and Ward, who records one fan claiming, 'It is the duty of every Englishman to sample the whores in every city where England plays football' (1994: 167). While this view was certainly not typical of the average carnival fan abroad, red-light districts were popular areas to drink and find cheap hotels, and visits to Amsterdam and Hamburg, with their famous red-light areas were always popular. Even here, the use of prostitutes by the fans was limited to a small number; most were content with mere 'window shopping' or strip clubs ('titty bars'). When female fans were present, even visits to 'titty bars' would be limited or avoided. It was also common for some members of the fan groups to bring their wives or girlfriends to away matches abroad, which could also limit their opportunities for engaging in this type of activity. However, being the wife or girlfriend of one of the carnival fans did not mean that they would not be engaged in sexual banter and flirtation by other members of the group. Even if one-night stands, visits to brothels and 'titty bars' were not on the cards, the prevailing sexist attitude remained, with attractive local women often commented on or subjected to chants of 'get your tits out for the lads'.

Female carnival fans

Although masculine and misogynist views dominated the culture and vocabulary of the fan groups, there were a number of women who attended matches in these groups regularly, and drank, sang and entered into banter in the same way as their male counterparts. Furthermore, despite the chauvinist attitudes, and 'movements' such as NWAF, women who were able to fit into the model of the 'genuine' carnival fan were largely respected and welcomed. Adhering to this model was vital though. They needed to adapt to the mannerisms of the fan groups, joining in with the banter, bad language and discussion of traditionally masculine topics, most notably fighting and disorder at football. They were also expected to have a good knowledge of the team, the club's history and terrace culture. Women were expected to drink heavily (preferably beer), sing raucously and dress 'appropriately' to fit in with group. They were also expected to be comfortable in situations where disorder occurred (it was not expected that they would fight – although some did). Not all the women in the carnival fan groups at Blackpool, England or United fitted this typology (Ruby for example attended many matches in high heels, while Becs often wore a skirt), but most of those who were accepted and welcomed into the world of the 'lads' conformed to these norms. Most of the data in this section is gathered from female members of the United carnival fan groups observed from 2008–11.

The women of the United carnival fan groups referred to in this book had all been attending matches for a number of years and had generally been accepted by the male members of the support, even those who subscribed to the 'no women at football' school of thought. Some of them were attending matches in the 1980s, and used to stand on the terraced Stretford End as teenagers when in their view, far fewer women attended matches.

Char: You have to accept that it is male dominated. If you don't like it, don't go. It took us a lot longer to, like, get accepted among the regular United fans ... But then you get that respect because you keep going ... It's more difficult to get accepted and recognized as a girl, but once you are, it's not an issue really.

Caz: It's not something you thought of 'cos you were, like, just going to the match.

Char: Like the lads, your first love is United isn't it?

Sally: If you were the sort of person who would feel isolated as a female then you just wouldn't go.

Gemma: I think when you're a woman you do need to know a little bit more [to be accepted] ... I didn't get any hassle about going to United until I was about sixteen. When I was a kid going with my Dad it was like 'we know who she is ...' before then I was just another kid going to the football.

They agreed that being female meant that they needed to try harder than a male fan in order to be accepted as 'genuine'. While they felt that the 'time-served' nature of their support over the years meant that they were now accepted by fans around them (and some argued that this process was actually a very quick one), they still felt judged when they met other fans who did not know them.

Gemma: Every now and again like, say you go on a coach to an away game and it's not a coach you've been on before and you don't know a lot of the people on it. And when you get on there's this kind of look as if to say, 'Who's brought their fucking missus along?' And it's like, 'Hang on, I'm not anyone's missus! I'm just here 'cos I want to go to the game'. And it's constantly a battle. When you meet new people and they haven't seen you before ... and if anyone had just brought their [male] mate along to the match it would just be 'oh, that's so-and-so's mate.' but when you step on a coach it's, 'oh fucking hell, someone's brought a bird, fucking going to have to watch my language, can't drink ... blah blah blah'.

This was particularly problematic away from the match, where fans (sometimes of other teams) who did not know them would question their commitment to United and even their knowledge of the game. Becs recounted a story of having to prove she understood the offside rule in a pub with beer mats while a group of male Liverpool fans attempted (unsuccessfully) to catch her out. She suggested the same treatment would not have happened to a male supporter.

Sally: I find as soon as you have any kind of constructive conversation with these people, demonstrating the knowledge that you have, they'll immediately switch and treat you like a bloke and have a proper football conversation with you.

Gemma: The words 'I was there' usually helps quite a lot.

They admitted that they also sometimes fell into the same trap when it came to requiring female supporters to prove themselves more than their male counterparts. This they agreed was unfair, as for them the issue was not whether the fan was male or female, but whether they were 'clued up' in their understanding of the game, the club and its fan culture. As we have seen, this template of what a 'clued up' fan looks and acts like is one based on traditional masculine norms, but for the female carnival fans, it was a template that should be adhered to, whether you were male or female. In particular the women singled out 'pink scarves and pink hats' (pink football merchandise specifically targeted at women), as well as women attending matches in 'skirts and high heels'. It was important, they felt to dress 'properly', in order to show that you are there to watch the game, not to be 'looked at' yourself. However, an equally bad crime was to attend a match just because your boyfriend was attending.

Sally: there are more women that are being taken by their boyfriends
Char: And they want shooting
Caz: And they're taking the tickets ... I don't think there's a woman in this room that's against the ethos of NWAF as in the sort of women that it's trying to say shouldn't bloody be there [at the game]. And we're all NWAF – apart from us! [laughs]
Gemma: I sort of feel guilty when that thought comes into my mind. Like before [a recent] game I went out with Gary before the game and he brought some girl that he was really interested in ... And she turned up in [the pub] in skirt and high-heeled boots and that and she was banging on about how much she loved United and blah blah blah. I was sitting there listening to her and I thought, 'oh you fucking dick' and then all of a sudden I felt guilty and I was just sort of like, 'I shouldn't be calling her a dick, I shouldn't be saying, 'oh you fucking nobhead', just because she's a woman ... Being a woman, I should be giving her a chance, whereas anyone else who was a man would be saying exactly the same thing to her ... So I felt like a double dick head in the sense that I should be being nice to her but then, I was like, why should I be nice to her? She's a fucking nobhead!

The resentment towards women who were seen as 'tourists' was even greater at away matches, where tickets were more difficult for carnival fans to obtain:

Rae: At an away game, when there's [only] 2,000 tickets, and some tart's fucking next to me ... like at Chelsea this year. There were more women at Chelsea, at that away game, than I've ever seen at any United away game in years. All with fucking big bags that take up the size of a fucking seat ...
Caz: And there's never any beer in them!
Rae: It's just fucking wrong ... How the hell did they get that ticket? But my exasperation with it is the lads that have let the tickets go to them.
Gemma: But that doesn't come back to them being a woman. That comes back to them just being a dick that's gone to the match that shouldn't be there.

Char: How many of those women are actually going to watch the football? Or
        are they going to be the centre of attention – 'look at me'. Why do you
        need to dress like that?
Sally: It is just their Saturday out.

For female carnival fans, this 'type' of woman was not a 'proper fan', and many of
them suspected that they were only at games because of their boyfriend or
because they were looking for a man. Gemma noted the number of women she
saw 'turning up on the United scene', usually with men, and then disappearing
completely, along with other women 'doing the rounds' (sexually) with the male
fans before disappearing. It was felt this type of female supporter made it harder
for the 'genuine' female fans to be accepted.

Caz also recounted a tale from a match where she had defended a pregnant
female supporter who was being abused by two male United fans:

> We were next to these two cockneys, jammed in next to us. And they start having
> a go at this pregnant woman saying 'fucking women shouldn't be at football' ...
> I mean what's the fun in taking the piss out of a pregnant woman? And they
> were being really fucking rude. So I went over there and said, 'Don't talk to
> people like that'. And he said, 'Who are you?' And I said, 'It doesn't matter who
> the fuck I am, who the fuck are you?' 'Oh yeah, fucking women shouldn't be at
> football ...' I didn't let him finish [throws an imaginary punch – room laughs]
> and his mate fucking ran away!

However, the women did not expect any kind of special treatment on their
grounds of their sex (although they did on occasion take advantage of their
gender and traditional chivalrous attitudes, particularly in situations where
disorder occurred or when they were trying to gain entrance to the stadium).
They all admitted to being incredulous, and also amused, when male fans who
did not know them apologised for swearing in their earshot, particularly while
singing football chants. This was something I observed on a number of occasions
at matches, despite the fact that on each occasion the female in question was
participating in the indecent chant herself. Only Sally said she would not chant
'the c-word', with another respondent saying that United's 'My Old Man' chant,
was the only time she ever used the word 'cunt'. At the opposite end of the
spectrum, some of the female research participants adopted the misogynist
internet phrase KHITC ('kick her in the cunt') when detailing how they would
deal with women they disliked, or when engaging in banter with other women.

The views on engaging in sexist chants varied; when engaged in a popular
football chant, it is difficult to make out exactly what words are being sung by
individuals so there is the option to alter or skip certain words or lines. Sally and
Rae said that during the 'Manchester Is Wonderful' chant, they just 'blanked out'
the 'tits and fanny', while Gemma, Caz and Char pointed out that it depended on
the context and, importantly, how drunk they were – the more drunk, the more
likely they were to sing the sexist words. Half the time they would sing the 'tits
and fanny' line, but on other occasions they would blank out the words or even
change the lyrics; 'it's full of Giggs, Fletcher and United', or 'it's full of Giggs, the

Hacci[2] and United'. However, it was not considered a serious problem, and Rae even commented of the original lyrics that, 'It's complimentary [everyone laughs] because it ranks [us women] alongside United!' Ruby didn't see any issue with the chant at all: 'I sing it. It's the words isn't it?'. Another song discussed was 'Hello, hello, we are the Busby Boys'.

> Gemma: It depends what it's being sung about. If we're singing about what's on the pitch, that's sound, but if we're singing it in a pub where it's like, 'woooaaahh we're all lads together watching the football', I'm like, 'er ... hang on a minute.

They all approved of chants referencing the fact the females were an integral part of United's support, most notably United's version of the Blaydon Races (above), and also:

> She wore, she wore, she wore a scarlet ribbon,
> She wore a scarlet ribbon in the merry month of May.
> And when, I asked, her why she wore that ribbon
> She said it's for United, and we're going to Wem-ber-lee
> Wem-ber-lee! Wem-ber-lee!
> We're the famous Man United and we're going to Wem-ber-lee!

Gemma spoke of the time that, in reference to this song, she wore a red ribbon to the final and wrote on her T-Shirt, 'I'm wearing it for United 'cos we're going to Wembley'. However, the group did not admit to feeling any particular feminine pride at such songs being sung in contrast to other traditional United chants.

They also did not consider there to be any problem with sexist abuse given to opposition players, fans or other women at football. For example, all would join in chanting 'she fell over' at an opposition player who was considered to have taken a dive. They would also sing 'get your tits out for the lads' to female physiotherapists, dancers or opposition fans, with the general consensus being that 'it's funny' (Caz: 'If you take that seriously, you're in the wrong place'). Similarly, the women recounted with amusement the time that United fans chanted 'Who let the dogs out?' when female cheerleaders ran onto the pitch at half-time during a match at Middlesbrough – 'Quality, I joined in with that!'. In terms of sexist abuse towards females on football internet message boards, most of the women visited and posted on the boards. While they were aware of the inherently sexist nature of the content of the boards, and were generally disparaging about those who posted such material, they did not consider it a reason not to visit the forums, as the seriously abusive threads were easily avoided and several of them found the forums useful for obtaining match tickets.

From my observations, sexism towards the female carnival fans at matches received mixed responses. On occasion it met with genuine anger from them, but usually was treated as being merely part of the normal match-day banter between members of the fan groups. In turn, some of the male fans would attempt to wind up the women by openly supporting and extolling the virtues of the NWAF 'movement'. Sexual advances towards female members of the fan groups were also common, both those made in jest and also more serious propositions. Again responses were varied: some were welcomed (and indeed encouraged) and considered complimentary and others were laughed off. On more than one occasion I witnessed a female supporter revealing her breasts upon a request by male carnival fans to 'get your tits out for the lads'. However, some female carnival fans were genuinely angry and upset by physical approaches towards them (even if they were made 'in jest'). One of the women recounted how she was genuinely relieved when a male fan she often travelled with was not attending a match because he would try to 'feel me up'. Of course, in addition to this, there were sexual relationships occurring between male and female members of the fan groups. A number of liaisons and affairs took place during the course of my research between fans, some of whom were married or in long-term relationships with partners (usually these partners did not attend matches). The camaraderie, heavy use of alcohol and general carnival atmosphere around matches probably contributed to the number of these 'flings'.

Another finding from observations and focus groups was that there appeared little difference in attitude towards 'hooligan' violence between female and male carnival fans. The female fans were no more likely than their male counterparts to condemn hooliganism and their views were in line with the positive attitudes towards football violence exhibited by many members of the fan groups detailed in Chapter 4. Some female carnival fans were clearly disturbed when serious violence took place near them, but no more so than many of the males in these groups. In some cases, the women appeared to be less frightened by violence, as they were less likely to be targeted by rival hooligans than the men they were with. Crowd crushes were of greater concern, with the average lesser physical size, strength and stamina of the females making them more at risk of injury in situations where creating a space around yourself in order to move and breathe freely became essential. In the many crowd crush situations that occurred during my research, it was common to see male supporters pay particular attention to how women in the crush were faring (as they did with any children in the crush), often trying to create space around them, shouting warnings to fans nearby, or appealing to police officers or stewards to get the women out of the crush. The angry shout of 'there's women and kids here', was regularly heard in situations where crowd crushes developed, particularly at turnstiles.

However, not all of the women were more fearful of crushes than the men, and two of the group admitted to regularly jibbing into matches without tickets, for which crowd crushes and pushing and shoving often assisted. Both Gemma and Caz on occasion adopted 'traditional' feminine responses to such situations to gain access to matches without paying: 'The amount of time I've got into games by putting on crying and …' [does mock crying impression]. Other tactics taking advantage of their gender to jib into grounds were recounted but cannot be discussed here (Caz: 'Don't put that in the book or I'll never be able to use it again. And remember, I know where you live!' [laughs]). Some women also admitted (or were observed) behaving aggressively at football matches (as opposed to merely being involved in disorder in situations where they felt the need to defend themselves). Again, this was comparable to male members of the carnival fan groups observed. In addition to some of the stories detailed here and in Chapter 4, during observations with United, Blackpool and England I also witnessed female fans confronting rival supporters with abusive and threatening language (on one occasion I was subjected to this by a female supporter of Middlesbrough), throwing missiles at rival supporters and police, kicking in seats at away matches, and slapping 'Love United hate Glazer' stickers on police officers. Caz was also involved in the deliberate tripping up of a police officer (Chapter 4) and another female fan had previously been given a football banning order for punching a steward. Although the women did not consider themselves 'hooligans', and avoided becoming involved in the 'mobs' that travelled to matches with the intention of confronting rival firms, many had been caught up in such violence and, as Gemma explained, did not always choose to try and hide or escape:

> It's all about the situation in which you find yourself. You never go to a football match thinking, 'right today I'm going here today because I want to kick off, and fucking put a fucking brick through the White Lion or whatever'. But every now and again you find yourselves in situations where it's, right, it's fight or flight. Or hide under a table or whatever, not get involved ... But you just sort of try to get involved with what's going on. You never go out and like cause aggression, although sometimes you'd like to.

This response was not typical of the women observed, most of whom chose flight ahead of fight when disorder occurred. However, this was also true of the male research participants. My findings were that in carnival fan groups, gender made little or no difference to whether an individual would become involved in disorder if it occurred.[3] The Leicester School famously identified the culture of 'aggressive masculinity' as being behind football violence. While it may be that this culture, and wanting to be part of it, influenced some of the reactions of the women when faced with disorderly situations, their actual gender appeared to be of little significance.

In terms of their relationship with police and stewards, the women generally felt that in the UK (but typically not abroad), they were treated more leniently than male fans, who were more likely to be subjected to abuses and intimidation.

> Becs: When we went to Liverpool and we were marched back to Lime Street ... the one copper was effing and blinding and saying how shit United were and all of that. He turned round and saw me and said 'Oh sorry, I didn't realise you were there', and apologised to me for all his bad language and said he didn't mean it to me because I was a woman. But it was all right to swear and to say he was going to kick the shit out of all of the men ... So yeah, I do think some police and stewards react differently to women.

My observations of how women were treated by police and stewards was that the differences were not as great as might have been expected. For example, Carly was punched in the face by an Italian riot officer at a match in Rome in 2007 (for trying to record police abuses on her camera), and in 2009 I saw Becs being thrown into a metal fence by a steward at an away match. Two of the women also recounted incidents where they felt they had been targeted *because* they were women (on both occasions by female police/stewards). One was arrested at Middlesbrough by a steward who claimed she had punched her in the face. She was prosecuted but the court case collapsed: 'I made her cry and made her say she'd made it up because she was embarrassed'. Another of the women complained that, 'There's this one female copper, a real bulldog of a woman who always seems to be at [team name]. She always gives me shit'.

It was clear that female fans did play an important role in the carnival fan groups, particularly at United. However in order to gain acceptance within these groups, the women had to adopt the traditional masculine culture of football. This was done with differing degrees of enthusiasm, but the women in the fan groups inevitably ended up reaffirming the sexist attitudes and behaviour as the dominant norm within carnival fan groups. The findings from my research reflected those uncovered by Katharine Jones's work on female fans in the UK. Jones found that the female fans she was researching typically excused sexist behaviour from male fans as being 'funny', or not being serious enough to cause a problem. She also highlighted that if the female supporters complained, their status as female would become relevant and their difference from the majority of male fans would be highlighted (2006: 16). As we have seen, highlighting this difference was something that the female carnival fans typically wanted to avoid and most appeared happiest when they were simply seen as 'one of the lads'.

Xenophobia, Islamophobia and racism

Football fans have historically suffered from a bad reputation when it comes to racial tolerance. Accusations of racism and xenophobia have frequently been levelled at English supporters, and numerous attempts have been made to try and rid the game of this reputation, including the Kick Racism Out of Football campaign and the Football (Offences) Act 1991, which criminalised 'racialist' chanting. From my own observations, an assumption that football supporters are more racist than other groups in society is wrong, but in a sport built upon rivalries between nations and regions, negative stereotypes of the opposition players and supporters were never far away and these sometimes took a xenophobic or racial form. On rare occasions this developed into serious racial abuse from large numbers of supporters (although never all) of a particular team. Significant differences between how different groups of fans behaved, based upon shared understandings of what was acceptable behaviour at any given time were also found. That fan behaviour when it came to racism was so influenced by this form of usually unspoken self-policing also suggests that expressions of racism from a fan group can vary over time, even if the attitudes of individual fans within that group towards issues of race remain more entrenched.

Research with fans of Blackpool in the 1990s indicated an underlying racist element among many of the carnival fans, and also an apparent acceptance that racist abuse from the terraces could, under certain circumstances, be acceptable.

It was impossible to say that this meant than fans from Blackpool were, for example, more racist than those from United, but it was clear that expressions of racism were at the time more acceptable in the stands at Bloomfield Road than Old Trafford. But even here, racist abuse towards black players or supporters was not commonplace; during my research with Blackpool fans, the only instance of so-called 'monkey chanting' towards black players (by many accounts a feature of matches during the 1970s and early 1980s) heard was by fans of Millwall at Bloomfield Road. The apparently once popular chant of 'you black bastard' was also absent, and on one occasion the South Paddock abused black veteran Cyril Regis with chants of 'you old bastard' for the duration of the game, completely ignoring the colour of his skin. However, there were several instances when I heard individual racial shouts or comments about black opposition players.

The most overt racism at Blackpool during my research was abuse of fans from towns perceived to have large populations of Asians. 'You're just a town full of pakis' would be chanted at opposition fans of both Preston and Burnley, and on one occasion against Bradford (after they beat Blackpool in a play-off). This chanting could not be discounted as the actions of a small minority, and the chants were of similar volume to non-racist chants throughout the games. Although it was impossible to accurately estimate numbers or proportions of the crowd singing, hundreds (possibly over a thousand on a few occasions) of fans were involved. It was noticeable that this chant was only sung at the most high tension matches, and I never heard it during league matches against the likes of Luton or Bradford where the numbers of Asian residents are also high. It appeared therefore that racist chants were perceived by most Blackpool fans to be in the main undesirable, and more 'serious' than standard abusive and indecent chants that formed part of every match. However, in local derbies and on the occasion of missing out on a promotion play-off final, this racial chant suddenly became acceptable and fans felt able to sing it at full volume without fear of reproach. In 2008, ten years after my observations at Blackpool finished, nine fans were banned by the club for engaging in this chant during a match against Preston, two of whom were subsequently found guilty under the 1991 Act and at subsequent derbies no such racial chants were reported.

Racism and Islamophobia was also a feature of some of the England matches at which research was carried out, particularly abroad. Racist chanting by small groups of English fans in bars and town squares was a feature of every England match I attended, but on only one occasion did this escalate into widespread chanting within the stadium. As with Blackpool, it appeared that the fans who engaged in these chants were aware that it would only be seen as acceptable by those around them in certain circumstances, and that fans wishing to engage in these chants were unlikely to risk starting them, instead preferring to wait for a 'critical mass' of those around to sing before joining in. Following the fatal stabbing of two Leeds United fans in Istanbul and subsequent violence prior to the UEFA Cup Final between Arsenal and Galatasaray, anti-Turkish chants occurred around England matches for the duration of my research with the national team. Previously I had witnessed England fans chanting 'If you all hate pakis clap your hands', but now this 'hatred' of Asians resident in England was used to insult the Turks. 'I would rather be a paki than a Turk' became a popular chant in bars and town squares frequented by England fans. While this was only sung by a minority of the carnival fans, it was sung openly and with regularity – the fans knew there was little chance that they would be challenged by other England supporters over their behaviour. During a match in Germany in 2001, England fans gathered outside a bar altered the lyrics and sang 'I would rather be a paki than a Kraut', resulting in one fan turning to his friend and commenting, 'no, I wouldn't!'. When England played Turkey in 2003 in Sunderland, anti-Turkish chants including this one were also heard inside the stadium, along with 'Die die Turkey fucking die' and 'If you all hate Turks clap your hands'. When speaking to an England fan about this latter chant, I was told that he did not consider the chant racist because it was against the Turkish national team, not the nationality itself. Following the September 11 and July 7 Al Qaeda terrorist attacks, Islamophobic abuse also started to seep into the songbook of groups of England fans, and chants of 'If you all hate Muslims clap your hands' were heard at a number of England games, although again predominantly by small groups of fans outside stadiums.

The behaviour of Blackpool and England fans could be largely contrasted with that of United fans, who appeared to have a much lower threshold for what racial abuse was acceptable, and I did not witness any racist chanting at United matches during the early years of my research with them. Although a number of the fans with whom I was researching expressed in private conversations anti-Turkish, anti-Asian or anti-Muslim views, the chanting of racist songs was almost unheard of, even away from the stadium. Indeed, even pro-English chants were rare at United matches. Prior to a match against Boavista in Portugal in 2001, a dispute broke out between two groups of United fans in one of the squares. One group of fans started chanting 'In-ger-lund', which was quickly drowned out by chants of 'Manchester' and then:

> David Beckham went to France, as a national hero,
> Got sent off, he came home, reputation zero,
> England fans, they're all twats, they get so excited,
> Shove your England up your arse, we are Man United!

The chant referred to the media and public vilification of then United player David Beckham following his sending off at the 1998 World Cup against Argentina. For many United fans, who were already infuriated about the treatment by England fans of United players representing the national team, and the perceived bias of the Football Association against United, this was the final straw in their relationship with the national team. For the duration of the 1998–99 season, United fans would goad opposition fans booing Beckham by chanting 'Argentina!'. Anti-England chants such as this, 'Portugal' (when Portugal knocked England out of the 2006 World Cup), and 'You can shove your fucking England up your arse', soon became commonplace at United. Argentina and Portugal flags were also waved and a banner was produced stating simply 'United > England'. This anti-nationalistic attitude was also reflected in the behaviour of United fans at European away matches; although xenophobic and occasionally racist attitudes were evident among some fans, the accepted norms of behaviour for United fans, on the terraces and in the popular bars, appeared deliberately anti-racist.

This prevailing non-racist norm among United carnival fans is flagged up by King (2000), and was something that many were very proud about. Many United fans contrasted the behaviour of their fans in this respect in stark contrast to those of 'small town' clubs such as Blackpool, and to the 'little Englander' mentality of those who followed the national team. However, Back *et al.* (2001: 280) criticise King for claiming that United's fan culture transcends the nation state, being representative of the city, not the country, but not recognising 'racist practice' among United fans. My own research revealed that while United fans were undoubtedly less tolerant of racist abuse than I had experienced with fans of Blackpool and the national team, some racist chanting and abuse did occur. During a match against Tottenham Hotspur, for example, some United fans were heard 'hissing' (this is done to symbolise the sound of gas at Auschwitz, as Tottenham are perceived to have a high number of Jewish supporters), and on a number of occasions, individual United fans were heard abusing locals at European away matches by calling them 'Kraut/froggy bastards'.

In 2008, the adoption by United fans of Tottenham's chant against black African player Adebayor, and widespread singing of this from the Stretford End, also suggested that racial chanting of a surreptitious nature may have been becoming more acceptable at Old Trafford:

> Adebayor, Adebayor,
> Your dad washes elephants,
> Your mum is a whore.

Although far from the more blatant forms of racism discussed earlier, the chant cast an antiquated negative racial stereotype upon the player and would certainly not have been sung had the player not been black. Whether this chant was acceptable split opinion from the United carnival fans. A minority considered the chant racist and did not engage in it. A larger proportion did not consider the song to be racist at all, including one black British supporter. Finally, another section of the support were unsure whether the chant was racist or not, but expressed concerns about its use because it was 'a Spurs song', and United fans should be above 'stealing' chants used by other clubs. I witnessed a number of instances of carnival fans contesting the use of the song on racial grounds, but the chant was considered acceptable by the fan base as a whole.

Another chant at United which also raises questions about racism and xenophobia was sung in support of United's South Korean player, Ji Sung Park and was even more popular:

> Park, Park, where ever you may be,
> You eat dogs in your own country.
> It could be worse, you could be scouse,
> Eating rats in your council house.

Other less popular songs suggested that the player regularly ate Labradors. United's carnival fan groups did not consider these chants to be racist or xenophobic, arguing that they were sung in support of the player, that they were just 'a laugh' and that some Koreans *did* eat dogs. On the whole, while United's carnival fans were observably more sensitive to racial issues, negative racial stereotypes and xenophobia did permeate their views and even their chants. Jay set out his views on the issue of racism in the Red Brigade in their forum: 'I will clearly state here and now, this is not a place for anyone in a PC [politically correct] brigade. We allow views of many extremes, in fact we even have a couple of blatant racists. However instead of banning them [from the forum] we take time to point out how daft they are while pointing a finger and sniggering at them'.

The forum contained numerous casually racist references, although identifying the genuine beliefs from the 'wind-ups' posted to provoke a response from those labelled the 'PC brigade' was often difficult. Racist comments away from the forum were less common, and face to face the match-goers of the Red Brigade on the whole appeared sensitive to both the issues and to how making such comments would reflect on them to the rest of the group. Furthermore, British Asians and also foreign fans were welcome at pre and post-match gatherings and at Euro aways United fans often welcomed supporters of the home team to drink with them. That said, individual black or Asian fans that were accepted as part of the carnival groups were on occasion subjected to banter about their colour or cultural background, and sometimes expected to join in with this. Only where this banter was engaged in by those outside of the immediate group of friends was it perceived (by both the 'victim' and others) to be racist rather than harmless fun.

While racism existed to a certain extent within all the carnival fan groups, it was usually expressed only under certain circumstances; if it was of a certain 'type' and in a particular context. At United, the standards of what was unacceptable were set higher, and individual racial comments or chants were much more likely to be challenged by other fans, meaning that for those wishing to engage in such chanting, it was simply often not worth the risk of embarrassment or even a physical confrontation. Self-policing therefore appeared the determining factor on whether, and to what extent, racism would be expressed at and around matches. Over the sixteen years of this research, it also appeared that racist chanting and abuse on the terraces (from both the teams under observation and the opposition fans) was reducing and becoming less acceptable. It was also noticeable that fan reaction to racist chanting about their team's players at matches in Europe was one of outrage and a belief that this demonstrated how much more 'civilised' fans were in England than parts of the continent. However, the process of racist chanting dying out was not uniform or without regional or team variation. Attitudes to what was acceptable at United, for example, had not progressed noticeably since 2001 and many fans believed that the Adebayor chant would not have been accepted earlier in the decade. Additionally, Islamophobic abuse and chanting following the Al Qaeda terrorist attacks (and probably fuelled by anti-Muslim sentiment in many tabloid newspapers) has undoubtedly increased.

My observations suggested that on the whole, football fans were not more inherently racist, prone to making racist comments or engaging in racial abuse than society more generally. At Blackpool or United matches I was no more likely to hear individual racist comments than in a pub on a non-match day, on in cricket or rugby crowds that I have been part of socially. Furthermore, there was no vocal or visible support for the likes of the British National Party from the carnival fans observed. Political extremism was simply not an influential factor on the outlook or behaviour of these supporters. The only occasion that it even became a serious topic of conversation was around an 'anti Islamic extremism' march by the English Defence League (EDL) in Manchester in 2009. The EDL appeared to be made up primarily of a loose-knit amalgamation of football fans called 'Casuals United', and a number of United fans were identified in the demonstration that day. Although they had no formal links with the British National Party (BNP), there were links in membership between the two organisations, some members of the march carried banners claiming 'No more mosques' and a few were seen making Nazi salutes. Although none of the carnival fans I knew joined the march, a number of United fans were active in the counter-demonstration organised by Unite Against Fascism and expressed excitement at the rumour that the United hooligan firm was gathering to confront the EDL group. Matches with England were slightly different from my experience with Blackpool and United, as small groups would gather and chant anti-Asian or anti-Muslim songs away from the stadium. However, these were a small minority of the overall support and again I did not witness recruitment by far-right groups or political parties (although some fans would admit to being pro-BNP).

A considerable amount has already been written on racism in football, and may provide a misleading picture of the prevalence of discriminatory attitudes within football crowds. One of the problems here is that the rare instances of racist chanting (which is usually by a small minority) tend to be reported, whereas the absence of such chants receives little attention. While in my research I came across a number of quite openly racist individuals, they were dwarfed by the number of fans who were tolerant and indeed welcoming of other races, nationalities and cultures. However the culture of participating in mass chanting to insult the opposition club, players and spectators that exists in football means that occasionally this minority become able to express these views more vocally than in non-football contexts. With the negative views on issues like 'asylum seekers', 'immigrants' and 'Islamic fundamentalists' that are prevalent in much of the popular press and reflected in the views and opinions of much of the public, it is a testament to the progress that has been made by anti-racist organisations involved in football, and more importantly, the self-policing of the fans themselves, that more chants and abuse of this nature are not heard in and around football grounds.

Attitudes to disability and sexuality

In addition to being largely white and male, the carnival fans observed were, with very few exceptions, able-bodied and openly heterosexual. With reference to disability, the carnival fans tended not to mingle with seriously disabled supporters. Practical reasons may explain this; wheelchair-bound fans typically were allocated separate areas inside the stadium from able-bodied fans, usually a single disabled section for both home and away fans. Outside the ground, much of the carnival fans' activities precluded seriously disabled supporters from joining in with their rowdy version of carnival, particularly at away matches and games abroad where disorderly and occasionally violent incidents could occur. One exception to this rule was on the South Paddock at Blackpool, where a supporter with clear learning disabilities was highly popular and participated fully in the creation of rowdy carnival in this area. He would on occasion write handwritten match reports of the game and while some of the fans around him would laugh at his efforts, his presence was welcomed by those around him. When he died prematurely, his mother was invited onto the pitch before the next match to thank the fans in the Paddock for making him feel at home and they in turn chanted his name to her. Disabled supporters (and senior fans with walking sticks) were on the whole treated with great respect by the carnival fans, regardless of the team they were supporting, and when identified in a crowd, they would sometimes make a deliberate effort to try to create space for them, holding back other fans unaware of their presence to assist their progress. However, at the same time the fans frequently used insults based on disability in banter with each other, or to abuse able-bodied opposition fans or players. On internet forums, the term 'spastic' was used continually, and 'mong' was regularly used as an insult at and around matches.

In banter between carnival fans, and when abusing fans or players from rival clubs (or locals when disputes arose), supporters would also frequently use homophobic insults. Fans would use terms such as 'gay', 'queer' and 'sausage jockey' to insult others. This became so frequent in banter and 'piss-taking' within the fan groups that some fans rather than denying the accusation would turn it around and claim that they were homosexual and that the accuser knew and secretly approved of this. Homophobic chants were also commonplace, and received none of the stigma of racist chants. Shock was expressed by many fans when it was reported that a number of Tottenham fans had been found guilty under the Football (Offences) Act for homophobic chanting at former player Sol Campbell. While homophobic abuse was on the whole tongue in cheek, rather than deliberately aimed at insulting or harassing gays, it would probably have made it very uncomfortable for an openly gay fan to join a trip with the carnival fans and would be likely to discourage a gay or bisexual supporter from 'coming out' for fear of constant ridicule. It was therefore little surprise that none of the fan groups observed contained openly gay supporters.

Conclusion

In terms of their views on most issues of discrimination and equality, carnival fan groups appeared to merely reflect those of any group of 'lads' who gathered together socially, either in the local pub or away from home on a stag party or 'lads' holiday'. Attitudes towards homosexuality and disability that were commonplace within the fan groups were the same as those witnessed in pubs, clubs, student halls of residence and even some academic conferences. Tongue-in-cheek insults of this nature as part of banter between friends were simply part of the carnival for the fans and remain likely to increase or decrease alongside the wider societal attitudes towards issues of equality. However, the dominant masculine attitudes that existed in carnival fans groups, and the wider match-going support, appeared to reflect the extremes of societal views on gender; football was 'a man's game' off the pitch as well as on it. This did not stop women joining these carnival groups, but those who did were expected to adopt these dominant masculine norms in terms of language and behaviour in order to be fully accepted.

Notes

1 5.40 p.m., 12/11/09.
2 A reference to the now defunct Hacienda nightclub in Manchester.
3 Female enjoyment of, or involvement in, disorder is not limited to football (see Hobbs, 2003: 132–6; Winlow and Hall, 2006: 103) nor is it a new phenomenon (Davies, 1999, 2009).

8

The impact of technology

Introduction

During the research, two significant technological developments occurred that had a huge impact upon football fan culture and behaviour, altering fandom considerably and probably forever. Although both the internet and mobile phones existed prior to the start of my observations in 1995, they had yet to make a significant impact upon supporter culture. By the early 2000s, in contrast, they were both playing a significant role for supporters, with most fans possessing and using mobile phones at matches, and many also posting on internet forums. Later in that decade, phones with cameras became prevalent and files recorded on these phones started to be posted on the internet, often on these message boards. This chapter focuses on these developments and how carnival fans utilised them in their expressions of fandom. New technology has revolutionised much of carnival fan culture, expanding networks, opening up more opportunities for expressions of the carnivalesque and providing a forum to discuss fan issues. It has also allowed carnival fans to provide a window into their subculture to those from the outside, meaning that even 'armchair' fans at home can be exposed to the behaviour and attitude of these match-going supporters. Whether these developments were considered beneficial by the fans is another matter that needs to be considered as technology also had the ability to create cliques, detract from the spontaneity of the match experience and possibly provide greater opportunities for 'hooligans' to congregate and confront each other away from the eyes of the police.

Internet forums

I started drafting this chapter on 23 November 2009. At 2.45 p.m. that Monday there were 840 users on Red Cafe, the biggest of the independent Manchester United internet forums. There were 679 online on the second biggest, Red Issue, 166 on Fred Tissue, forty-five on Red Issue's subscription-only 'Sanctuary' and thirty-two on the invite-only Red Brigade forum. These are the forums that during the course of my research I was a member of and posted on, but there were dozens of other active independent United forums (and FC United sites) and also the official club site. In addition there were generic football chat forums that some fans used. And this was a slow news day regarding United; there are no player transfers taking place, no important games just around the corner and United's last game was two days previous. When United suffered a shock defeat to Burnley earlier that season, 3,973 different users were on the Red Cafe message board (around 1,500 more United fans than were present at the match). Their record number of users online at a single time is currently 5,755, with Red Issue's currently standing at 2,570. Blackpool fans are also now well catered for, with new messages being posted on A View from the Tower almost every minute, and a number of other active message boards. Football internet message boards are exceptionally popular and, from my research, highly influential on match-going fan culture. The majority of the research in this chapter will be drawn from my experiences with fans of United, as the technology was only just starting to have an impact when my research with Blackpool finished. For many match-going United fans, internet message boards played an important role in their support of the team. Not all of the carnival fans posted on these message boards but the vast majority of the fans with whom I spoke in recent seasons posted on at least one forum, or at least 'lurked' (i.e. read what others were posting but did not post themselves). Furthermore, as we will see, for some posters on the Red Brigade message board, this particular forum had actually created a physical social network for the fans to join at matches.

Message boards were primarily used to allow fans to discuss football issues; a supporter would join the board and choose a 'username' with which he or she could post messages and engage in debate with other posters. These debates were organised into different 'threads' (topics of discussion). Some message boards were split into a number of different sub-forums – examples being 'Ticketing and travel' (where fans could exchange tickets and find lifts/spaces on coaches/cars to matches), 'Football chat' (although this inevitably turned up in most threads, whether relevant or not), 'Current events', 'Not safe for work' (links to pornography), 'Entertainment' (film, TV, music) etc. – but others had all these topics discussed in different threads on the same forum. Returning to the Red Issue forum of 23 November 2009, threads being discussed at the time included: 'Wigan refund fans', 'U2 confirmed for Glastonbury' (music), 'Great players who are total cunts when you meet them', 'Seven Sisters tube fatality in 1981' (hooliganism), 'Swap 2 Fulham away tickets for 1 West Ham', 'The Royle Family' (TV), 'Should quad bikes be banned?', 'Did anyone else have Bryan Robson's soccer skills book?', 'The Hacienda Christmas party' and a poll on whether David Villa would be a good signing. Additionally, there were a number of 'wind-up' threads (which will be discussed below). This was a typical spread of thread topics.

Another feature of the football message board was that the majority of posters benefited from anonymity. Since posters could choose their own username, and only the administrator for the board knew their e-mail address, almost all posters chose a name that enabled them to be anonymous. Popular usernames on the message boards were drawn from real names, past and present players, geographical areas and various references to popular culture or football. On the Red Issue message board on 23 November 2009, the following active posters appeared under 's':

Sal3, SaleRed, Salford M6, Salford91, salfordred31, salfordsgc, SAR, sbp, Schoolboy Error, scoreboard paddock, scousebasher, seat157, seb12, seggy, serbianwarcriminal, sevendust, Sevy, Sharpey, shaunwudyrider, sheephead, Sheriff Buford, Shev, shyamg22, sic, Sicarios, Sifter, simonw, Sinder22, sins, sir alex's hairdryer, SirMattBusbyWay, SiWard, skinno, Skinsman, skydealsRus, SmellyDirtBox, smokingbertcooper, Solofantastico, soul2soul, sox9, spaceman spiff, sparky85, Spear, spud, srmufc, Stephen Parr, Steve1974, steve5345, stevey, Steve_Naive, stevy, Stoned Moses, street_creduk, stretforddave, stretfordender, Stretford_M32, stured, Superman, SupremeMonarch, Swagger, Sweet Sweet Pootang and Symun.

This meant that posters usually did not know who they were debating with. This did not prevent discussions on the message boards becoming heated and indeed many debates would resort in posters abusing, insulting or threatening each other. Many carnival fans suggested that it was the relative anonymity of the message boards that encouraged this behaviour and that the posters would act differently face to face. 'He's alright in real life', was often posted to defend forum members being criticised online by those who had not met them.

Another outcome of this anonymity was that when supporters met for the first time at matches, one topic of discussion was if the other posted on a forum; if the two fans posted on the same forum, they would inevitably reveal their username and discuss other posters. Fans also admitted making judgements immediately on fans they had just met depending on the forum they said they posted on, similar to that which might be made upon asking what newspaper someone reads. As the message boards at United became more and more central to the subculture of the carnival fans, posters would occasionally arrange to meet each other at matches (usually to exchange tickets) and usernames started to become used to introduce new fans. My own username on the United forums was Pancho_Scores with reference to former United player and namesake Stuart Pearson. It was common for me to be introduced to other fans, or talked about in the third person as 'Pancho' as a result of this. Likewise, on numerous occasions I knew fans only by their username, particularly if I only met them at matches. Even when I did know a fan's real name, often it was easier to use their username because this would be more familiar to other fans or because the poster could be confused with a number of other fans of the same name. The message-board username therefore acted as a nickname for many fans, albeit sometimes a clumsy one – I was once introduced to 'Mr Red, White And Black' and on another occasion went on a sleeper train to Kiev organised by someone I only knew as 'Big Jim Holton' (the name of a former United player). Pseudonyms used in this book are made up of a mix of real names, nicknames and forum usernames, in keeping with the names used when these individuals met in person.

Due to the size of United's fan base, there were dozens of popular message boards that drew fans from all over the world, some easier to find than others. While some appeared high on internet search engines for 'Manchester United

Forum/Messageboard', others were hidden away, some were closed to newcomers and others were 'invite only'. Those that appeared high on internet searches tended to have a more varied membership, with many overseas supporters, some of whom had never attended a match, and also a number of fans of other teams. Forums that were more difficult to find tended to be frequented by regular match-goers and carnival fans. While the divisions between the two types of forum were not as clear-cut as they first appeared, different forums had different reputations. Forums such as the official United forum and Red Cafe, were avoided by many of the carnival fans because they were considered to be full of 'out-of-towners', 'Johnny-come-latelies' and 'gloryhunters'. Carnival fans who posted on these sites often become frustrated at the lack of knowledge of match-going issues shown by the posters. In contrast, non-match-going fans who found their way on to sites such as Red Issue, were rarely made welcome and their lack of experience of attending matches was often ridiculed. Forums dominated by carnival fans tended to focus more on topics about match-going, for example discussions of events on previous away trips, complaints about the match 'atmosphere' and arrangements for travelling to future matches. Those dominated by non-match-goers tended to focus on on-pitch issues (such as the team selection and form of different players). Both types of forum devoted a lot of time to the discussion of social issues and current events that were unrelated to football.

One key theme in many of the United forums was the 'wind-up merchant' (or WUM). This was used to refer to specific threads/posts that did not reflect the actual views of the poster but were instead designed to illicit an angry response from others. In other forums this practice is known as 'trolling', and posters were advised 'not to feed the troll' by responding to such posts. Some posters in fact became known themselves as WUMs due to the sheer number of posts of this nature. Some even had more than one username, which would enable them to start 'wind-ups' without damaging the reputation of their 'real' log-in. The prevalence of WUMs, multiple log-ins and posters who misrepresented their identity makes carrying out ethnographies of the internet (or 'netnographies') exceptionally difficult where the researcher wants to gather data about the people who are posting, rather than merely their internet personas. While some researchers into football crowd behaviour have rightly started to become more aware about the role of the forums (e.g. Millward, 2006), what is posted on them should always be handled with care. As a result, this chapter focuses on how the forums shape the activities of fans at matches, rather than what posters claim on the internet. Fortunately, through my research with the Red Brigade, I was able to get to know the posters in 'real life', and compare this with their internet persona. Often the impression that I got from an internet persona was fundamentally different to how that person appeared and behaved at matches; usually fans commented that posters were much friendlier in person than online.

'Wind-ups' are of course not limited to internet message boards, and have been identified as part of British humour in particular. Kate Fox, for example, states that the first rule of arguments in pubs is not to take them seriously (2005: 102) and as we have seen, this is also true of the observed behaviour of carnival fans around matches. Fox notes that the typical WUM conversation between friends will occur when, 'A bored regular will deliberately spark off an argument by making an outrageous or extreme statement and then sit back and wait for the inevitable cries of "bollocks!" The instigator must then hotly defend his assertion, which he secretly knows to be indefensible' (*ibid.*). Internet WUMs work in a similar way, and on many United forums made up a large portion of the posts. Some were elaborate and would last for weeks, drawing hundreds of responses. One poster for example started a thread entitled 'RORO', in which he claimed that he was a top sports lawyer who knew the identity of a number of incoming signings for United, but that all he could reveal was the letters of their initials. Another WUM claimed that CSKA Moscow fans had just 'trashed' a pub in Manchester city centre and were attacking any United fans they met. Others would deliberately spark off arguments by claiming that United fans needed to sit down at matches more, or should stop/start singing particular songs. Another form of WUM was for a poster to deliberately lie about their own life, for example by claiming that he had just discovered his 'missus' in bed with his father-in-law and asking for advice. This would inevitably lead to another thread being started by someone claiming to be either the father-in-law or the wife in question and ridiculing the sexual prowess of the poster of the initial WUM. As with conversations in pubs and on journeys to and from matches, the talk on the internet forums was centred around humour. The key difference was that the insults traded tended – when posters did not know each other personally – to be perceived more seriously.

It would also appear that internet forums are becoming used by journalists to gain an insight into the views of supporters on various issues that is accessible from the office. As was noted in Chapter 4, *The Independent*'s report on the crowd disorder at Barnsley vs. United quoted 'one poster on an online United fans forum' blaming the disorder on the 'Moston Rats' (*The Independent*, 29/10/09). The posters on Red Issue were amused to see that the post had been used by a broadsheet newspaper, especially as it was considered to be wildly inaccurate. In another incident, a poster who threatened violence against visiting supporters was quoted to demonstrate that violence was likely at that particular match. However, the poster in question was a well-known 'WUM' whose speciality was inventing stories of unlikely crowd violence to amuse the rest of the forum. Posters were aware that journalists and police frequented the forums attempting to pick up useful information, and on occasion would deliberately post false or misleading information in an attempt to trick or humiliate them. Increasingly, however, police intelligence about planned disorder is drawn directly from these forums. At a number of recent football banning order hearings,[1] anonymous posts on fan forums and the social-networking site Facebook have been presented as evidence that individuals were in hooligan gangs and that disorder was planned in particular locations. When United travelled to Manchester City in 2010, a post on Red Issue stating that a fan intended on taking a red flare into the ground resulted in increased security at turnstiles and a subsequent crowd crush.

As detailed in Chapter 3, observations suggested that at United the internet has yet to have a significant impact in how fans develop and circulate chants. However new social media platforms such as internet forums and social networking sites have enormous potential to influence and alter fan culture. They also have the potential to reduce the power and influence of carnival fan groups upon the creation of 'atmosphere' at grounds by providing access to the development of new ideas to those outside these networks. The true potential power of the internet upon football was witnessed in the 2009–10 season, when United fans embarked upon a protest against the club's owners following the issuing of a bond prospectus restructuring the debt they had placed upon the club. Within hours of the documentation's release, it had been dissected and discussed by fans on the internet, leading to a protest inside the stadium. A week later, an administrator on Red Issue known as 'Chatmaster' suggested that fans protested by wearing green and gold colours rather than red, black and white. The idea circulated round the message boards, Facebook and via the Supporters' Trust e-mail database in days. The first green and gold scarves were seen at the next match and by the end of the season in the region of 50,000 scarves (in addition to hats, shirts and flags) had been bought by United fans. Chatmaster's internet handle, but not his real name, was frequently mentioned in media reports of the protest.

The Red Brigade

The forum that provided the focus for much of my research was an 'invite-only' message board called Red Brigade. The Red Brigade forum was launched in 2007, initially as a breakaway forum for posters who were disillusioned with another message board. The most common reasons given for the breakaway were that the original forum was too heavily regulated by the moderators, leading to a number of the posters being banned, and that there was continual tension between match-goers and non-match-goers. The Red Brigade population then grew, with invitations to join being sent to posters whose posts were rated by the regular Brigade members from other forums (usually by their 'private message' facilities). Additionally, Brigade posters recommended new members from their circle of match-going friends. Although not all of the Brigade posters were match-goers – and indeed several were not even United fans – this became the most popular method of recruitment because it was felt those posters could be trusted not to be internet 'WUMs' or 'Moles' (internet personas created purely to infiltrate and disrupt forums) and because the Brigade prided itself on being a forum for match-going fans. In 2009, there were over 230 registered users on the forum, although many of these were not active posters. Trips to matches (and other social events) arranged on Red Brigade could bring as many as thirty posters together, making them a coherent sub-group within United's carnival support. On match days this group was often also bolstered by other carnival fans who were friends of active posters.

As a result of this emphasis on face-to-face socialising and attending matches, the Red Brigade had a very strong and distinct identity, both online and around matches. A number of high-profile and senior members of the Brigade provided a focus for match-day 'meets', most notably Jay, who was instrumental in setting up the forum. The Brigade also had its own flag, which would be hung up outside hotels and bars where its posters were drinking, and as well as inside away grounds where United were playing. The Red Brigade message board was split into a number of different forums, including General Chat, Football, Other Sports, Tickets, Gashpad (pornography links), Betting and Food & Drink (where members posted recipes and pictures of meals they had cooked). General Chat tended to be the most popular sub-forum, and contained most of the discussions about plans for trips to matches along with comments about fan issues such as new chants and atmosphere. In addition to this there was also a Match Reports forum where members would post reports, photos and videos from previous matches, usually domestic and European away games. This part of the site performed an important role in allowing the fans to relive moments of carnival from the past, and also in helping new members identify other posters for future meetings. The fact that the Red Brigade forum was both small and closed to outsiders meant that, in contrast to public forums, anonymity was not a key feature of the forum. This led to the same kind of tongue-in-cheek abuse and personal banter online that would be heard between the fans at a match. At times, when reading posts online from members whom I knew well, I could subconsciously hear them speaking the words. This was also noted by Little Jim, who in response to one of my own posts asked, 'Is it weird that I can actually hear you saying this?'.

Mobile phones

The second technological development that had a profound influence on altering the behaviour of carnival fans was the mobile phone and camera phone. In 1995, I did not know a single carnival fan who possessed a mobile phone for personal use (or brought one to matches) but by 2011, it seemed that every member of the United carnival fan groups brought one to matches. If a fan lost their phone, or it was broken or ran out of batteries, this was considered to be out of the ordinary, and the fact they were phone-less was discussed as a potential problem for the rest of the day. The mobile phone's major role for the fans was in organising meeting at matches. For home games, they would text each other to discuss which pubs they were drinking at, and at what time they were meeting. Prior to the use of mobile phones, meeting up before a match was typically done by either arranging in advance or by arriving at the 'usual' pub or club at a certain time. To a certain extent this still went on even in the mobile phone age, and many of the Brigade would simply turn up at a normal location before a match, expecting to bump into their friends. However, this meant that late changes to plans could result in fans not meeting up as expected, and prior to the mobile phone, this could mean that fans would not meet each other as planned, possibly for the duration of the whole day. During the course of my own research with Blackpool fans, because I was not fully integrated into the local network of supporters, this meant I often missed out on late changes to plans. One advantage of this was that

I got the opportunity to meet more supporters, as talking to other Blackpool fans was preferable, and more useful, to standing on my own in a pub. Typically the groups of Blackpool supporters I travelled to games with were those I simply 'bumped into' in the usual places, often in the Tangerine Nitespot before a home match. For away matches, it would be a case of meeting on the train from Blackpool, or in pubs close to the train station or the stadium.

Planning to meet up prior to away matches, particularly infrequent or high-risk ones, was the most valuable use of the mobile phone for carnival fans. Fans would often discuss possible pubs to meet in on the internet forums in the match build-up. However, not all carnival fans posted on these forums, not all were willing to disclose where they would be drinking (particularly if they thought police or 'tourist' fans may be viewing) and plans could change at the last minute, so basing a plan on decisions made in advance was not always wise. Fans travelling to away matches would arrive at the host city at different times and may have different ideas on where they wanted to drink, some wanting the noise and activity of a pub that had been taken over by their team's supporters while others preferred a quieter environment to sit down and drink with their friends. Additionally, sometimes the fans would have their plans changed for them at the last minute, should a pub close its doors to away fans, or should the fans be escorted to a different pub by the police. As a result, if you arrived early in the host city, sending a text to those following saying which pub you were in was considered good manners. Likewise, upon arrival in the host city, texting those who you expected to arrive ahead of you, 'Where are you?' would usually enable you to join the rest of the group.

The mobile phone has therefore taken a lot of the organisation and effort away from groups of carnival fans gathering together for away matches. It was no longer necessary for fans to take a certain train or football special in order to ensure that they would be part of the travelling support (although this was still popular for 'the craic') so long as they had the mobile number of someone in the network of carnival fans that day. It also meant that groups of fans could be more selective in terms of the pubs that they frequented and the company they kept. At United, certain sub-groups of carnival fans often kept themselves separate from other groups, often because they felt they were too rowdy or were likely to cause trouble and/or attract the attention of the police. This was also the case for the hooligan groups, who used mobile phones to try and meet away from the attentions of both the police and non-hooligan fans. The mobile phone therefore provides new challenges for those looking to control and manage football crowds; while on the one hand it may reduce the problem of huge numbers of fans all travelling by one mode of transport (which can pose public order risks), it allows travelling supporters to travel separately and meet in more obscure locations. This means that police will often not know where fans are gathering and can spend considerable time on a match-day attempting to track down groups of supporters they consider may be a risk to public order. Mobiles also proved invaluable for matches abroad where alcohol bans were in place, as carnival fan groups could split resources, locate an establishment breaching the ban and then advertise its location to their friends. Word would then spread and quite obscure and hidden-away bars, cafes, kebab shops or restaurants could be full of hundreds of fans within hours. Again, the local police would often be completely unaware of these gatherings. In Rome in 2007, the mobile phone played a key role in a group of between 250–300 United fans being able to gather in a group and walk up to the stadium, where they were confronted by local hooligans.

Two of the older members of the Red Brigade gave their views on how mobile phones and the internet had changed their match-day experience. As far as they were concerned, the technological developments had been nothing other than beneficial and there was none of the nostalgia for days gone by that I was expecting:

Jay: You only have to take a look at the crowd we've got here today to see the importance of the internet. Before the internet if some of the old crowd didn't come along I might just have a quiet pint with the missus beforehand and that were it, that was your match-day experience … It's probably the best thing to happen to counteract the loss of the old style of football. We've lost the standing, we've lost the pay-on-the-turnstiles, at least we've gained something …

Author: So in the past what did you used to do in terms of meeting up with your mates when you were going to a match? You couldn't go on the message board, you couldn't text to see who was around …

Denis: Ours was coaches. 'Cos we didn't live in town [Manchester]. That was our … we just got leathered on the coach. So you went with the same people… you didn't necessarily like them all, you know what I mean? It's just that you were United supporters, you drank beer and you went to the match … [Denis then stopped going on the coach so that he didn't have to travel with 'some of the dick heads' and ended up in the same situation as Jay, with a limited pool of mates he would regularly go to the game with]. So I would say it's been a massive positive … and I was talking to a few young fellas, and they were saying that they would still be going with their Dad or a [his emphasis] mate if it weren't for the internet where they met like-minded people and now we all meet here, don't they? For a good drink up. It's a good match-day experience, it's been a definite positive.

Author: So you think it means you can be more discriminate about the people you go to the game with?

Denis: Yeah, I absolutely think that … You're always guaranteed your match-day experience now, aren't you, just enjoying company?

Jay: Same couple of pals I'd go with all the time. Sometimes one couldn't go. Sometimes both on the odd occasion – you just had to trundle along on your own then. And then I might even give the pub a swerve. I'd think 'I'll just get there in time for kick-off', I'd go in, go back home …

Camera phones

Mobile phones also performed important cultural functions for carnival fans away from the match day. Text messages in particular would be used to advertise spare tickets or to request tickets for matches. They would also be used to swap jokes (both football related and otherwise), pass comment on football gossip or observations and to circulate the words to new chants. With the advent of integrated cameras, the fans also started to use the mobile phone to record elements of their carnival to show at a later date or post on the internet to a wider audience. During my research I saw photos and videos being taken on mobile phones of fans chanting in pubs, trains and in stadiums, of police escorts, of fights and general crowd disorder, of riot police, and of the actual match itself. This type of carnival fan 'tourism' was not engaged in by all, and indeed some criticised those who used their phones in this way usually because they considered it to be inappropriate; the taking of photos and videos while the match was taking place in particular was considered to be the type of activity the 'tourist' fan would engage in, while the traditional fan should be merely supporting the team. Some carnival fans also objected to the use of photographs and videos because if incidents of disorder occurred, they had the potential to implicate them (although I was aware of no actual instance of this occurring). However, there were usually enough carnival fans recording incidents that some footage of the group's behaviour could be found. Some of the Red Brigade in particular spent time taking and sharing photographs to construct Match Reports of away trips (particularly abroad) to post on the forum. Where video clips were posted on public forums or on sharing websites such as YouTube, these could provide a window into the behaviour of the carnival fans for the armchair fans or 'tourists' who were not normally present at these type of matches. Although the use of such videos to circulate new chants was from my observations not yet influential in creating or circulating new chants for the regulars, it may be that such videos were useful for those outside of these social networks who attended away matches irregularly and wanted to be part of the experience and contribute to the atmosphere.

Another way in which the use of camera phones was starting to influence the match-day experience of carnival fans was through videos of perceived abusive behaviour by stewards and police. Digital cameras and camera phones, along with the increased use of CCTV in stadiums and the increased coverage of matches on television, means that football crowds are now recorded far more than in the past. While some fans objected to this, such coverage was useful when groups of fans came into confrontation with the authorities. In the past, when disorder occurred between fans and police and the two parties disagreed over who was the aggressor, the media and the authorities tended to believe the police account. This gave the impression that when English fans went abroad in particular, large numbers of them travelled with the intention of 'causing trouble' and would embark upon unprovoked violence and disorder, leading to a police response. The views of many fans that disorder was started or escalated by local fans or by aggressive policing or stewarding were normally discounted as being merely the 'excuses' of hooligans (Stott and Pearson, 2007: 33–5). In 1997, however, English fans at the World Cup qualifier in Rome were shown live on television being baton-charged by riot police, and it was clear from the scenes that most of those were not previously disorderly. This was to prove the watershed moment for the British media, who became aware that English fans could be victims as well as aggressors.

After 1997 much media condemnation of English hooligans continued (most notably in Marseilles and Charleroi), but journalists were forced to acknowledge that the situation was not as clear cut as had been previously assumed. While this has not led to a reassessment of the behaviour of English fans *before* this time, where video footage of violent or disproportionate policing exists, fans can expect to receive support they could not have dreamt of in the past. Ten years after England fans were baton-charged on the terraces of the Stadio Olympico in Rome, United fans suffered a similar fate. The official response from the Rome police and the club was that it was the fault of drunken hooligans, but television footage clearly showed innocent fans being beaten, some as they tried to escape, assisted friends or lay on the ground. Again, thanks to the television coverage, the blame was correctly apportioned to the indiscriminate and aggressive policing and sub-standard stadium management. One victim of the police attacks in Rome was Carly, a United carnival fan who was attempting to video the police's aggression when she had her camera snatched from her hand by a police officer. She was then punched in the face and repeatedly struck about the head by a baton. Fortunately, another supporter further up the terrace had been recording the same group of police, and captured the whole assault. The video appeared on the YouTube website soon after under the title 'Lucky old lady' (mistakenly assuming Carly's hair was grey rather than peroxide blonde – she was in fact in her early twenties) and for a time she became a local celebrity, appearing on Italian television and receiving an apology from the mayor of Rome, a new phone, and a VIP visit to the next Roma vs. United match.

Carly's story is an extreme example of the power of new technology in this area, but camera phones in particular empowered fans in their relationship with the police (the same is true of political protests such as the London G-20 in 2009). When incidents occur in football crowds, particularly involving police or stewards, it is likely that some fans will attempt to record it, potentially capturing incidents of violence against fans that can be used in legal action against the aggressor. The presence of this technology may also mean that police and stewards are more careful in dealing with fans and more likely to 'play things by the book'; on a number of occasions at matches I heard officers on the ground shout 'camera' (or an equivalent code word) to warn other officers that their actions were being recorded. On occasion this may have the effect of reducing the peace-keeping (as opposed to law-enforcing) ability of the police in these situations, but it also provides significant protection for fans. When I was assaulted by stewards at a match in 2009 (see Chapter 5), I felt relief about the presence of CCTV cameras and thinking this could have prevented a more serious assault on me by the stewards in question. When the same supervisor verbally abused and threatened a fan of another team several weeks later, this was captured on camera phone and the footage sent to the Football Supporters' Federation and the club in question. The club who prior to seeing the footage had dismissed the fan's complaint, then dismissed the steward.

Carnival by proxy

The powerful combination of camera phone and internet message board is increasingly being used by carnival fans to connect those at the match and those left at home. Internet-compatible phones mean that increasingly fans can browse and post on message boards on trips to the football. On occasion, fans even posted from the match itself, although they were often ridiculed for this. For obscure European away matches, the connection between the travellers and those at home was particularly important. When United played in Turkey in 2009 for example, only five of the Brigade travelled, with the rest considering the trip too expensive, time-consuming or dangerous. However, the thirst for information about those who had travelled was not diminished. The trip provided the first face-to-face meeting with a Turkey-based member of the forum, and so text messages were sent to those in Istanbul requesting photographs of 'Captain Kebab' (many members had assumed he did not exist and was merely a WUM). A photograph of him posing with the Brigade was duly texted and posted on the forum the evening before the match.

The drama that was to occur on the terraces in Turkey (see Chapter 4) was also played out on the Red Brigade forum as it occurred. The initial post was made approximately five minutes after the violence had occurred and the debate continued by text and internet for the following hour. Much of the information, for example about fighting with Turkish fans, was incorrect, having been distilled through previous knowledge of matches in Istanbul and texts from fans in Turkey who had not witnessed the incidents first-hand. However, the picture became clearer over the next hour and eventually the real story emerged:

Posted by Jay –   Just spoke to Dougal. Everyone is bladdered. Denis was apparently in the game, and Dougal thinks he may have butted someone. Apparently he hasn't be nicked, but he's lost his wallet and phone ... and they don't know where he is.

Posted by Moston –   Got a text from 2 people at half time saying his head was cut and he'd been nicked ... Hopefully the folk are right that are saying he hasn't been nicked anyway ... I'd not want to get stuck out there.

Posted by DirkDiggler – A fair few been nicked, it went off with the turks then on each other about 3 hours before the game, ive heard that those that got arrested most were let straight go.

Posted by Moston –   He was with young Billy when something happened at half time and that's all I can make out ... been a struggle getting in touch with folk but the texts I got where thus: 'Denis's been nicked' and then Billy text me with 'Bad news. Denis has been in nicked in Turkey for scrapping. Can you let Jay know just incase he needs to be contacted. He also got his head cut open'.

Posted by Jay – Pancho says he was nicked ... then they slung him out ... then he was back in the ground. He said he was fine except for a cut head and being completely bladdered.

Posted by Moston – Pancho seems a sensible head ... I'm inclined to trust his tale of events ...

Posted by Jay – Just had it confirmed by Pancho ... it was a red on red. An altercation with some cunt in the pub beforehand ... Denis found him on the terrace later. The other bloke came off much worse.

Posted by Jay (some time later) – Good news! Dougal has found him bowling around large as life ... somewhat pissed ... but in good form.

Posted by Great_Gonzo – Any updates? My phone SIM is fucked so cannot receive any texts etc etc, so any updates would be appreciated.

The next day, following much initial concern and then relief from the members of the Brigade still at home, Moston posted a photo of Denis on the terrace to prove he was unhurt. Denis and the rest of the travellers were still in Istanbul, the excitement of the night having been played out almost in real-time over the internet.

Retro fandom in the digital age

New technology and its convergence is clearly having a huge impact upon the expression of fan culture by carnival fans, but it is likely that the impact of this is most keenly felt at the clubs with big and geographically diverse supports, such as United and Liverpool. Indeed, groups like the Red Brigade, are probably at the forefront of the use of new technology in their fan culture and the way in which they use the internet in particular may not be representative of carnival groups, even at United. However, as younger fans become more influential fans within these groups over time, this may well change and the camera phone and the internet forum are likely to become an even more significant way in which fan culture is expressed. Currently, however, the use of technology by carnival fans is used in limited circumstances and for limited purposes.

Noticeably, carnival fans appeared to be using new technology to express and share a version of fan culture that was extremely traditional or, for younger fans, decidedly 'retro'. Among the United carnival groups in particular, younger fans attempted to reproduce a stylised version of fandom from the 1970s and 1980s, viewing recent fandom experiences through a cultural filter based on their understandings of the nature of fandom in this period. Experiences that were believed to reflect this period were considered to be 'good' expressions of fandom, those that did not were considered to demonstrate the decline in the quality of fan culture. At United, much of this view was drawn from video clips of fandom from the 1970s (which remains the most influential period upon fan culture among United carnival fans), although some was also drawn from the tales of older members of the fan groups and hoolie-lit. A search of YouTube will uncover videos of rowdy fan behaviour at recent matches mixed in with clips of the retro period, with each reinforcing the view that the older period represented 'genuine' fandom which has at every opportunity to be repeated in order to authenticate the new carnival fan groups' own expressions of fandom. Ironically for carnival fans, the mobile phone and the internet forum provided effective tools not to introduce new forms of fandom, but to re-enact their view of traditional fandom.

Conclusion

The greatest change in terms of fan behaviour observed over the sixteen-year period of this research came from the introduction of new technology. Mobile phones and the internet, and the powerful combination of both, provided a new way for carnival fans groups to communicate, congregate and express themselves. Internet forums in particular assisted like-minded fans to identify and integrate themselves into carnival groups and mobile phones enabled fans to be more selective in terms of who they attended matches with, possibly accentuating subcultural identities and divisions with a club's wider support. It would appear that this technology has strengthened the hand of the carnival fan groups, who at Manchester United and England remain at the forefront of the influential fan forums, and many of the developments are currently being used largely to reinforce traditional views of fan expression and behaviour. However it is likely that the true potential of technology and convergence has yet to be seen in football crowds, with the opportunity for fans who do not travel in groups to away matches to gain influence over chant generation and trends in fashion and behaviour that are currently controlled by the carnival fans.

Note

1 *Etherington and Punter* v. *Chief Constable of West Yorkshire Police*, Leeds Crown Court 6–8/10/10; *Chief Constable of Avon and Somerset* v. *Bargh*, Bristol Magistrates' Court 27/01/11.

9

Conclusions

Football as carnival

For a large number of football fans who travel home and away with their team, fandom is analogous to carnival. For the fans observed during the period of this research, a key motivation, if not the *primary* motivation for travelling to matches was to experience and take an active role in the carnivalesque. For these 'carnival fans', gathering in large groups, singing, drinking and being rowdy was at least as important than what was actually happening on the pitch. As we have seen, viewing football fandom as an expression of the carnivalesque is not a new concept (Giulianotti, 1991, 1995; Brown, 1993; Hughson, 2002; Jones, 2006), but we should be careful about how we use this analogy, particularly bearing in mind the fact that football supporters (even match-going ones) belong to many different groups and subcultures who sometimes have little in common other than the team they are supporting on the pitch. I do not claim that all football fans are carnival fans (and it should be reiterated that this is not a label that is used by the fans themselves), rather that these are a distinct subculture within English match-going support, who from my observations dominated the consti-tution of the teams' support away from home but formed only a small part of overall football support. Many football fans did not want to engage in carnival-esque activity and for some it provided a practical inconvenience and distraction from the 'serious business' of watching the team, or enjoying a safe and well-regulated family day out. However, while only forming a small part of the club's overall support, this subculture were disproportionately influential on creating 'atmosphere' at matches, and without their networks and activities football grounds would be much quieter and less passionate environments.

We must also be careful about using the carnival analogy due to the wildly varying understandings of what carnival means. Most late twentieth century academic discussion about carnival has been based upon Mikhail Bakhtin's version of carnival in early modern Europe and it is this understanding that forms the basis for my own use of the term. Carnival is the 'second life' of the people (Bakhtin, 1984), a time of 'ecstatic collectivity' (Stam, 1988: 135), when the world is turned 'upside down' (Curtuis, 1953; Burke, 2002) or 'inside out' (Bakhtin, 1984). It is a period of transgression from the norm (Presdee, 2002) that sits between order and complete lawlessness (Presdee, 2002: 32) and that is frequently recalled, and anticipated with great excitement (Caillois, 1950). It was these general themes of change, transgression and collective ecstasy that were so heavily ingrained in the views of the research participants about what constituted a rewarding football experience. But we should not take this analogy too far. It was tempting to engage on a flight of fancy by viewing the subculture of the carnival fan through the lens of Bakhtin, where hierarchy and status is reversed; on a Euro away does the jibber become king and the prostitute queen? In reality of course, while the successful jibber will certainly gain reputation and will have his/her moment of glory, failure was as likely, and those who make the important practical decisions on these football trips – e.g. where to travel to, which hotels and bars to stay at – tended to be the senior, reputationally established fans who had access to tickets. As for the prostitute, she remained an abused figure of ridicule and fun even during the duration of the trip. Indeed, the powerful in terms of status largely remained in this position during the football carnival (as we have seen, policing of football crowds is often more draconian than 'normal' life), and Stam would argue that the reaffirmation of the dominant masculine culture that took place during these trips means they were not 'a Bakhtinian celebration of people's culture' (1988: 135).

However, this in and of itself does not mean that these collective experiences were not a reworking of carnival. There is considerable dispute as to how accurate Bakhtin's depiction is, with some suggestion that his view is 'nostalgic and overly-optimistic' (Stallybrass and White, 1986: 18) particularly in terms of the suspension of the normal rules of hierarchical rank and the redistribution of social roles. Indeed, Stallybrass and White argue that, 'carnival often abuses and demonizes *weaker*, not stronger, social groups – women, ethnic and religious minorities, those who "don't belong"' (*ibid.*: 19). They also point out that carnival varied from place to place (*ibid.*: 178). When using the metaphor of carnival to explain the motivations of this subculture of fans we need to accept that we are not using a static singular concept, but instead a collection of ideas focused on the concepts of collectivity, pleasure, transgression and change. These were the aims of the carnival fans as, it is claimed, they were the ideals behind carnival. Football matches and the social space around them provided an opportunity to achieve these goals, but the extent to which they succeeded depended on issues such as numbers, environment, policing and, occasionally, the result of the match itself. The majority of matches did not result in anything like 'the world turned upside down', but this was probably true of many carnivals in early-modern Europe. Nevertheless, in order to understand this subculture of fans, it is essential to acknowledge this driving force behind many of their individual and collective actions and decisions.

Another caveat is that football was not necessarily the *only* expression of the carnivalesque for the fans. Here, of course, the author cannot speak with complete authority, having not observed the research participants extensively in their non-football environments. However, stories that were told to me of some of the carnival fans being 'off their face' on stag parties and Saturday nights out indicated that football was for some only one opportunity to pursue the carnivalesque. To a greater or lesser extent, drugs, drink and occasionally prostitutes were used outside of the football environment by groups to assist in achieving this state of change and transgression, and I would agree with the views of Hobbs (2003), Presdee (2002), Tomsen (1997) and Winlow and Hall (2006) that contemporary urban leisure is an expression, remnant or reworking of carnival. However, for the research participants, football crowds had the potential for the *ultimate* expression of collective ecstasy, and for some fans, particularly older fans or those with child-care commitments, football provided one of the only real opportunities to 'get away from it all'. Whether it possesses a cathartic function necessary for 'social survival' (Presdee, 2002: 33), or an unconscious desire to escape from the misery and 'cultural frustration' of civilisation (Freud, 1961) was beyond the capability of this research but it was clear that for carnival fans, participating in a football carnival was viewed as an essential part of life generally.

The term 'carnival fan' in this book is therefore one that should be used with care, and it should be acknowledged that with all attempts to label different subcultures of football fans, there are individuals that may flit between one label and another depending on the match or season in question. For example at certain matches (e.g. cup finals), those normally viewed as 'tourists' or 'day trippers' would engage in carnivalesque activity, as on occasion would 'hooligans' who wanted to take their family to such an important match rather than spend the time around it in their firm. Similarly, the carnival fan was not *always* looking to create a carnival – sometimes for example they may be the only one of their group with a ticket, and simply travel to and from the stadium in order to watch the match. But from my observations the term had more meaning in its ability to describe a culturally cohesive group, than the term 'hooligan'. This latter term appears to be becoming increasingly redundant as a label to describe those who actually fight at football matches; many of those identified as 'hooligans' did not engage in regular violence, whereas 'non-hooligan' (often replica-shirt-wearing) fans were witnessed on many occasions becoming involved in both disorder and quite serious interpersonal violence. However, while carnival activity was engaged in on occasion by tourists, anoraks or hooligans, for the fans detailed in this book, engaging in the carnivalesque was their primary motivation throughout a season.

Whither the carnival fan?

One opinion of the carnival fans that was repeated at Blackpool, United and England was that their style of support was on the wane and that the 'craic' of going to football with your mates was not as good as it had been in the past. This view was even shared by younger fans who could not have remembered previous eras of football fandom but who had received this perceived wisdom from older fans (a view particularly reinforced on internet message boards). The atmosphere at games was also perceived to be diminishing, with fewer fans chanting, more women and 'tourists', and more fans leaving early. Reasons given by the carnival fans were the difficulty of getting tickets, increasing price of tickets, removal of the terraces (making it more difficult for friends to stand together) and the increased regulation in and around football grounds by the police. One overriding perception was that this 'taming' of the football fan was primarily the result of the traditional working-class fan being excluded, mainly due to pricing of tickets. The limitations of this research (both the time spent in each field and the number of clubs researched) makes it difficult to reach robust conclusions about this common perception, but my observations casted doubt on its validity. While it is probably true that there are large sections of traditional working-class fans that have been excluded from the modern game, this does not necessarily mean that carnival fandom is on the wane. There was certainly no clear link from my observations between class background and fans who engaged in the carnivalesque type of activity detailed in these pages.

Indeed, my observations suggested that the carnivalesque form of fandom was retaining its dominance at matches away from home in particular. First, larger numbers of fans have the ability to travel to away matches now than previously. The advent of budget airlines means that Euro aways can sometimes be cheaper than trips to the other side of the country, and carnival fan groups now have the ability, through cheap travel, opening borders, and access to cross-border information and technology, to express their version of the carnivalesque regularly in places as far-flung as Russia and Turkey. The idea of travelling in huge numbers (even without tickets) to engage in a football carnival around a match is increasingly ingrained in the culture of England fans in particular, with as many as 70,000 travelling to Frankfurt for the 2006 World Cup, half of whom would never get access to the stadium but were satisfied drinking, singing and decorating the town squares with their flags. Indeed, in contrast to earlier observations with England fans, the 2004 European Championships and the 2006 World Cup saw the organisers welcoming ticketless fans to just come and enjoy the party, with large-scale events and match-screenings set up specifically to accommodate them.

Second, it may also be that as a response to the perceived 'bourgeoisification' of football support more generally, these fan groups are escalating their carnivalesque activity in order to differentiate themselves from the 'tourists'. Finally, while the pricing-out of working-class fans may have reduced carnivalesque expressions of fandom at home in the past (e.g. on the terraced Stretford End), there was little evidence from my observations that it would reduce the power of carnival fan groups more generally. It should be reiterated that the carnival fans observed at all clubs were not primarily drawn from the working class in terms of income, although they did express what might be considered traditional working-class attitudes. Part of the attraction for some of the middle-class fans was precisely the fun and excitement of acting in this way; some fans were observed selling on their own ticket in order to be able to 'jib' into a ground, or sneaking alcohol into a ground or pub rather than paying the full price, and the driving force behind this behaviour was often more a statement of transgression than an economic necessity. In this sense many of the carnival fans could be said to fit the depiction of the class tourist from Pulp's' 'Common People'.[1]

However, there are dangers for the future of the carnival fan groups. It may be that other opportunities for expressions of the carnivalesque are starting to become more enticing for those who currently see football as the main opportunity to engage in collective hedonism and expression. For example the number of music festivals is increasing, and are typically much less regulated in terms of alcohol and drug consumption than football matches. Thanks to budget airlines, stag parties, package holidays and weekend 'benders' abroad are often cheaper than a trip to the football. Even a Saturday night out in a home town can also provide opportunity for carnival with greater access to beer and women – and for some– the opportunity for violence, than the football match. All of these opportunities could lead to the number of fans who use football as a way of expressing the carnivalesque to drop. Finally, another risk to the power of the carnival fan groups comes from online social networking. This has the potential to reduce the influence and the power of the carnival fan groups as it has the power to open up information and networks currently guarded jealously by these groups to a team's wider fan base. While my observations suggested that online social networking was thus far being used to reinforce the existing culture of the carnival fan, it clearly has the potential to allow non-carnival fans to begin to participate more fully in, for example, new football chants, or changes to behaviour or dress sense.

Recommendations for those managing football crowds

One finding from this ethnography was that the carnival fan groups can be difficult to manage at times. Quite often their motivations are at odds with those attempting to manage and control football crowds and I have documented dozens of instances when disputes and confrontations have occurred between the fans and police or match-day stewards over issues both inside and outside the ground. As a result it might be attractive for clubs to try to reduce the numbers of carnival fans who attend matches and replace them with more conformist 'tourist' fans, 'anoraks' and families. After all, my observations suggested that the carnival fans only rarely bought official club merchandise (certainly in comparison to other fan groups), tended to travel independently, arrived late at grounds, ignored their designated seat, persistently stood contrary to ground regulations, engaged in (and created) abusive, homophobic, sexist and occasionally racist chants and also had a tendency for ignoring lesser games (with some only attending away matches, thus denying the home club gate revenue). On occasion they were also abusive towards other customers and club employees, 'jibbed' into matches for free and became involved in disorder and even violence. For the actual amount of money they spent on the club they support in contrast to the trouble that seemed to surround them, clubs might be tempted to think that they are not worth it, and instead concentrate on more compliant fan groups.

However observations at all clubs demonstrated that these fans performed a vital role in creating football's unique 'atmosphere'. This atmosphere is beneficial to clubs in the following ways. First, it makes them commercially more attractive, both to non-carnival spectators (who seemed to enjoy there being atmosphere around them at matches even if they did not participate) and to broadcasters. As Taylor notes, 'the most remarkable and gripping feature of football has always been its supporters, with their outlandish garb, fierce enthusiasm and idealistic investments of time, energy and money ... In the end the crowd is the supreme authority without which the golden core of the game has no currency' (1992: 185, 188). It was noticeable that visually striking, but illegal activity, such as mass pitch invasions and the lighting of distress flares in stadiums was often focused on to demonstrate the passion of the fans or the importance of a match in marketing campaigns by both clubs and broadcasters. Second, 'atmosphere' was considered to be beneficial to the team on the pitch, with players and managers frequently urging the supporters to increase the noise in the stadium. Football without the carnival fan would certainly be less unruly, but it would be quieter and possibly less commercially attractive. And this is assuming that it would even be possible to exclude the carnival fan groups from matches; we have seen that a lack of tickets will not always mean fans will not travel if there is the opportunity to engage in a football carnival around the match, and also the regularity with which *non-carnival* fans will engage in carnivalesque activity around significant football matches. There may even be a tentative argument that the carnival fan groups can be beneficial in public order terms by providing 'hooligans' with an acceptable route out of the hooligan firm activities. Additionally, if the views of the fans were to be believed, in wider public order terms it was likely that many of the problems associated with the carnival fan groups would simply be displaced and the carnival fans would merely look to express their version of the carnivalesque elsewhere.

The recommendation for football clubs, governing bodies, local authorities and the police is therefore that carnival fan groups need to be recognised as a distinct sub-group within the wider football supporter base, and this understanding needs to be at a much more developed level than considering them merely as 'maverick' or 'Category B' fans in terms of their potential for becoming involved in disorder (which as we have seen, varies widely within the groups themselves). The overall perceptions, interpretations and motivations of these groups need to be understood in order to ensure that they continue to perform their positive function within match-going support, while at the same time attempting to separate these groups from those who may attend football with the intention of causing disorder. Engaging the carnival fans is not, however, an easy task. As this book has documented, attempts by clubs and local authorities to create or control the carnival are often not appreciated and are sometimes rebelled against. Observations suggested that the more 'official' the carnival was, the less support it would get from the carnival fans, which again fits in with Bakhtin's notion of carnival; there needs to be a sense that the carnival fans are transgressing the norms of accepted behaviour in order for the carnival to be alluring. 'Flag days' at Manchester United or Blackpool's 'carnival atmosphere initiative' were largely ignored by carnival fans, and often purposefully opposed.

That said, attempts by authorities to create a space (not just geographically, but also socially and legally) for carnival were more successful and this, observations and other research have suggested, can also assist in the successful policing and management of football crowds. For this to work, police and local authorities have to be seen by the fans to be part of the carnival, even if in little more than an observational capacity. As we have seen, positive interaction with fans is vital to public order, and where police are seen to be assisting fans in creating and maintaining their carnival, the fans will often isolate real 'hooligans', and be more accepting of tolerance limits placed upon them. As these pages have, it is hoped, shown, the carnival fan groups are exceptionally resourceful and resilient, and show no sign of abandoning football however much they may resent its increasing commercialisation. The carnival will continue; the only question appears to be, by whose rules?

Note

1 'I want to live like common people. I want to do whatever common people do.'

References

Ackroyd, S. and P. Thompson, *Organizational Misbehaviour* (London: Sage, 2003).

Adler, P. and P. Adler, 'Moving backwards', in J. Ferrell and M. Hamm (eds), *Ethnography at the Edge: Crime, Deviance and Field Research* (Boston: Northeastern University Press, 1998).

Adorno, T., *Against Epistemology: A Metacritique* (Oxford: Blackwell, 1982).

Allen, J., *Bloody Casuals* (Glasgow: Famedram, 1989).

Armstrong, G., 'Like that Desmond Morris?', in G. Armstrong, D. Hobbs and T. May (eds), *Interpreting the Field: Accounts of Ethnography* (Oxford: Oxford University Press, 1993), pp. 3–44.

—— *Football Hooligans: Knowing the Score* (Oxford: Berg, 1998).

Armstrong, G. and M. Young, 'Fanatical football chants: Creating and controlling the carnival', in G. Finn and R. Giulianotti (eds), *Football Culture: Local Contests, Global Visions* (London: Frank Cass, 2000), pp. 171–211.

Atkinson, P., *The Ethnographic Imagination: Textual Constructions of Reality* (London: Routledge, 1994).

Back, L., T. Crabbe and J. Solomos, *The Changing Face of Football: Racism, Identity and Multiculture in the English Game* (Oxford: Berg, 2001).

Bakhtin, M., *Rabelais and His World* (Bloomington: Midland Books/Indiana University Press, 1984).

Becker, H. and B. Greer, 'Participant observation and interviewing: A comparison', in W. Filstead (ed.), *Qualitative Methodology: Firsthand Involvement with the Social World* (Chicago: Markham, 1970).

Berger, P. and T. Luckmann, *The Social Construction of Reality* (Harmondsworth: Penguin, 1962).

Bittner, E., 'The police on skid row: A study of peacekeeping', *American Sociological Review*, 32(5) (1967): 699–715.

Bourgois, P., *In Search of Respect: Selling Crack in El Barrio* (Cambridge: Cambridge University Press, 2006).

Brabbie, E., *The Practice of Social Research* (London: Wadsworth, 1989).

Brimson, D. and E. Brimson, *Everywhere We Go* (London: Headline, 1996).

Bromberger, C., A. Hayot and J. Mariottini, 'Allez L'OM, forza Juve: The passion for football in Marseille and Turin', in S. Redhead, *The Passion and the Fashion: Football Fandom in New Europe* (Aldershot: Avebury, 1993), pp. 103–51.

Brown, A., 'United we stand: Some problems with fan democracy', in A. Brown (ed.), *Fanatics! Power, Identity and Fandom in Football* (London: Routledge, 1998), pp. 50–67.

—— 'Ratfink reds: Montpellier and Rotterdam in 1991', in S. Redhead (ed.), *The Passion and the Fashion: Football Fandom in New Europe* (Aldershot: Avebury, 1993), pp. 33–44.

Bruyn, S., 'The new empiricists: The participant observer and the phenomenologist', in W. Filstead (ed.), *Qualitative Methodology: Firsthand Involvement with the Social World* (Chicago: Markham, 1970), pp. 283–7.

Bulmer, M., 'The merits and demerits of covert participant observation', in M. Bulmer (ed.), *Social Research Ethics* (New York: Holmes & Meier, 1982), pp. 217–51.

Burgess, R., *In the Field* (London: Routledge, 1991).

Burke, P., *Popular Culture in Early Modern Europe* (Aldershot: Ashgate, 2002).

Caillois, R., *L'homme et le sacré* (Paris: Gallimard, 1950).

Cohen, S., *Folk Devils and Moral Panics* (London: Routledge, 2002).

Collinson, D., *Managing the Shopfloor: Subjectivity, Masculinity and Workplace Culture* (Berlin: William de Gruyter, 1992).

Coomber, R., 'Protecting our research subjects, our data and ourselves from respective prosecution, seizure and summons/subpoena', *Addiction Research and Theory*, 10(1) (2002): 1–5.

Crabbe, T., 'The public gets what the public wants: England football fans, "truth" claims and mediated realities', *International Review for the Sociology of Sport*, 38(4) (2003): 413–25.

Crolley, L., 'Lads will be lads', in M. Perryman (ed.), *The Ingerland Factor: Home Truths from Football* (Edinburgh: Mainstream, 1999), pp. 59–70.

Crow, G., R. Wiles, S. Heath and V. Charles, 'Research ethics and data quality: The implications of informed consent', *International Journal of Social Research Methodology*, 9(2) (2006): 83–95.

Curtuis, E. R., *European Literature and the Latin Middle Ages* (New York: Pantheon, 1953).

Dal Lago, A. and R. De Biasi, 'Italian football fans: Culture and organisation', in R. Giulianotti, N. Bonney and M. Hepworth (eds), *Football, Violence and Social Identity* (London: Routledge, 1994).

Davies, A., 'Those viragoes are no less cruel than the lads: Young women, gangs and violence in late Victorian Manchester and Salford', *British Journal of Criminology*, 39(1) (1999): 72–89.

—— *The Gangs of Manchester* (Preston: Milo Books, 2009).

Deehan, A., 'Alcohol and crime: Taking stock', *Policing and Reducing Crime Unit. Crime Reduction Research Series*, Paper 3 (London: HMSO, 1999).

Department of Health and Social Security, *Drinking Sensibly* (London: HMSO, 1981).

Drury, J., S. Reicher and C. Stott, 'Transforming the boundaries of collective identity: From the local anti-road campaign to global resistance?', *Social Movement Studies*, 2 (2001): 191–212.

Dunning, E., 'The social roots of football hooliganism: A reply to critics of the "Leicester School"', in R. Giulianotti, N. Bonney and M. Hepworth (eds), *Football, Violence and Social Identity* (London: Routledge, 1994).

Dunning, E., P. Murphy and I. Waddington, 'Anthropological versus sociological approaches to the study of soccer hooliganism: some critical notes', *Sociological Review*, 39(3) (1991): 459–78.

Dunning, E., P. Murphy and J. Williams, *The Roots of Football Hooliganism* (London: Routledge, 1988).

Durkheim, E., *The Rules of Sociological Method* (London: Macmillan, 1964).

Elias, N., *What Is Sociology?* (London: Hutchinson, 1978).

Elias, N. and E. Dunning, *The Quest for Excitement: Sport and Leisure in the Civilising Process* (Dublin: University College of Dublin Press, 2008).

Emerson, R., *Contemporary Field Research: A Collection of Readings* (Boston: Little, Brown and Company, 1983).

Engels, F., *The Condition of the Working Class in England* (Oxford: Oxford University Press: 2009).

Erikson, K., 'A comment on disguised observation in sociology', *Social Problems*, 14 (1967): 366–73.

Feenan, D., 'Researching paramilitary violence in Northern Ireland', *International Journal of Social Research Methodology*, 5(2) (2002): 147–63.

Ferdinand, J. M., G. Pearson, M. Rowe and F. Worthington, 'A different kind of ethics', *Ethnography*, 8(4) (2007): 521–44.

Ferrell, J. and M. Hamm, 'True confessions: Crime, deviance and field research', in J. Ferrell and M. Hamm (eds), *Ethnography at the Edge: Crime, Deviance and Field Research* (Boston: Northeastern University Press, 1998), pp. 2–19.

Festinger, L. and D. Katz, *Research Methods in the Behavioural Sciences* (New York: Holt, Rinehart & Winston, 1953).

Fleisher, M., 'Ethnographers, pimps and the company store', in J. Ferrell and M. Hamm (eds), *Ethnography at the Edge: Crime, Deviance and Field Research* (Boston: Northeastern University Press, 1998), pp. 44–64.

Fonarow, W., *Empire of Dirt: The Aesthetics and Rituals of British Indie Music* (Middletown: Weslayan University Press, 2006).

Fox, K., *Watching the English: The Hidden Rules of English Behaviour* (London: Hodder & Stoughton, 2005).

Frake, C., 'Ethnography', in R. Emerson (ed.), *Contemporary Field Research: A Collection of Readings* (Boston: Little, Brown and Company, 1983), pp. 60–7.

Frankfort-Nachmias, C. and D. Nachmias, *Research Methods in the Social Sciences* (London: St Martin's Press, 1992).

Freud, S., *Civilization and Its Discontents* (New York: W. W. Norton & Company, 1961).

Friedrichs, J. and H. Ludtke, *Participant Observation: Theory and Practice* (Westmead: Saxon House/Lexington Books, 1975).

Frosdick, S. and P. Marsh, *Football Hooliganism* (Cullompton: Willan, 2005).

Gadamer, H., *Truth and Method* (London: Sheed and Ward, 1989).

Garfinkel, H., *Studies in Ethnomethodology* (Cambridge: Polity Press, 1984).

Geertz, C., *The Interpretation of Cultures* (London: Hutchinson, 1973).

—— 'Thick description: Toward an interpretive theory of culture', in R. Emerson (ed.), *Contemporary Field Research: A Collection of Readings* (Boston: Little, Brown and Company: 1983), pp. 37–59.

—— *Works and Lives* (Cambridge: Polity Press, 1988).

Gibbs, J., 'Alcohol consumption, cognition and context: Examining tavern violence', in A. Campbell and J. Gibbs (eds), *Violent Transactions: The Limits of Personality* (Oxford: Blackwell, 1986), pp. 133–52.

Giulianotti, R., 'Scotland's Tartan Army in Italy: The case for the carnivalesque', *Sociological Review*, 39(3) (1991): 503–27.

—— 'Football and the politics of carnival: An ethnographic study of Scottish fans in Sweden', *International Review for the Sociology of Sport*, 30(2) (1995): 191–223.

—— *Football: A Sociology of the Global Game* (Cambridge: Polity Press, 2000).

Goffman, E., *The Presentation of Self in Everyday Life* (Harmondsworth: Penguin, 1984).

Hall, S., 'The treatment of "football hooligans" in the press', in R. Ingham, S. Hall, J. Clarke,

P. Marsh and J. Donovan (eds), *Football Hooliganism: The Wider Context* (London: Inter-Action Inprint, 1978), pp. 15–37.

Hammersley, M., 'Are ethical committees ethical?', *Qualitative Researcher*, 2 (2006): 4–8.

Heidegger, M., *Being and Time* (Oxford: Oxford University Press, 1962).

Hobbs, D., *Bad Business: Professional Crime in Modern Britain* (Oxford: Oxford University Press, 1995).

—— *Doing the Business: Entrepreneurship, Detectives and the Working Class in the East End of London* (Oxford: Clarendon, 1996).

Hobbs, D., P. Hadfield, S. Lister and S. Winlow, *Bouncers: Violence and Governance in the Night-time Economy* (Oxford: University Press, 2003).

Hornby, N., *Fever Pitch* (London: Victor Gollancz, 1992).

Hughson, J., 'Among the thugs: The "new ethnographies" of football supporting subcultures', *International Review for the Sociology of Sport*, 33(1) (1998): 43–57.

—— 'Australian soccer's "ethnic" tribes: A new case for the carnivalesque', in E. Dunning, P. Murphy, I. Waddington and A. Astrinakis (eds), *Fighting Fans: Football Hooliganism as a World Phenomenon* (Dublin: University College Dublin Press, 2002).

Husserl, E., *Ideas: General Introduction to Pure Phenomenology* (London: Allen & Unwin, 1931).

—— *The Idea of Phenomenology* (The Hague: Martinus Nijhoff, 1964).

Inglis, S. (ed.), *The Best of Charles Buchan's Football Monthly* (London: English Heritage and Football Monthly, 2006).

Jacobs, B.A. 'Researching crack dealers: Dilemmas and contradictions', in J. Ferrell and M. Hamm (eds), *Ethnography at the Edge: Crime, Deviance and Field Research* (Boston: Northeastern University Press, 1998), pp. 160–77.

James, M. and G. Pearson, 'Football banning orders: Analysing their use in court', *Journal of Criminal Law*, 70(6) (2006): 509–30.

Johnson, J., 'Trust and personal involvements in fieldwork', in R. Emerson (ed.), *Contemporary Field Research: A Collection of Readings* (Boston: Little, Brown and Company, 1983), pp. 203–15.

Jones, K., '"Get your kit off" isn't sexist: Women's responses to gender abuse in English football crowds'. Paper presented at the annual meeting of the American Sociological Association, Montreal, Quebec 10 August 2006 (www.allacademic.com /meta/p105543_index.html).

King, A., 'Football fandom and post-national identity in new Europe', *British Journal of Sociology*, 51:3 (2000), 419–42.

—— *The End of the Terraces: The Transformation of English Football in the 1990s* (London: Leicester University Press, 2002).

—— *The European Ritual: Football in the New Europe* (Aldershot: Ashgate, 2003).

Kurt, R., *As the Reds Go Marching on* (Edinburgh: Mainstream, 1995).

Lakoff, G. and M. Johnson, *Metaphors We Live by* (Chicago: University of Chicago Press, 1980).

Lipsey, M., D. Wilson, M. Cohen and J. Derzon, 'Is there a causal relationship between alcohol use and violence? A synthesis of evidence', in M. Galanter (ed.), *Recent Developments in Alcoholism: Volume 13 Alcohol and Violence* (Dordrecht: Kluwer, 1997), pp. 245–82.

MacAndrew, C. and R. Edgerton, *Drunken Comportment: A Social Explanation* (London: Thomas Nelson, 1969).

Marsh, P., *Aggro: The Illusion of Violence* (London: Dent, 1978).

Marsh, P. and K. Kibby, *Drinking and Public Disorder* (London: Portman Group, 1992).

Marsh, P., E. Rosser and R. Harré, *The Rules of Disorder* (London: Routledge, 1978).

McElhone, F., *Football Crowd Behaviour: Report by a Working Group Appointed by the Secretary of State for Scotland* (Scottish Education Department/HMSO, 1977).

Millward, P., 'We've all got the bug for Euro aways', *International Review for the Sociology of Sport*, 41(3) (2006): 357–75.

—— 'Glasgow Rangers supporters in the city of Manchester: The degeneration of a "fan party" into a "hooligan riot"', *International Review for the Sociology of Sport*, 44(4) (2009): 381–98.

Morris, D., *The Soccer Tribe* (London: Jonathan Cape, 1981).

Murphy, P., E. Dunning and J. Williams, *Football on Trial* (London: Routledge, 1990).

Norris, C., 'Some ethical considerations on field-work with the police', in D. Hobbs, and T. May (eds), *Interpreting the Field: Accounts of Ethnography* (Oxford: Oxford University Press, 1993), pp. 122–44.

O'Neill, M., *Policing Football: Social Interaction and Negotiated Disorder* (Houndmills: Palgrave Macmillan, 2005).

O'Neill, T., *Red Army General* (Preston: Milo Books, 2005).

—— *The Men in Black* (Preston: Milo Books, 2006).

Patrick, J., *A Glasgow Gang Observed* (London: Methuen, 1973).

Pearson, G., 'Legal responses to football hooliganism' (Ph.D. dissertation, University of Lancaster, 1999).

—— 'The English disease? The socio-legal construction of football hooliganism', *Youth and Policy*, 60 (1998): 1–15.

—— 'The researcher as hooligan: Where "participant" observation means breaking the law', *International Journal of Social Research Methodology*, 12(3) (2009): 243–55.

Pearson, G. and A. Sale, 'On the lash: Revisiting the effectiveness of alcohol controls at football matches', *Policing and Society*, 21(1) (2011): 1–17.

Pearson, Geoffrey, *Hooligan – A History of Respectable Fears* (London: Macmillan, 1983).

—— 'Talking a good fight: Authenticity and distance in the ethnographer's craft', in D. Hobbs and T. May (eds), *Interpreting the Field: Accounts of Ethnography* (Oxford: Clarendon Press, 1993).

Percy, M. and R. Taylor, 'Something for the weekend, sir? Leisure, ecstasy and identity in football and contemporary religion', *Leisure Studies*, 16(1) (1997): 37–49.

Pernanen, K., 'Alcohol and crimes of violence', in B. Kissin and H. Begleiter (eds), *The Biology of Alcoholism: Social Aspects of Alcoholism* (New York: Free Press, 1976).

Pihl, R. O., 'Alcohol and Aggression: A Psychological Perspective', in E. Gottheil, K. Druley, T. Skoloda and H. Waxman (eds), *Alcohol, Drug Abuse and Aggression* (Springfield: Charles Thomas, 1983), pp. 292–313.

Polsky, N., *Hustlers, Beats and Others* (Chicago: Aldine, 1969).

Presdee, M., *Cultural Criminology and the Carnival of Crime* (London: Routledge, 2002).

Redhead, S., *The Passion and the Fashion: Football Fandom in New Europe* (Aldershot: Avebury, 1993).

—— *Post-Fandom and the Millennial Blues: The Transformation of Soccer Culture* (London: Routledge, 1997).

—— 'Little hooliganz: The inside story of glamorous lads, football hooligans and post-subculturalism', *Entertainment and Sports Law Journal*, 8(2) (2010).

Reynolds, P., 'Moral judgements: Strategies for analysis with application to covert participant observation', in M. Bulmer (ed.), *Social Research Ethics* (New York: Holmes & Meier, 1982), pp. 185–216.

Rookwood, J., 'Fan perspectives on football hooliganism' (Ph.D. dissertation, University of Liverpool, 2008).

Rookwood, J. and G. Pearson, 'The hoolifan: Positive attitudes to football "hooliganism"', *International Review for the Sociology of Sport*, 47(2) (2012): 149–64.

Roversi, A., 'Football violence in Italy', *International Review for the Sociology of Sport*, 26(4) (1986): 311–32.

Sale, A., 'Chaos and order? Etnografia dell'ordinario conflitto tra tifosi e polizia in Italia e Gran Bretagna' (Ph.D. dissertation, University of Milano-Bicocca, 2010).

Sales, R., *English Literature in History 1780–1830: Pastoral and Politics* (London: Hutchinson, 1983).

Schutz, A., *The Phenomenology of the Social World* (London: Heinemann Educational, 1972).

Sellitz, C., H. Jahoba, M. Deutsch and S. W. Cook, *Research Methods in Social Relations* (London: Methuen, 1965).

Shepherd, J., M. Irish, C. Scully and I. J. Lesley, 'Alcohol consumption among victims of violence and among comparable UK populations', *British Journal of Addiction*, 84 (1989): 1045–51.

Silverman, D., *Interpretating Qualitative Data* (London: Sage, 1993).

Sinclair, S., *The Blackpool Rock* (Preston: Milo, 2009).

Stallybrass, P. and A. White, *The Politics and Poetics of Transgression* (London: Methuen, 1986).

Stam, R., 'Mikhail Bakhtin and left cultural critique', in E. Kaplan (ed.), *Post-modernism and Its Discontents* (London: Verso, 1988), pp. 116–45.

Stott, C., O. Adang, A. Livingstone and M. Schreiber, 'Variability in the collective behaviour of England fans at Euro2004: "Hooliganism", public order policing and social change', *European Journal of Social Psychology*, 37 (2007): 75–100.

Stott, C., P. Hutchinson and J. Drury, '"Hooligans" abroad? Inter-group dynamics, social identity and participation in collective "disorder" at the 1998 World Cup Finals', *British Journal of Social-Psychology*, 40 (2001): 359–84.

Stott, C. and G. Pearson, 'Football banning orders, proportionality and public order', *Howard Journal of Criminal Justice*, 45(3) (2006), 241–54.

Stott, C. and G. Pearson, *Football Hooliganism: Policing and the War on the English Disease* (London: Pennant Books, 2007).

Stott, C. and S. Reicher, 'How conflict escalates: The inter-group dynamics of collective football crowd "violence"', *Sociology*, 32 (1998): 353–77.

Sugden, J., *Scum Airways: Inside Football's Underground Economy* (Edinburgh: Mainstream, 2002).

Taylor, Lord Justice, 'Hillsborough Stadium Disaster Final Report' (London: HMSO, 1990).

Taylor, R., *Football and Its Fans: Supporters and Their Relations with the Game, 1885–1985* (Leicester: Leicester University Press: 1992).

Taylor, S. and R. Bogdan, *Introduction to Qualitative Research Methods* (New York: Wiley, 1984).

Thorne, C., 'Political activist as participant observer: Conflicts of commitment in a study of the draft resistance movement of the 1960s', in R. Emerson (ed.), *Contemporary Field Research: A Collection of Readings* (Boston: Little, Brown and Company, 1983), pp. 216–34.

Tomsen, S., 'A top night: Social protest, masculinity and the culture of drinking violence', *British Journal of Criminology*, 37(1) (1997), 90–102.

Trow, M., 'Comment on "Participant observation and interviewing: A comparison"', in W. Filstead (ed.), *Qualitative Methodology: Firsthand Involvement with the Social World*

(Chicago: Markham, 1970).

Tuck, M., *Drinking and Disorder: A Study of Non-Metropolitan Violence*. Home Office Research Study. No.108 (London: HMSO, 1989).

Van Maanen, J., 'The moral fix: On the ethics of fieldwork', in R. Emerson (ed.), *Contemporary Field Research: A Collection of Readings* (Boston: Little, Brown and Company, 1983).

—— *Tales of the Field: On Writing Ethnography* (Chicago: University of Chicago Press, 1988).

Ward, C., *Steaming in: The Journal of a Football Fan* (London: Pocket Books, 1994).

Webb, D., 'Bakhtin at the seaside: Utopia, modernity and the carnivalesque', *Theory, Culture & Society*, 22(3) (2005): 121–38.

Weed, M., 'Ing-Ger-Land at Euro 2000: How "handbags at 20 paces" was portrayed as a full-scale riot', *International Review for the Sociology of Sport*, 34(4) (2001): 407–24.

White, J., *Are You Watching Liverpool?* (London: Mandarin, 1994).

Whyte, W. F., *Street Corner Society* (Chicago: University of Chicago Press, 1973).

Williams, J., 'Who you calling a hooligan?', in M. Perryman (ed.), *Hooligan Wars: Causes and Effects of Football Violence* (Edinburgh: Mainstream, 2001).

Williams, J., E. Dunning and P. Murphy, *Hooligans Abroad* (2nd edn, London: Routledge, 1989).

Williams, T., E. Dunlop, B. Johnson and H. Ansley, 'Personal safety in dangerous places', *Journal of Contemporary Ethnography*, 21(3) (1992): 343–74.

Willis, P., *Learning to Labour: How Working Class Kids Get Working Class Jobs* (Aldershot: Gower, 1977).

Willis, P. and M. Trondman, 'Manifesto for ethnography', *Ethnography*, 1(1) (2000): 5–16.

Winlow, S. and S. Hall, *Violent Night: Urban Leisure and Contemporary Culture* (Oxford: Berg, 2006).

Winlow, S. and S. Hall, 'Retaliate first: Memory, humiliation and male violence', *Crime, Media, Culture*, 5(2) (2009): 123–45.

Index

Note: 'n.' After a page number indicates the number of a note on that page.

Lightning Source UK Ltd.
Milton Keynes UK
UKOW07f1559150115

244509UK00003B/48/P